GENERATION OCCUPY

REAWAKENING AMERICAN DEMOCRACY

MICHAEL LEVITIN

COUNTERPOINT
Berkeley, California

Generation Occupy

Copyright © 2021 by Michael Levitin
First hardcover edition: 2021

Library of Congress Cataloging-in-Publication Data
Names: Levitin, Michael, 1976– author.
Title: Generation occupy : reawakening American democracy / Michael Levitin.
Description: First hardcover edition. | Berkeley, California : Counterpoint, 2021.
Identifiers: LCCN 2020053403 | ISBN 9781640094499 (hardcover) | ISBN 9781640094505 (ebook)
Subjects: LCSH: Occupy Wall Street (Movement) | Protest movements—United States—History—21st century. | Income distribution—United States—History—21st century.
Classification: LCC HN59.2 .L4948 2021 | DDC 303.48/409730905—dc23
LC record available at https://lccn.loc.gov/2020053403

Jacket design by Lexi Earle
Book design by Jordan Koluch

COUNTERPOINT
2560 Ninth Street, Suite 318
Berkeley, CA 94710
www.counterpointpress.com

Printed in the United States of America

10 9 8 7 6 5 4 3 2 1

For my parents

There is a mysterious cycle in human events. To some generations much is given. Of other generations much is expected. This generation of Americans has a rendezvous with destiny.

—FRANKLIN DELANO ROOSEVELT
in his acceptance speech at the
Democratic National Convention
in Philadelphia, 1936

True peace is not merely the absence of tension; it is the presence of justice.

—MARTIN LUTHER KING JR.,
Stride Toward Freedom:
The Montgomery Story, 1958

CONTENTS

GENERATION OCCUPY

1

OCCUPY GENERATION

A DECADE AFTER OCCUPY WALL STREET IGNITED A DISCUSSION about wealth inequality, corporate greed and the corrupting influence of money in politics, people still ask: *What happened to Occupy?* The movement that sprang to life in lower Manhattan on September 17, 2011—the 224th anniversary of the signing of the U.S. Constitution—sparked occupations in a thousand towns and cities that seemed, for several months, to rewire America's political DNA. Polls showed two-thirds of the country backed the ideas and principles of the movement, and for a brief autumn Occupy captured the global stage as its message resonated around the world.

Then, like a storm, it was over. Collapsed both from its own lack of structure and from the state violence that suppressed it, Occupy vanished almost as quickly as it had arrived. One thing most people remember is that Occupy introduced the vocabulary of the 99 percent and the 1 percent, putting the crisis of inequality on the map. But that's about it. The movement created no electoral organization, achieved no legislative success and made no real impact on American political life, or so the story line went. To date, no one has provided an accurate answer to the question, *What happened to Occupy?*

I would contend we are no longer the country we were before Occupy Wall Street revived the labor movement, remade the Democratic Party and reinvented activism, birthing a new culture of protest that put the fight for economic and social justice at the forefront of a generation. Far from a passing phenomenon, Occupy inaugurated an era of political change in which the demands of the majority continue to grow louder and more focused. It began with the kids. The kids came out and they didn't go home. They targeted Wall Street, the source of our dysfunctional democracy, and issued a singular demand that was all of the demands: Justice. Fairness. Equality. Their slogan—*We are the 99 percent*—inspired hundreds of thousands to move away from their screens and into the streets and squares where the vision of Occupy replaced the unfulfilled promise of Obama's Hope and Change. They had no leaders. There was no plan. This was not a protest. It was a rebellion, a revolt whose time had come. The seeds they planted took root overnight and quickly spread and multiplied, germinating in the country's consciousness. No one thought young people would remain camped out in parks forever. Nor did anyone expect the movement to reshape the political and cultural arenas in the ways that it did.

I DIDN'T COME TO NEW YORK LOOKING FOR A REVOLUTION. I CAME to catch a flight leaving JFK for Berlin, where I had a wife waiting to divorce me. I believe in the adage that when one door closes, another one opens. It may not be the one you expect, but the trick is to walk through it anyway.

Perhaps I had been waiting for Occupy—we had all, to some degree, been waiting for it—and when it finally appeared, I felt I had no choice. It was right there in front of us, staring our generation in the eyes, daring us to act as no moment ever had, to put our convictions and our bodies on the line. We weren't used to doing such things, *our generation*. You could call us the

Obama Generation. The iPhone Generation works, too. We were the Anti-Globalization and the Millennial Generation, the Unaffordable Rent and College Debt Generation. We were also, of course, the September 11, Iraq War, Financial Crisis and Great Recession Generation.

We were the Occupy Generation. Generation Occupy.

As far back as I can recall I had been in search of our generation. I grew up in the 1990s, that formidably inactive decade when we inherited a million choices and a spirit of prosperous unworry despite the sinking ship we knew we were already on. Our generation? We had underachieved to the point that we were already like a forgotten, irrelevant chapter in the nation's story, an in-between period of minimal consequence, pressed like an island between two continent-like centuries. Generations, like individuals, define themselves as much through their inaction as through their actions: not by what they do but by what they fail to even *try* to do. I had always felt so much more was expected of our generation—at least the expectation that we would do *something*. Which is why, when our moment finally arrived, not a bone in me could turn away.

Like so many at Occupy, I came from a family of liberal Democrats. My grandparents on my father's side were Russian Jews who fled Berlin in the 1930s and who understood firsthand the value of freedom and democracy. My mother's parents were Democratic Party organizers who helped launch the celebrated career of the senator from California, Alan Cranston. I grew up in the hippie hills of Sonoma County, an hour north of San Francisco, with a mother who reported on the United Farm Workers in the seventies and marched for nuclear disarmament in the eighties, and a beatnik writer–house painter stepfather from Oklahoma who had resisted the Vietnam draft. Instilled in me was a belief that American government at its best played an active role helping to improve and secure society, from the New Deal under Franklin Delano Roosevelt to the Civil Rights era of Lyndon B. Johnson. I learned to trust in the virtues of a liberal, patient style of politics: the faith that for all our system's flaws and disappointments, the United States managed not only to bumble along and function but also, on occasion, to progress.

My first political memory was the November night in 1992 when Bill Clinton won the presidency and parties up and down our road carried on past dawn. The Reagan-Bush years were over, a baby boomer was in the White House and suddenly the 1960s were looking vindicated while the 1990s, *our generation*, were about to take off. Born in 1976, I came to adolescence in time to glimpse the Berlin Wall falling and Patriot missiles shooting across the Baghdad sky. By the time I reached college, the planetary crisis had descended upon us. In Vice President Al Gore's 1992 book, *Earth in the Balance,* science already presented clear evidence of man-made global warming. While studying history at the University of California, Santa Cruz, I found my place in environmental activism. I helped organize a UC-wide boycott of Mitsubishi—at the time, and incredibly still, one of the world's largest destroyers of tropical rainforest—and campaigned to stop Pacific Bell, the state's telephone monopoly, from producing tens of millions of annual phone books from British Columbia's ancient boreal forest. At one point I joined the radical outfit Earth First! and was arrested in Humboldt County with three hundred other protesters for blockading a road into the Headwaters Forest, the largest privately owned stand of old-growth redwood trees on Earth. The resistance in the nineties felt real, it felt serious, and for a moment, it seemed, our generation stood poised to shift the nation's priorities and become masters of our future.

Then the window closed. The 1994 midterms that swept Newt Gingrich and the Republican Revolution into Congress marked the end of what many Americans considered to be legitimate democratic governance. The GOP's Contract with America sought to undo decades of labor, health and environmental laws, and the party's attempt to shut down the federal government was a watershed moment signaling that Republicans had stopped playing by the rules. Corporate Democrats, meanwhile, gave away the store, as Clinton sacrificed U.S. manufacturing jobs to NAFTA and embraced a neoliberal agenda that favored deregulation and unconstrained globalization, abandoning American workers to Wall Street profit and greed. The internet bubble in the late nineties fueled obscene levels of economic growth and inequality, and after his fourteen-month drama of impeachment for a lie about a workplace affair in the West Wing, Clinton finished off the decade with two signature bills. The Financial Services Modernization Act repealed core elements of Glass-Steagall, a law that had successfully separated commercial and investment banking since the Great Depression, while the Commodity Futures Modernization Act prevented the regulation of derivatives by any federal agency. Taken together, the legislation enabled big banks to refashion themselves into credit default swap casinos, paving the way for the 2007 housing crash and financial crisis that would unravel the economy.

What happened next was the moment historians will invoke as they examine the fulcrum between the twentieth and twenty-first centuries: the stolen presidential election of 2000. This is really where the story of Occupy Wall Street begins, for in the maiden autumn of the millennium it was the United States Supreme Court that stopped the Florida vote recount and, discarding its role as the impartial third branch of government free of partisan concerns, put a thumb on the scale to hand the forty-third presidency to George Walker Bush. Ten months later, airplanes flown by nineteen al-Qaeda terrorists, mostly from Saudi Arabia, took down the Twin Towers in New York City in the largest attack on American soil since Pearl Harbor. I had just moved to New York to attend Columbia Journalism School and found myself reporting at an AIDS clinic in the Bronx on the bright September morning when the first plane struck the World Trade Center. That evening, President Bush promised "to find those responsible and to bring them to justice," saying, "we will make no distinction between the terrorists who committed these acts and those who harbor them . . . to win the war against terrorism." His words presaged America's defining military blunder as it embarked on two wars in the Middle East—the second one based almost entirely on White House lies and misinformation—ushering in the twenty-year era from which we are still searching our way out.

We knew already then and can see with greater clarity today that 9/11 put us on the backside of history. That is to say, it fundamentally changed the way America viewed itself—its vulnerability, its incompetence, and its inability to respond honestly and intelligently to a crisis. If the coronavirus pandemic of 2020 delivered a tragic coda to two decades of systemic American decline, September 11, 2001, was the opening gong. The attacks on New York City and Washington, D.C., launched the country's twenty-year war in Afghanistan, and the eight-year destruction of Iraq at a cost of forty-five hundred U.S. and half a million Iraqi lives while draining $5 trillion from the U.S. Treasury. But disastrous imperial ventures that introduced torture as official American policy, with legacies like Abu Ghraib and Guantanamo, were only one hallmark of the Bush years. The other was a housing market gambling spree steered by the world's biggest banks, which bet the long-term security and well-being of Americans against a get-rich-quick mountain of derivatives, collateralized debt and mortgage-backed securities. When the house of cards came crashing down in September 2008, it took the world's economy with it.

Two months later, a youth-led Democratic coalition elected Barack Obama as America's first Black president, signaling our generation wasn't ready to give up hope. Ten million Americans would lose their homes and many more their pensions and life savings in the foreclosure and financial crises that wiped away $10 trillion in household wealth. As many as nine million people lost jobs in what became the most prolonged recession since the Great Depression. Everyone knew who to blame for the corporate greed and criminal profiteering that wrecked so many lives and destroyed the economy: Wall Street. Suffering, angry, fed up—the people demanded justice.

But instead, as the refrain would go, "Banks got bailed out, we got sold out." Flanked by his Democratic supermajority in the House and Senate, Obama faced down the global financial crisis but missed the transformational opportunity for which he had been elected. He rescued the auto industry. He signed the Reinvestment and Recovery Act to help rebuild the ravaged economy. But the unforgivable sin for which history will judge Obama is clear: he let the banks off the hook. It was one thing to stuff his Treasury Department with executives and lobbyists from Citigroup and Goldman Sachs. But two months into his term, when President Obama sat down for a reckoning with the most powerful CEOs on Wall Street and issued them a slap on the wrist, he lost much of the public's trust. Instead of facing retribution for high crimes committed, the banking chiefs received hundreds of billions of dollars in taxpayer-funded bailouts, few strings attached. From that bailout, they lavished tens of billions in bonuses on themselves, board members, and traders, and repurchased company stock rather than investing it to rebuild the economy. Finally, Obama's Justice Department handed down exactly zero jail sentences against the bankers who unlawfully enriched themselves at the nation's expense.

By this time, it didn't take a policy wizard to understand that Wall Street was calling the shots, not our elected leaders in Washington. This message was further confirmed in January 2010 when the Republican-majority Supreme Court wrapped up a rotten decade with its 5–4 decision on *Citizens United*, authorizing unlimited election spending by corporations, which the court considered "people" with a First Amendment right to free speech. That same winter, a far-right populist movement calling itself the Tea Party emerged in opposition to the bailouts and what it considered government corruption and overspending. Bankrolled by the Koch brothers and other right-wing interests, the movement reshuffled the political deck, getting a generation of GOP anti-Washington ideologues elected to Congress and statehouses nationwide. Unemployment in 2011 remained close to 10 percent as the country spiraled deeper into a recession. The silence around these injustices was deafening, and the suffering mounted. America was still waiting for something to save it, although it didn't know quite what. Then, suddenly and mysteriously, the tables turned.

I HAD BEEN WORKING FOR SIX YEARS AS A JOURNALIST IN BERLIN, and when my wife and I split up, I took a magazine job in San Francisco.

That is where I was living when the revolutions began. They started in Tunisia in December 2010, when a twenty-six-year-old vegetable vendor named Mohamed Bouazizi set himself on fire to protest corruption after police had confiscated his cart and then refused to hear his complaints in court. Days before, WikiLeaks had released a trove of U.S. diplomatic cables critical of President Zine El Abidine Ben Ali, the country's autocratic ruler of twenty-three years. Bouazizi's self-immolation lit a democratic flame that caught fire across the country as millions of Tunisians demanding jobs and freedom poured into the streets. For weeks, facing tear gas and bullets, they filled the capital and towns nationwide, refusing to go home until, on January 14, 2011, Ben Ali fled the country and the protesters declared victory. The Arab Spring was underway.

I didn't grasp the real significance of what was taking place until a much larger and more visible rebellion erupted a few weeks later on the streets of Cairo. There, hundreds of thousands of Egyptians had pitched tents to occupy Tahrir Square in the heart of the capital where they vowed to remain until their dictator of nearly three decades, the U.S.-backed strongman Hosni Mubarak, stepped down. State forces killed hundreds of Egyptians and injured thousands during the eighteen-day standoff, which spun out of control when pro-Mubarak assailants swept through Tahrir on camel- and horseback, sabers raised, striking down unarmed civilians. The regime laid bare its brutality as the whole world watched, and soon after, on February 11, millions of protesters occupied the city's bridges, squares and streets until Mubarak, without international support to turn to, resigned.

I found myself driving around the hills of San Francisco that winter listening to National Public Radio day and night during the hopeful early months of the Arab Spring. The revolutions spread to Libya, where a rebel army attempted to oust Muammar Gaddafi, then on to Yemen, Bahrain and Syria. After the American housing bubble burst in 2007, and the markets crashed and millions lost their homes and jobs, I had expected to see unrest break out in our own country. Perhaps I was naive; I just assumed the upheaval would begin in America. That a worldwide revolt demanding economic justice, political representation and an end to corruption could spring from the repressive regimes of the Arab world took me, as it took many, by surprise.

Then, on May 15, 2011, attention shifted suddenly to Europe where the protests of the Indignados, known as the 15-M movement, erupted across austerity-stricken Spain. Tens of thousands of young people marched and built encampments in city squares nationwide as millions more demanded "Democracia Real Ya!"—*Real Democracy Now!*—from a government they said had failed to represent them. That same month, union strikes and violent anti-austerity protests paralyzed Greece, where the national debt was soaring and half the population under thirty was out of work. Whereas Europe in the debt crisis had opted for harsh belt-tightening measures that cut social spending and drove people to revolt, Washington provided a temporary remedy with a $1.4 trillion Troubled Asset Relief Program, or TARP, and stimulus recovery bill. But trouble had been brewing that winter and spring in our backyard, too, after tens of thousands of Wisconsin protesters stormed and occupied the state capitol in Madison to oppose Governor Scott Walker's "budget repair bill" that crushed collective bargaining rights for public-sector workers.

The upheavals were coming fast and they were coming everywhere, it seemed. In July, hundreds of thousands of Israelis swarmed the streets of Tel Aviv to create a sprawling tent city where they called for greater social justice and affordable housing. The next month, London police shot and killed a young Black man named Mark Duggan, setting off a week of riots across the U.K., where anti-austerity protests had been growing throughout the year. There were loud stirrings in South America, too, as Chilean students marching by the tens of thousands occupied and shuttered universities to demand better-funded schools.

With the global recession bearing down and nations in both hemispheres suddenly on the brink, no country, not even our own, looked immune to revolution. No visible or defining leadership had emerged; there wasn't any singular cause or message tying the rebellions together beyond a generalized anger, economic frustration and people's widespread disbelief in the legitimacy of their elected governments. A hunger for change was in the air. It was global, palpable, urgent, as though a fissure had opened and suddenly we could all see through the cracks of capitalism and political corruption everywhere. What seemed to drive the 2011 protests more than anything was a new sense of clarity: people no longer feared the truth because they were speaking it out loud, together.

I still had the divorce to take care of, so I bought a ticket to Germany leaving in late September from New York, and that August I got in my car and started driving east from California. I was shooting a documentary about the impacts of climate change that were already being felt across the United States. That summer, Hurricane Irene washed through Vermont, flooding from the Missouri River inundated Midwestern cities like Omaha and Pierre, and a punishing drought killed cornfields from Colorado to Iowa as cattle fell dead across the fiery, bone-dry landscape of Texas. I drove past retreating glaciers in Montana and spoke to workers in Wyoming's coal country. Traveling for a month through recessional America, all I heard on the radio was talk about a looming government shutdown as Congress debated the so-called debt ceiling. There was plenty just then for Americans to be outraged about: the financial crash, the foreclosure chaos, the bank bailouts, the unemployment crisis, and not one individual in power held to account for any of it. At the same time, Republican lawmakers obsessed with budgets and defeating Obama refused to discuss a jobs program. Like the August heat that summer, the public's 84 percent disapproval rating of Congress broke records. Yet somehow the arbiters in Washington failed to hear. They failed to see. To them, America was still sleeping, tired and unmovable.

Until the day, midway through September, when the giant woke up.

NO GOING BACK

SEPTEMBER 24, 2011

IT WAS ON THE LAST LEG OF MY ROAD TRIP EAST THAT SUMMER, somewhere outside of Cleveland, when I started hearing radio reports about the protest happening in New York City's financial district. People were camped out, they were calling it Occupy Wall Street and a man interviewed said, "I'm here to protest a criminal financial system that gambled away our economy, that kicked millions of Americans out of their homes and jobs and got away with it—because the banks and the corporations own our government, not the people." The man's words cut through the traffic sounds of Manhattan to reach me out on the Ohio plains, causing me to speed up. When I got to New York, I still imagined I'd be stepping on a plane in two days to Berlin. But then I went down to have a look at the park and something inside of me shifted.

The gathering that came into view centered around a large, red, steel sculpture anchored at the southeastern corner of Zuccotti Park. As I entered the square, what struck me first was how quiet and intriguingly still it all seemed.

People crowded on the steps spilling off Broadway into the park where hundreds more spread out, some sitting, some standing, others bunched together atop marble benches that formed a jigsaw pattern under the bright green canopy of trees. Some were talking but mostly they all just seemed to be waiting, watching, surveying the scene with a seriousness I couldn't quite place. The intensity on the young faces was new, a kind of shared language that required no words, and it was the silence that struck me most: the noiseless anticipation assembled there across hundreds of brows glowing with preparedness, as if merely awaiting a sign, a signal, to act. The crowd held that fixed pose and time seemed to stop moving as I stood among the others, suspended between past and future, wondering if this was what the beginning of a revolution looked like.

When I arrived that Saturday afternoon, the occupation was exactly one week old and people had just returned to Zuccotti on a march from Union Square, where they were protesting the state execution of a Black man named Troy Davis in Georgia. Things got rowdy when police tried to block the protest and arrested around eighty people, "kettling" them inside orange plastic nets. It was then that a New York City police officer, Anthony Bologna, shot a stream of pepper spray into the faces of several unarmed white women who fell to the sidewalk shrieking in pain. Smartphones with cameras had only recently become popular; now every young person was carrying one, but never before had they been used as instruments of evidence to document police brutality for millions of waiting viewers. Within hours of being posted to YouTube, the "pepper spray cop" video went viral. It was the greatest gift the NYPD could have bestowed on the nascent movement. For the first time, the public was forced to watch and listen to what was happening in the streets, and it generated an outpouring of sympathy that would catapult Occupy Wall Street onto the national stage.

In the park, a man climbed onto one of the marble benches as a crowd gathered around him. Swarthy and well built, he spoke slowly, clearly, enunciating his words in a husky voice while hundreds pressed in to listen and the human microphone reverberated outward. "This is about reclaiming public space. This is about empowering ourselves to speak!" said the man, who brought a semblance of order to a scene that appeared otherwise unfocused. As I stood on the park steps, I felt drawn to the magnetic pulse of whatever this new thing was—an instinctual desire to be part of it, tribal almost, as though I had discovered a group I knew I belonged to but hadn't until that day found. I cringed at the same time that I exhilarated in the crowd's performance. The speak-and-repeat theatric with its unifying echo made me feel uncomfortable at first, reciting the man's words along with the others, because it reminded me of some kind of cult where one person leads and the rest follow. Except no one here, not even the man speaking, seemed to be leading, nor did anyone appear to be following. As I began to participate it was clear that I wasn't witnessing a protest or demonstration but something more purposeful than any gathering of Americans I had ever seen. Our generation had finally showed up.

When I got there on Monday morning, the square was already buzzing: bloggers typing, cooks serving, conversations voluble. There was a manic throb and hum to the place as people drifted in from the morning march at the stock exchange. Dozens kneeling on the stone ground painted words on cardboard signs that scattered a sprawling tapestry of messages across the surface of the park: "Dissent Is Patriotic"—"It's Not A Crisis, It's A Scam"—"End Corporate Personhood"—"No Such Thing As Too Big To Fail"—"Make The Banks Pay"—"Debt Is Slavery"—"Bail Out Main Street Not Wall Street"—"Lost A Job, Found An Occupation." I watched the beginnings of a library being formed at the base of the park's granite wall and joined different working groups discussing next steps for the movement. "People get 'the 99 percent,'" a female protester told me, "they just need to be brought in to participate." A tall man with curly hair and an auburn beard was trying to organize teams of activists to ride the subways. "We entertain, we bring music, performance, energy, humor, excitement. Many people on the subway are trapped in their jobs or in their fear of losing their jobs and we show them that something is happening which speaks to that deep fear," he said.

The voices in the square were calling for a new America, and as I sat wedged into a circle of bodies, raising my hands and wiggling my fingers to show approval of what was being said, everything seemed possible. Once one o'clock came around I had to decide, with the song refrain banging in my head: *Should I stay or should I go?* I got up and tried to leave several times but couldn't. Something rooted me to the spot; I was unable to pull away from the park and the promise that it held. The divorce could wait. Realizing it was now or never, I phoned the airline and canceled my flight. That afternoon, alongside many hundreds, I marched for the first time to the New York Stock Exchange on Wall Street for the closing bell, then found an open patch of concrete on the southwestern edge of the park where I established my piece of camp.

That night heavy clouds and mist loomed over lower Manhattan and a cold wind swept down through the canyon of buildings to reach us in the shadow of the half-built Freedom Tower. High above, construction lights glared and the clanking sound of machinery produced a steady thrum as I opened several large cardboard boxes and laid the overlapping strips of carton on the ground, then unfolded my sleeping bag. It was my first night in Zuccotti Park and people were up late wandering the camp, smoking, talking in small groups. When the rain came we dashed under tarps, flattening ourselves on the stone floor in an attempt to stay dry, but the water quickly soaked through the carton beneath my sleep sack and I began to shiver. A quiet overtook the camp; others seemed to fall asleep easily as if they had done this before—as if they knew what camping out in a goddamn rainstorm in the middle of New York City felt like. My teeth were chattering and soon the shaking got uncontrollable, though I recognized it wasn't the cold that was bothering me so much as the hysteria I suddenly found myself in. Minutes dragged into hours as I lay there wet, in a silent craze, gazing up into the mist that filtered down through the delicate branches of the honey locust trees, trembling in my bag with the realization of what I had done—what my decision to stay actually meant. Panic gripped me, a sudden, unfamiliar pulse of fear running through my body. The fear that this time I had stepped in too far, and too deep, to return.

Perhaps I was feeling that way because of what the filmmaker Michael Moore had told us earlier in the evening when he showed up unannounced at the park. Wearing his trademark ball cap, horn-rimmed glasses and sneakers, Moore gathered a swarm of cameras and flashing lights as the people followed him down the steps from Broadway, into the darkness under the trees, where he spoke to the crowd of hundreds. Not everyone had awoken to the facts, he said. But we had. We were the first line of rebellion, the opening shot fired by the 99 percent against the 1 percent, and as Moore spoke, the people repeated his words through the people's mic that fanned out in a thundering chorus of voices around him.

"It had to happen somewhere," said Moore.

"IT HAD TO HAPPEN SOMEWHERE!" the crowd echoed.

"Might as well have been here."

"MIGHT AS WELL HAVE BEEN HERE!"

"They know what's coming on Wall Street," he went on, pointing at the offices above us, "because it's not just the hundreds or thousands that have come down here to Liberty Square. It is millions of Americans who have suffered as a result of the decisions made by the people in these buildings."

He paused to gather himself, then shouted:

"I want to see a perp walk! I want to see the people responsible for destroying the lives of millions of people put in handcuffs"

"IN HANDCUFFS!"

"And led away."

"AND LED AWAY!"

"And brought to justice."

"AND BROUGHT TO JUSTICE!"

"Immediately!"

"IMMEDIATELY!"

"It's time to make them pay! Tax them!"

"TAX THEM!"

"Tax them!"

"TAX THEM!"

"Tax them!"

"TAX THEM!"

"How much? Not enough! How much? Still not enough! They're thieves, they're gangsters, they're kleptomaniacs who have tried to take our democracy and turn it into a kleptocracy—*their* kleptocracy!"

"*THEIR* KLEPTOCRACY!"

"The four hundred richest Americans own more wealth than one hundred and fifty million combined. They may think they're going to get away with this because they have so much more than everyone else. But they're afraid of one basic thing: there's only four hundred of them and there's at least one hundred and fifty million"

"ONE HUNDRED AND FIFTY MILLION!"

"Two hundred million."

"TWO HUNDRED MILLION!"

"Two hundred and fifty million."

"TWO HUNDRED AND FIFTY MILLION!"

"Of us!"

"OF US!"

"You don't have to be into sports to understand the outcome of that game," continued Moore. "They think their power is derived from their bank accounts, but our power is derived from the people—*all* of the people"

"*ALL* OF THE PEOPLE!"

"Not the four hundred."

"NOT THE FOUR HUNDRED!"

"All of the people!"

"ALL OF THE PEOPLE!"

"Do not despair because there's only a few hundred of you here right now," he concluded. "All great movements start with just a few people. You're in the hard part here, but everyone will remember three months from now"

"THREE MONTHS FROM NOW!"

"Six months from now."

"SIX MONTHS FROM NOW!"

"A hundred years from now."

"A HUNDRED YEARS FROM NOW!"

"That you came down here and you started this movement."

AS I LAY SHIVERING IN MY SLEEPING BAG WITH THE RAIN FALLING on me and the filmmaker Moore's battlefield words rippling in my head, I panicked because I understood what he had said was true. I wasn't playing revolutionary any longer in the California woods. This time I'd got what I wanted: I joined a revolt that seized its strength from the epicenter of financial greed, and yes, we came unarmed for battle, yes it was a festive takeover of these gray slabs of cement we called Liberty Square, occupied on the same block of land ten years and six days after the century's first catastrophe. Now it was the staging ground for a different kind of battle, and as I squirmed in my soaked bag under the darkness of the tarp, I felt angst and foreboding because our mutinying army was engaged in resistance against the highest forms of power. I rolled around on the hard park floor, unable to sleep, and it must have been dawn or shortly before when a soft-voiced man dressed like a fairy, with a feather dangling from his ear, walked me from Zuccotti across Broadway, sat me down with a coffee, and let me ramble. I was caught in the madness and we both knew it. A readjustment was setting in. I could feel myself teetering but there was no longer any choice to make. I shook with dread though it wasn't quite that. More like a premonition, because I knew there was no going back.

2

OCCUPY ECONOMY

INEQUALITY ILLUMINATED: AWAKENING THE 99 PERCENT

SEEDS OF THE MOVEMENT: ALEXIS GOLDSTEIN

SOMETIMES IT TAKES AN INSIDER WHO BECOMES AN OUTSIDER TO help the inside understand what the outside is saying. And when it came to conveying Occupy Wall Street's message of economic justice to the media—and, finally, to the corridors of decision-making power in Washington—no one played the inside-outside role to greater effect than the equities and derivatives analyst Alexis Goldstein.

Like many Occupy protesters, Goldstein grew up liberal. Raised in a Maryland suburb just outside Washington, D.C., she discovered activism in high school when she joined an environmental group fighting to stop pesticides being sprayed near schools. She later lobbied against but failed to halt the construction of a highway through a biologically sensitive area in her region. Then, while studying computer science at Columbia University, she "did a one-eighty and disengaged politically." Very unlike most Occupy protesters,

Goldstein was aggressively recruited by Wall Street banks and, upon graduating in 2003, took a job as a programmer for Morgan Stanley. "It was great," she recalled of her early experience working for the global investment bank. The company "really makes you feel wanted. They invest in you with technical and financial training. I drank the Kool-Aid: I became economically conservative."

Goldstein, who has gentle, round features and straight, shoulder-length brown hair, went to work building complex programming systems that enabled hedge funds to interact with banks. Gradually she began to fall under the influence of her fellow employees who complained nonstop about taxes. "There's this huge sense of martyrdom on Wall Street, where you work so hard and you aren't happy so you feel entitled to every dollar you earn. It doesn't matter that you're making so much more than everyone else: you compare yourself to your colleagues and one easy way out of feeling bitter at your firm is to say, 'I'm paying too much in taxes, look at this horrible government and the politicians that are bleeding me dry.'" Goldstein absorbed her peers' chatter about wasteful and exploitative unions—including the oft-repeated company myth that if you wanted to move an office computer at Morgan, the union had to do it, "then five people would come: one to unplug it, one to hold the monitor, one to hold the clipboard . . . I couldn't tell you which mysterious union it was or if it was real, but it was seen as this bad evil thing exploiting our very well-paid industry." What formerly progressive views she held became reactionary ones, even if Goldstein didn't understand the particulars of what made her angry—like the Supplemental Nutrition Assistance Program, or SNAP, which her co-workers bashed for helping keep people afloat through food stamps. "I just had this idea that there were people who weren't working and had it easier than me," she said. "It was very easy to find some external thing to hate on, and I hated on everything. It's the animating force of the culture."

Goldstein lasted three years at Morgan Stanley before she took a job building equity derivatives software at Merrill Lynch, where she would have a front row seat to the financial collapse. On the day it happened, September 15, 2008, she recalled seeing the CEO, John Thain, come to the trading floor, "where there's this giant LED board full of the different stock indexes, and they were all watching it crash." Bank of America rescued Merrill that very day by purchasing it for $50 billion; Goldstein's colleagues worried the bank could still be nationalized in lieu of a bailout, but it soon received billions through TARP, along with nearly a hundred billion in government guarantees against its toxic assets, alleviating those concerns. When Goldstein asked her boss if he thought the public would ever forgive the industry, he told her, "The public forgot after the savings and loan crisis" of the eighties, which cost tax-payers more than $130 billion, "and the public is going to forget about this, too. Things will go back to normal, we just have to wait it out." By mid-2010, Goldstein was done waiting: helping wealthy people get wealthier made her miserable, and so she quit. She took on some technical consulting jobs and taught programming classes. Then, in September 2011, when Occupy Wall Street came into view, Goldstein found herself in an unexpectedly useful role: she had intimate knowledge of the tools used by the big banks to take down the global economy and, more importantly, she had ideas about how to help rein in the power of those institutions.

"I think I didn't really come to terms with my own culpability in this larger system until Occupy," she told me, and "when it happened I was very skeptical. I thought cops would just shut it down. But then I got curious enough and after the [September 24] pepper-spray incident, I went to check it out. The day I showed up at Zuccotti Park, [author] Naomi Klein was there giving a talk, and after several rounds of the people's mic, I asked her a question: 'Should we bring back Glass-Steagall?' Klein said it would be a good demand. Then someone said, 'What's Glass-Steagall?'" That's when Goldstein realized maybe there was something she could contribute. She came to the next general assembly—the twice-daily forum which served as the movement's decision-making body—where she offered to do a teach-in, explaining finance industry basics along with some proposals for what she thought should change. And just like that, Goldstein began turning Wall Street expertise into Occupy Wall Street cred.

She helped form a working group, Occupy the SEC, which called for re-forms to the federal Securities and Exchange Commission. By the second week of the movement Goldstein was being called for studio interviews on top cable news programs to discuss the structural flaws that had led to the financial cri-sis and the kinds of practical regulatory measures that could limit the power of the big banks. "The press seemed flabbergasted that someone at Occupy could read and write," she recalled. Goldstein would go on to become one of the most visible spokespeople at Occupy Wall Street, someone who accurately diagnosed the crimes of the 1 percent and fueled the public's widening out-rage over corporate greed. She soon teamed up with another former banker, Caitlin Kline, who had worked as a credit derivatives trader, and together they designed a road map aimed toward one primary goal: tightening the finan-cial regulations in Washington. The previous year, Congress had passed and Obama had signed into law the Dodd-Frank Wall Street Reform and Con-sumer Protection Act, a bill shaped by literally thousands of lobbyists on Capi-tol Hill that sought to curtail some of the excesses of the Too Big to Fail banks, but did little to actually reform the industry. Within the broad package of laws in Dodd-Frank, Goldstein and Kline targeted one specific rule—named after the former Federal Reserve chairman Paul Volcker—that would restrict com-mercial banks from making some of the riskiest and most speculative types of investments with their customers' money. "We weren't politicians, we didn't have power," said Goldstein, "but there was an opportunity for one regulation, the Volcker Rule, to see if we could make it better."

In the winter of 2012, during the public comment period before the pro-visions of the Volcker Rule would go into effect, Occupy the SEC wrote and submitted a three-hundred-page comment letter that answered a lot of ques-tions about the law's complexity and proposed modifications to strengthen it. Goldstein had dissected the policy through a strictly financial lens, treating it the way a banker would. "We put on our Wall Street hats and thought, 'How would we evade this rule to get around it?' Then we wrote about how to change the rule so people couldn't get around it." Occupy the SEC put forth a series of aggressive yet reasonable proposals to close some of the loopholes, and specifically to restrain the banks from dangerous proprietary trading; incredibly, the halls of power started to listen. "As protesters have moved off the streets, a small minority of Occupiers has waded deep into the weeds of the federal regulations, legal decisions and banking practices that make up the actual architecture of Wall Street," wrote Suzy Khimm for the *Washington Post*, "and they're drawing on the technical expertise of the financial industry's own refugees, exiles and dissidents to do so." Goldstein and her colleagues traveled to Washington to meet with some of the most important federal regulation officers involved in implementing the Volcker Rule—at the Federal Deposit Insurance Corporation, the Federal Reserve, the Office of the Comptroller of the Currency, the Securities and Exchange Commission—and explained their rationale for strengthening the law. They drew attention within the establishment, impressing a number of congressional insiders. When lawmakers ultimately tightened the rule, it was in some of the precise ways Occupy the SEC had advised. "I don't know if it was because of us or others who recommended the same things," said Goldstein, "but [proposals] that we suggested were implemented."

Goldstein never returned to big finance; on the contrary, she became a senior policy analyst for Americans for Financial Reform, a D.C.-based nonprofit working to hold the banks, regulators and policymakers accountable for industry abuses. Assessing the movement's long-term legacy, Goldstein likened the "viral spreading of occupations across the country" to a new type of software model, in which "here's the template for what you can do—now go do it in your hometown." With offshoots rooted in more than six hundred U.S. cities and communities, the "Occupy diaspora," as she called it, scattered the seeds of Occupy everywhere, planting a generation of resistance that, a decade later, had "sprouted" across America. "So many people I met at Occupy are involved in some of the most important movements now: the immigrant rights movement, the labor movement, the climate movement," she said. While leaderless in structure, Occupy Wall Street in an elemental way empowered people like Goldstein to lead, because it "taught us that you don't have to wait for someone else to solve the problem: you can come together with people and do it now. I think so many movements since Occupy continue to do that. We've learned that as a society you have to fight all the time—you have to know what you want and constantly agitate for it. People say, 'What did Occupy accomplish, what did it change?' All I know is it changed me. It changed me profoundly. And I'm not the only one."

A NEW NARRATIVE

IN THE WAY THE MOVEMENT AWAKENED GOLDSTEIN, IT ALSO SIG-naled an awakening for the country. Occupy Wall Street reshaped how Americans viewed the economy, inspiring a long-overdue discussion of issues of income inequality, corporate greed, an unjust tax structure and capitalism itself. Occupy posed an emphatic challenge to the status quo, pointing a finger directly at the wealthy as the source of the problem. The eruption on Wall Street was the first visible sign of Americans' widespread recognition that the economic system is rigged for those at the very top. Occupy's slogan—*We are the 99 percent*—crystalized the public's shared sense of injury: Wall Street got bailed out and Main Street was left to rot as Washington subverted instead of advanced the interests of the majority. The movement didn't merely change the national conversation: it opened Americans up to the realization that our crony capitalist system was created by design to enrich only a small fraction of the wealthiest Americans.

Occupy accomplished much of this because it told a compelling story. Only a decade ago we had no common vocabulary to discuss America's growing income gap and its effects. The extent to which corporate power had defeated lawmakers and regulators was largely unremarked in the media, and more importantly, in people's everyday discussions in the office, the school, the gym, the church, the street. The enduring power of the Occupy movement was never its physical occupation of parks and public spaces, which lasted only a few months. Rather, it was the transformation—the *occupation*—of the language Americans used to describe their economic and political reality. In its narrative about a generation left behind, Occupy Wall Street's visceral rhetoric enabled people to confront economic injustice in a way that hadn't been done during most of the preceding century.

"In the nineteen fifties and sixties we talked a lot about race. Then starting in the seventies we talked a lot about gender," the historian Adam Hochschild told me, "but this was the first time we really started in a big public way to discuss class and inequality. I think framing it as the 99 percent and the 1 percent was tremendously important because the creation and the growth of any kind of political movement needs a vocabulary, it needs images. The rhetoric of the 99 percent was important branding and that vocabulary has stayed with us ever since." While the movement's language of defiance had a clear economic focus, it also reflected a kind of universality. People didn't camp in Zuccotti and parks nationwide to protest against this or that company or cause or specific injustice; they were angry about all of it, and their rebellion forced a debate that had been in the making for decades.

Marianne Manilov, a grassroots organizer and strategist in San Francisco, said, "Occupy did what many organizations had been trying to do for a long time: it centered the narrative around people not having enough. The narrative of inequality—that our country is now one where the majority of people are one paycheck away from not having food and living in their cars—is the biggest gift that Occupy gave to our country." By describing America's economic and political unraveling in terms the public hadn't heard before, Occupy rewrote the modern script for protest. As the feminist author Susan Griffin put it, "The act of telling a story is so radical—it's the forerunner of change," and at its core, "Occupy was telling a story, breaking through the silence, breaking through the passivity. That's the most important thing Occupy did."

Creating a novel voice for its generation, Occupy Wall Street engaged in a Socratic dialogue with the establishment—seizing its power not through answers it professed to hold, but through questions it dared to ask. Questions that were on many people's minds, yet never declared in the public sphere until the balmy night of September 29, 2011, when the movement's NYC General Assembly convening in Zuccotti Park approved the Declaration of the Occupation of New York City, an assemblage of several dozen accusations that read like questions, such as: Why have worker wages plunged to new lows as executive pay has climbed to new heights; and why are communities poisoned by polluted water and air while the corporations that polluted them reap profits; and why are students graduating into a shattered jobless economy saddled with tens of thousands of dollars in debt; and why are corporations able to shape most laws in Washington; and why are workers stripped of the right to negotiate as they lose pay and benefits and watch their jobs get shipped overseas; and why can drug companies charge unfathomable sums in reckless pursuit of profit at the expense of human health; and why don't all citizens have a universal right to healthcare; and why have big agricultural companies killed small farms only to contaminate our food supply with pesticides, antibiotics and genetically modified organisms; and why do corporate media misinform and manipulate; and why aren't there strong consumer protections laws safeguarding the public; and why has our privacy been turned into a commodity; and why is workplace inequality and discrimination legal; and why are corporate prisons profiting off the mass incarceration of human beings; and why is the United States Defense Department funded with more money annually than the entire American public education system; and why did we waste trillions of dollars and countless lives fighting two unnecessary and unwinnable wars in Iraq and Afghanistan; and why has our government embraced torture; and why do Wall Street bankers control our Treasury Department; and why did the American people bail out and save from nationalization the very banks that destroyed the economy but ten million homeowners lost their houses and life savings and received no bailout; and why did the Supreme Court determine that corporations have the same First Amendment right to free speech as people, enabling them to spend unlimited sums purchasing our elections; and why were oil companies and the fossil fuel lobby permitted to destroy life on Earth for the sake of corporate profit and short-term shareholder gain?

Activists at Occupy Wall Street realized from the outset that mainstream media either would not or could not explain the anomalous uprising against inequality and corporate greed. Affirming Upton Sinclair's iconic line that "it is difficult to get a man to understand something, when his salary depends on his not understanding it," members of the news industry ignored the movement for as long as they could—one full week—as they stood on the sidelines, scratching their temples, wondering what the kids were about, assuming the motley encampment would just up and disappear. As Todd Gitlin wrote in his colorful chronicle of the movement, *Occupy Nation: The Roots, The Spirit, and the Promise of Occupy Wall Street*, "A top official at National Public Radio had justified an initial decision not to cover the protests in Lower Manhattan, insisting that there had not 'been "large numbers" of protesters; there have not been any "prominent people" involved; there has not been any great disruption; (and) the protesters have failed to articulate a clear point or aim.'"

In the absence of coverage, Occupy did the explaining: we *became* our own media. As master marketers creating the first global internet- and social media–powered movement of its kind, Occupiers trafficked in meme-ready slogans and sound bites that left scarce room for ambiguity: *99 percent vs. 1 percent*; *People Over Profits*; *Wall Street Greed*; *Tax the Rich*; *Jail the Bankers*; *End Corporate Rule*; *Stop the Foreclosures*; *Money in Politics*; *Economic Justice Now*. We replaced the antiseptic language of "tax shelters" and "capital investments" and "market efficiency" and "cost-cutting growth" with a simple declaration: *We are the 99 percent*. We abolished terms like *consumers, constituents, taxpayers, voters, buyers, spenders, customers* and *the electorate*, reclaiming the clearest definition of all: *people*. We described the power structure in layman's terms because we weren't talking to the elites; we were talking to each other and to the great mass of Americans who had been cheated of their future.

The press clamored to know: "What are your demands?" We had plenty of them: end *Citizens United*; cancel student debt; reinstate Glass-Steagall; raise the minimum wage; establish single-payer healthcare; reform criminal justice; transition to clean energy. The list went on and on. We had too many demands and we demanded them all at once, because we knew that you don't solve a systemic crisis with a changed law here, an improved regulation there. To appropriate one of Ronald Reagan's lasting quips: the system *was* the problem. And so our presence became our demand. In the words of Occupy Wall Street organizer Nicole Carty, "Occupy shifted the whole conversation and gave us a new framework for understanding inequality. We're still talking about the 1 percent." As another protester from the Zuccotti Park era, Dana Balicki, told me: "Without us, I don't know if there would be a story about income inequality to tell. We were a spectacle—we literally said, 'I'm going to sit here until you notice me.'"

For progressive media voices especially, the movement produced a shift in the national narrative that drove to the heart of financial and political power. "Nobody ever talked about the degree of income inequality the way Occupy did. Nobody talked about corporate personhood the way Occupy did," said Egberto Willies, host of the radio show *Politics Done Right*. In the aftermath of *Citizens United*, Americans became acutely aware just how much money corporations and wealthy individuals were pouring into the political system to shape electoral outcomes. According to the Sunlight Foundation, which mapped the influence of money in politics, between 2007 and 2012, several hundred U.S. corporations spent nearly $6 billion in combined campaign contributions and lobbying at the federal level. In return, they received close to $4.5 trillion in federal business and legislative support. By connecting the dots and tracing the influence between Wall Street corporations and lawmaking in Washington, "the Occupy movement started talking about money in politics in a way that people could understand," Willies said, and it moved the mainstream economic debate to a new place.

For the comedian Lee Camp, host of the RT America news show *Redacted Tonight*, Occupy "had massive implications and impacts that are still rippling across America and across the world," most importantly because "it changed the way our culture as a whole speaks about a lot of these issues—the 99 percent, the 1 percent, the ruling elite." These topics "weren't commonplace conversations in America. For the most part you didn't have people standing around the water cooler talking about how rich the tiny percentage at the top are," said Camp, and "that should be the goal of just about any protest movement: to cause a mental awakening and to change the paradigm of thought that is allowable and acceptable in our culture. In that way Occupy was a massive success."

Occupy's populist language gave voice to the sense of outrage that millions felt but had not been able to articulate. As Sarah Jaffe wrote in *Necessary Trouble: Americans in Revolt*, "Messages don't succeed because they say something new and exciting that no one has ever heard before; instead, they succeed because they explain something that people feel but have been at a loss to explain. With the discussion of inequality, the shock, the lack of an explanation for the events of the past few years, finally ended. It was, in a way, like a fog had cleared. Our problem was not simply that we were struggling, but that our struggling benefited someone else." The facts of economic injustice were plain enough to understand; people just needed to hear them spoken in clear words. The slogan *We are the 99 percent* "expressed a solidarity," wrote Jaffe, "that terms like 'middle class' or 'regular people' or 'Main Street' or even 'working class' did not."

Martin Kirk, co-founder of The Rules, an organization that tackled inequality in the developing world, agreed that Occupy drew its raw storytelling strength from its ability to articulate feelings that had long been suppressed. "When we talk about narrative, we're really talking about psychology: the psychology of belief, why people believe what they do," Kirk told me. "What Occupy did—and this was its real power and why it will go down in the history books as a success story—is it galvanized opinion around a certain set of beliefs." Kirk, who participated in Occupy London, recalled being stunned that "within two days, Occupy had something like eighty percent brand recognition in the U.K. It was unfeasibly quick, and why did it spread so quick? It didn't teach anybody anything at a fundamental level that they didn't already know," he said. "The reason is because people's minds were ready and open for it. They were already thinking about all those memes and people said, 'Got it—that's what I think, it's an expression of what I already know and what feels true to me,' and that galvanized a political consciousness around a radical proposal, which was radical in the mainstream world of politics but to the population at large it wasn't radical at all: it was common sense."

Following the movement's short-lived experience of the encampments, most media and observers focused on what Occupy had failed to achieve politically as a movement. The irony, Kirk added, was "it achieved an astonishing feat that ad agencies spend billions of dollars each year trying to achieve in terms of its communication power. You can hear the echoes of Occupy in everything people say—the whole concept of rethinking the economic system, not just replacing a policy or two." Tapping into growing doubts about the basic merits of capitalism, "Occupy said the battle isn't between this person and that person horizontally: it's between the rich at the top and the rest of us. It's a mythic, age-old struggle that we know in our souls, but it was also one that had no modern expression," said Kirk. "Occupy said we need new rules of the game, and it exposed that this opinion is pervasive around the world—and that everybody knows it."

AMERICA'S LONG DEBATE ABOUT THE RICH AND WHAT TO DO WITH THEM

TO UNDERSTAND OCCUPY WALL STREET'S IMPACT ON THE ECO-nomic psyche of the nation, it helps to look back to the Progressive Era of the early 1900s. At the height of the Gilded Age, in the 1890s, the top 10 percent of American households owned more than 70 percent of the nation's wealth. Robber barons led by Andrew Carnegie, J. P. Morgan, John D. Rockefeller and Cornelius Vanderbilt had amassed a grossly disproportionate share of the riches while the great mass of people remained mired in poverty after the depression of 1893. At the prodding of muckraking journalists and progressive politicians, President Theodore Roosevelt backed the passage of the country's first antitrust laws, breaking up the big oil and railroad monopolies that had operated unregulated and unfettered in the decades since the Civil War.

Roosevelt's efforts to constrain the excesses of the titans of industry were an important, if modest, starting point in addressing the problem of economic inequality. But others, such as Eugene V. Debs, wanted to go beyond reform to a worker's revolution, to an economy structured in the interests of the many, not the few. To socialism. In his 1907 retirement speech from the *St. Louis Post-Dispatch*, the publisher Joseph Pulitzer famously urged Americans to take on "predatory plutocracy or predatory poverty," which he saw as inextricably entwined. Unless America could level up the bottom to improve the lives of the country's poorest, and level down the top to reduce the concentration of extreme wealth, the founders' dream of creating a fair and prosperous society would falter. "There was this widespread sense that we couldn't just attack poverty—we needed to attack the concentration of wealth as well," said labor journalist Sam Pizzigati, author of *The Rich Don't Always Win: The Forgotten Triumph over Plutocracy That Created the American Middle Class, 1900–1970*, "and unless we did both—leveled the bottom and top at the same time—we were going to fail."

The Progressive Era produced significant gains for working Americans, from election reforms to the women's right to vote. In 1913, Congress and the states ratified the Sixteenth Amendment, which created the federal income tax. By 1917, the top marginal tax rate for the wealthiest jumped from 7 percent to 67 percent, making America's the most progressive taxation system on either side of the Atlantic. "At that point, no other country on the planet taxed the affluent so heavily," wrote Emmanuel Saez and Gabriel Zucman in *The Triumph of Injustice: How the Rich Dodge Taxes and How to Make Them Pay*. In 1918, President Woodrow Wilson spearheaded a profit tax on corporations to help the war effort, taxing "abnormal profits" beyond 8 percent as high as 80 percent. His administration levied a new estate tax of 20 percent on the wealthiest families. It also passed the Clayton Anti-Trust Act and the eight-hour day for railroad workers, which led to the eight-hour day for all industrial workers.

In 1929, the Roaring Twenties came to a screeching halt with the Wall Street Crash, sending the economy into a decade-long tailspin. With one in four out of work, the plight of the people became so desperate that it threatened the survival of the republic. The scale of human suffering experienced in the Great Depression brought about a change in the national consciousness. In the words of economist Richard Wolff, author of *Democracy at Work: A Cure for Capitalism* and host of the national radio show *Economic Update*, "No family escaped [the Depression], every family had a father or uncle or cousin affected, who used up savings, who leaned on family, and everybody was immediately and profoundly touched in a negative way so that you had a remarkable upsurge" in political and social agitation. Wolff said, "Americans were angry, they were bitter and they didn't take it lying down, so they did something extraordinary: they decided to join labor unions."

The 1930s would represent a high point for organized labor. The Congress of Industrial Organizations mobilized millions of unskilled and semi-skilled workers, from auto to steel to chemicals, and in its drive to "organize the unorganized," the CIO led the most dynamic chapter of popular economic resistance the country had ever seen. According to Wolff, "there was never anything like it before, and there's been nothing like it since," as workers rushed to join the movement. The union—which was prepared to form an alliance with the American Communist and Socialist parties—took workers' demands to President Franklin Delano Roosevelt. In Wolff's depiction of the historic encounter, "They went to Roosevelt and politely told him, 'We all voted for you and you've got to help us in this Depression. Capitalism has collapsed and if you don't do something you won't be president much longer, because we represent millions and millions.'" Heeding the message, Roosevelt pressured the country's wealthiest individuals and corporations to provide the financial support needed to sustain the people through a time of prolonged hardship. The potential alternative, he warned them, was to face a revolution. His proposal split the moneyed power brokers, half in his favor, half advocating a strong dose of repression. In the end, Roosevelt got the financial backing he needed to begin repurposing the federal government to serve the economic needs of working people.

Applying a Keynesian approach that stimulated growth through government spending, Roosevelt created the Social Security system, the unemployment compensation system, a public pension program, a federal minimum wage and a jobs program that put fifteen million Americans to work between 1934 and 1941. He did it by taxing corporations and the rich at vastly higher rates than they are taxed today. In 1936, his administration increased the top marginal income tax rate to 79 percent; it rose to 81 percent by 1940, and when Roosevelt addressed Congress at the height of World War II, he delivered a frank message about inequality: "Discrepancies between low personal incomes and very high personal incomes should be lessened, and I therefore believe that in time of this grave national danger, when all excess income should go to win the war, no American citizen ought to have a net income, after he has paid his taxes, of more than $25,000 a year" (a bit over $1 million today). Congress and FDR settled on a top marginal income tax rate of 94 percent in 1944. The elites' share of national wealth dropped sharply as a result, and critical social programs laid a foundation for the modern American middle class. "A politician proved that you can tax the rich and tax the corporations and use the money to improve the lives of average Americans, both middle class and poor," said Wolff, "and here's the result: the politician was reelected three times and he was and remains the most popular president in the country."

Under Republican president Dwight D. Eisenhower, America kept the top income tax rate at 91 percent on incomes over $400,000, while the average overall tax rate for the rich remained around 55 percent. Corporate profits, taxed at about 50 percent from the 1950s into the early 1960s, generated a large share of Washington's revenue. As Saez and Zucman reported of the period, "For any dollar of profit made in America, half went straight to government." The tax structure contributed to a massive leveling off of inequality in the postwar years, as "we went from being a country that was majority poor to the first nation in the world that had a mass middle class," said Pizzigati.

The rich fought back, and in their efforts to undo Roosevelt's New Deal programs they achieved some success. But a number of the most important programs survived, among them the Federal Deposit Insurance Corporation, the Securities and Exchange Commission, the National Labor Relations Board, the Social Security Administration, and the Tennessee Valley Authority. Meanwhile, the anti-communist fervor of the Cold War and Joseph McCarthy's red-baiting witch hunts in the Senate, demonizing left-leaning citizens and politicians as communist sympathizers and disloyal Americans, all but silenced those who would speak for the working classes. During that era, Pizzigati added, "if you talked about soaking the rich, you suddenly became suspect, a subversive. There was a real change in the public discourse."

The backlash against any talk of socialism left the field of economics open to free-market thinkers of the Chicago school of economics, disciples of Milton Friedman and Friedrich Hayek. Their influence allowed them to reshape the way Americans viewed the economic system. "A society that puts equality before freedom will get neither," Friedman famously said. Sixty years later, we see what freedom without an emphasis on equality has led to. The less government intrusion in the workings of the market, the neoliberals claimed, the fairer the outcome would be for both worker and employer. That theory has not stood the test of time, the reality being exactly the opposite. In the early sixties Americans embraced John F. Kennedy's maxim, "a rising tide lifts all boats." In 1963, Kennedy proposed cutting the top marginal income tax rate from 91 to 65 percent; the measure that passed under Lyndon Johnson as the Revenue Act of 1964 reduced the top marginal rate to 70 percent.

The next decade saw the onset of privatizations, further tax cuts and increased fealty to the corporate bottom line. By the 1980s, the 1 percent still garnered only about 10 percent of America's total pre-tax income until Ronald Reagan eviscerated public spending, crushed labor unions, deregulated industry and turned the free-market global economy into a playground for the rich.

Tax shelters and stock buybacks became the hallmarks of the era, as the number of American billionaires rose to eighteen. In 1986, supported by Democratic senators including Joe Biden, Al Gore, John Kerry and Ted Kennedy, Reagan signed into law the Tax Reform Act, which slashed wealthy America's income tax rate to 28 percent, the lowest level in the industrialized world.

That bill, more than any other piece of legislation, was responsible for the widening of the income gap in America. Quintile by quintile, one can chart the movement of the national income from people lower down the ladder to those higher up. The top 20 percent prospered under Reagan, leaving the rest treading water or falling further behind. Reagan's tax cuts led directly to Bill Clinton's neoliberal reconfiguration of the Democratic Party—one that, like the Republican Party, served the interests of Wall Street, not Main Street. Clinton created the most jobs of any president in the last forty years and oversaw America's greatest economic expansion as the country basked in the post-Soviet flush of globalization. He presided over deficit cuts that balanced the budget while gutting the federal welfare system and social spending programs. Although he provided some measure of fiscal relief for the working poor, the people Clinton was most attuned to were the oligarchs-in-waiting on Wall Street.

"This new narrative of 'Don't look at the rich, let's just concentrate on lifting up the poor' became the dominant narrative of the Democratic Party," Pizzigati told me. "For Clinton the message was 'Don't worry about the penthouse—we need to help people in the basement, and if you talk about what's happening in the penthouse you're just creating a distraction from the real task at hand.'" Clinton left Reagan's basic trickle-down economic model intact even as he raised the top marginal income tax to just under 40 percent. For the New Democrats on Wall Street, if the rich got richer it was fine so long as everyone was better off. "Where before we talked about leveling up and leveling down as two sides of the same coin, now people in the U.S. who considered themselves liberal started talking about economic growth," Pizzigati said. "It didn't matter so much how the pie was divided—what counted was growing that pie, and if you grew that pie, everyone could have a bigger piece even if the pie was divided unequally." Clinton's decade of triangulation as a skillful centrist enabled Democrats to claim to represent the interest of working people while their true allegiance was to the moneyed class.

President George W. Bush will be best remembered for his legacy of military destruction abroad and economic destruction at home. But he also presided over two rounds of extreme tax cuts for the super wealthy—dubiously called the Economic Growth and Tax Relief Reconciliation Act, signed in 2001, and the Jobs and Growth Tax Relief Reconciliation Act, signed in 2003—which gifted an average of more than half a million dollars each year to the top 1 percent over eight years, and increased wealthy Americans' annual after-tax income more than 5 percent. As the Center on Budget and Policy Priorities reported, the Bush tax cuts, contrary to Republican promises, "did not improve economic growth or pay for themselves, but instead ballooned deficits and debt and contributed to a rise in income inequality."

With the housing market destroyed, and the American and world economy in free fall after the financial collapse of 2008, Barack Obama was elected president on a promise to transform the economy and put the needs of a new generation first. But it didn't work out that way. Obama proceeded to bail out the financial class, showering Wall Street institutions with hundreds of billions in taxpayer dollars while offering nothing to the millions of Americans who had lost homes, savings and pensions. Following the Clintonian model, Obama engaged in futile debates with stonewalling Republicans over deficits and stimulus spending while glossing over the fraudulent actions of the corporate class that had led to the economic meltdown. In neglecting the millions devastated by the Wall Street debacle, Obama paved the way for Occupy. His failure to respond would be their call to action.

"So that's where we were early in the twenty-first century, and here comes Occupy, which says the reverse: it says we have to worry about the 1 percent and we can't have a decent society as long as this 1 percent is gaining in wealth and power in the United States. Occupy essentially dethroned the narrative that took hold in the second half of the twentieth century," said Pizzigati. As a result, "the trope of the 1 percent has now become a standard part of American political discourse and that, to me, is a fantastically important achievement. The key legacy of Occupy is that it fundamentally changed the narrative around the economy and equality: we're having the debate now that we should have had thirty years ago, and what you see now are people who are working on behalf of those at the bottom of our economic order, and tying their fate to the concentration of wealth and income at the top."

For Maurice Mitchell, national director of the Working Families Party, Occupy's ascent came at the moment when the neoliberal model of economic growth was collapsing, yet no one dared to admit it. Even in the depths of the Great Recession, as millions of jobs were being shed and livelihoods ruined, the talk in Washington still centered around budget deficits and belt-tightening policies. "Neoliberalism was common sense. I remember distinctly before Occupy how President Obama was big on austerity—like *big* on austerity," said Mitchell, who recalled the Bowles-Simpson bipartisan commission that Obama assembled to deal with the economic fallout. "It was supposed to be this thoughtful, even-handed commission and [instead] it was far right austerity that talked about cutting entitlements and created this narrative that 'serious people,' the adults in the room, were willing to do the politically challenging work that involved cuts." The conversations were mirrored on both sides of the Atlantic as lawmakers from Brussels to Washington remained unwilling to budge on spending. "In the U.S. and Europe, all of the elites, the Davos crowd—everybody was about austerity," Mitchell told me. "And then Occupy happened and everybody was about income inequality. The logic shifted, the debate shifted."

At their best, social movements "surface contradictions that have been baked into our system but have become so commonplace that we're no longer able to see them. They render visible the invisible and pose questions that for whatever reason have become unanswerable," Mitchell added. "Occupy didn't come out of nowhere. It was a grassroots and people-centered response to the neoliberal logic that had re-hardwired the thinking of political and economic elites everywhere." By overturning basic assumptions about the ways the economic system was supposed to work, Occupy "dealt a serious blow to austerity," sparking a debate that Americans were finally ready to have.

FLIPPING THE AXIS, BREAKING THE TABOO: CONFRONTING CAPITALISM

IN REFRAMING THE SOCIOECONOMIC PARADIGM AS A STRUGGLE BE-tween the 99 and the 1 percent, the Occupy movement flipped the economic debate on its side. Americans tended to see themselves somewhere between liberal and conservative on a left-right ideological spectrum. This horizontal axis served an important function, for the ruling class especially, because it made it appear as though we were all in the same boat: our views may differ by issue, but in the end we all inhabited the same basic plane of representative democracy. Occupy said the opposite. By putting inequality at the center of its worldview, the movement flipped the economic-political debate on end, turning the horizontal axis into a vertical one. Suddenly, instead of two poles of left and right, Americans saw themselves between two poles of top—the 1 percent—and bottom, the 99 percent.

"The left-right axis was completely inadequate to discuss the issues that Occupy raised," said Marc Armstrong, co-founder of the Public Banking Institute, a non-profit working to establish publicly owned banks at the city and state level. Occupy's resounding message was to say, "We're not all in the same boat, we're not on equal footing, we're being economically targeted and it's the 1 percent who are able to direct the economy by directing politicians and policies to their benefit, not the benefit of the 99 percent." Awakened by the uprising on Wall Street, Americans across the political spectrum agreed that they had stopped sharing in the rewards of the economy, and were getting the shaft at the expense of those at the very top. "This major assumption that we're all on the same playing field was thrown out the window with Occupy," which provided "a top-down perspective on how the upper classes exploited those below them in the economic system," Armstrong told me. "Occupy opened the door. Talking about economic injustice and classism is the new frame of reference, and all these things are being discussed now."

In 2016, Donald Trump's right-wing populism played on white working-class grievance, scapegoating liberal bicoastal elites—in Washington, in academia, in the "fake news" media—while Bernie Sanders castigated the billionaire class from the populist left. Both stressed a top-down measure of one's economic standing in society, a perspective that Occupy introduced and one that is clearly not going away. Even contentious social issues, among them abortion, guns, LGBTQ rights and immigration, reflect the influence of Occupy's emphasis on a vertical, class-conscious measure of wealth concentration and inequality. In the view of Leah Hunt-Hendrix, an Occupy Wall Street organizer who founded the activism donor network Solidaire, "In gun control conversations people are asking who's profiting, looking at the gun lobby and the manufacturers. Or in the opioid epidemic, a [corporate] family is making money while everyone is getting addicted and dying." To Hunt-Hendrix, "Occupy helped orient people toward thinking about who profits. Its focus on inequality, the 1 percent and corporate power really located what the problem is, and that we have a common enemy."

Occupy Wall Street's message even found support among conservatives. "Before it was Democrats versus Republicans, and Occupy reframed it so we're talking about the vast majority of people versus the tiny elite," said the journalist J. A. Myerson. "If politics is about which team you're on and which team you see yourselves opposing, the reintroduction of class consciousness, which hadn't really been talked about for eighty years, since the thirties, was a pivotal contribution. The public consciousness around the 99 percent and the 1 percent is an influence that can't be overstated." Michael A. Gould-Wartofsky, author of *The Occupiers: The Making of the 99 Percent Movement*, also remarked on the class unity that protesters forged, through "the tales they told of lives lived on the edge, amid unstable incomes, unpayable debts, and unaffordable public goods, such as housing, health care, and education ... the Great Recession, after all, had narrowed the gulf between middle class, the working class, the poor and the near-poor, convincing many that they had more in common with each other than they did with those at the top, and creating the conditions for a cross-class alliance of historic proportions."

The Occupy movement embodied the even more subversive concept—which no mainstream voices since the Roosevelt era had had the temerity to suggest—that capitalism is broken. According to Richard Wolff, from the onset of the Cold War, "raising systemic objections to capitalism was to commit suicide: it was the height of dangerous, inappropriate behavior." Occupy's declaration of under-regulated capitalism and the greed of the 1 percent as the source of America's illness turned the class divide into "a kind of centerpiece slogan" that concentrated on the fundamental injustice of how *the system* works. Occupy broke through a wall of silence.

"The 1 percent versus the 99 percent is a kind of statement that was taboo for decades before Occupy made it appropriate," said Wolff, because "with Occupy it became possible to be articulate and noisy about economics when that was precisely what you couldn't be. One of the important things Occupy did was to crowbar back into the allowable consciousness of the left the vital term of capitalism: to name the system that is the problem. Granted, it's an abstraction, a summary term, but it's precisely because of those qualities that it is absolutely vital to name it—because it allows disparate complaints, criticisms, flaws, weaknesses and injustices to be gathered together and called a name that can become the target for what needs to be changed."

Reclaiming control of language was a first step, and by tapping into the resentment that had been growing for decades, Occupy Wall Street challenged the moral legitimacy of the rich and powerful. "What the vocabulary is—literally what words and concepts are comfortable in people's minds—shapes in part where conversations can go, whether they happen in a big conference or late at night in someone's dorm room or over a sandwich at a workplace," Wolff added. "It's very different when people understand they're up against a system and a structure—not this or that particular event or individual or even enterprise or government agency—but that there's a *system*, a logic, a content to this word. It describes that particular way of organizing society by which we live our lives as the problem, and it means that you can explain to people their own historical moment."

RESHAPING THE ECONOMIC LANDSCAPE

AS AMERICANS RESPONDED TO THE ECONOMIC DEBATE INSPIRED BY Occupy Wall Street, a new generation of economists was compiling data to make sense of the country's alarming shift in wealth and income inequality. It wasn't as if the 1 percent was a new concept; researchers had been studying the impacts of inequality for decades prior to Occupy. But elite financial institutions like the International Monetary Fund and World Economic Forum downplayed its risks—essentially by looking the other way while promoting unfettered economic growth. During what was considered the golden age of capitalism, from the 1950s through the 1970s, the "virtuous cycle" of the free market produced rising wages, which led to rising consumption, which led to increased demand, which led to more investment and greater productivity: the ultimate macroeconomic success. The problem came when workers' salaries stopped rising to meet the rising costs of an affluent society. Wealth became increasingly concentrated in fewer and fewer hands, and debt became a pervasive feature of middle-class American life.

In 1992, toward the end of George H. W. Bush's presidency, the Congressional Budget Office committed additional resources to examining wealth disparities. But even as inequality research evolved during the Clinton years, the widening income gap was largely viewed as a necessary cost of the fruits of globalization—not as a deteriorating condition that required treatment. As economists worked to rationalize growing inequities in the context of globalization, "what they were imparting was that inequality is the result of trends that you could not and would not want to alter—in other words, inequality is the inevitable byproduct of positive dynamics of technology and globalization, and therefore the only appropriate policy is to adjust by giving people more skills," said Lawrence Mishel, former president of the Economic Policy Institute and senior author of *The State of Working America*, published biennially from 1988 to 2012. But "I don't believe inequality has anything to do with automation, and to the extent that it's about globalization, it's not as though globalization just fell from the sky: the shape and pace of globalization has been driven by policy decisions."

The economist Dean Baker—who co-founded and co-directs the Center for Economic and Policy Research, and was credited with being among the first to identify the American housing bubble years before it burst in 2007—told me that when he worked in the nineties alongside Mishel at EPI, measurements for wealth were "top-coded" at $400,000. This meant that whether a person's income was $400,000 or $10 million, it was labeled the same way: it simply exceeded $400,000. But that all started to change in the early 2000s, when a new wave of economists led by Thomas Piketty and Emmanuel Saez began collecting and studying tax returns to get a clearer picture of the wealth gains and the role that the top 1 percent—and even the top .01 percent and higher—were playing in the political economy.

"Other works showed upward distribution of wealth, but Piketty and Saez actually had the tax returns and showed the extent to which the gains for growth had really been concentrated in the 1 percent," said Baker, author of *Rigged: How Globalization and the Rules of the Modern Economy Were Structured to Make the Rich Richer.* Their research was a game-changer, because "they had access to data that showed [the gains] didn't just go to the upper-middle income person above four hundred thousand dollars, but to those with one million and ten million and more high-end people. It showed a vast upward redistribution not only to the top 1 percent but even more to the top tenth of 1 percent." In the words of Mishel, the new economists provided "a very specific take on income inequality, which immediately puts it into a different frame than what a lot of mainstream reporters and economists had done."

As the 2000s wore on, the income gap grew exponentially. In 2007, the 1 percent accounted for nearly a quarter of all U.S. income. By the time of Occupy in 2011, four hundred Americans owned more wealth than the bottom half of the population, and the 1 percent was en route to capturing 95 percent of all income growth during the Great Recession. As more research came to light, rising concern about inequality not only permeated U.S. culture but also became quickly absorbed into the lexicon of the same leading financial institutions—the World Bank and the IMF—that for decades had ignored it. Four months after the protests ignited at Zuccotti Park, the World Economic Forum at Davos placed economic inequality atop its list of global security threats. Suddenly, financial experts were speaking up, lending further credence to the inequality debate. From Federal Reserve Chair Janet Yellen to the Nobel Prize–winning economists Joseph Stiglitz, Paul Krugman and Robert J. Shiller, wealth and income disparity became regular talking points. The wealth gap not only posed a threat to working people, but to the future of democratic society.

The journalist Timothy Noah, author of *The Great Divergence: America's Growing Inequality Crisis and What We Can Do About It*, wrote at the time, "If we don't get growth in income inequality under control, the next generation will see about 25 percent less upward mobility than the current one." The billionaire investor Warren Buffett openly criticized the nation's tax code and came out in favor of higher taxes on the wealthy. President Obama called inequality "the defining challenge of our time" and Pope Francis labeled it "the root of social evil." In the period after Occupy, the conversation around the 99 percent and the 1 percent was so ubiquitous it practically became a cliché.

A universal reference for wealth disparity and its discontents, Occupy radically challenged our national economic myth of America as an egalitarian meritocracy where an enterprising person could rise from the poorest of circumstances. The idea was that if you worked hard, even in the face of enormous disadvantage, you could one day be comfortable and, perhaps, wealthy: today's bricklayer was tomorrow's billionaire. But amid the worst financial crisis since the Great Depression and with inequality reaching heights unseen since the Gilded Age, Occupy dispelled that myth. In effect, we were all now bricklayers constructing palaces for a handful of billionaires. Among the questions that Occupy asked, one struck the deepest chord: Did the sons and daughters of working- and middle-class people truly have the same shot at realizing the American Dream as kids born into privileged families—and was there even such thing as an American Dream any longer? "In the wake of Occupy there was much more interest in pursuing topics having to do with inequality," said Baker, and a focus that received particular attention was the way class status tends to remain fixed over generations. "If we want to think that the U.S. is this opportunity society where people can rise up regardless of what their parents' circumstances are, that's actually not true."

In the wake of Occupy, a majority of Americans across the income spectrum showed consistent support for government action to reduce inequality. "Tax the rich" became a common refrain among voters and many Democratic candidates as poll after poll indicated at least two out of every three Americans—including close to nine in ten Democrats, two-thirds of Independents, and half of Republicans—called for higher taxes on corporations and the wealthy. In some cases local government acted directly to tackle inequality, particularly in the realm of "pay ratio politics"—like Portland, Oregon, which in 2016 established the country's first "inequality tax" forcing corporations to pay a steeply graded business surtax if their CEO-to-worker pay ratio reached 100 to 1 or higher (the higher the ratio, the higher the tax). "The pay ratio movement is growing," said Pizzigati, "and I think that's a direct offshoot of the spirit of Occupy."

An expanding body of economic research has also revealed the clear rationale for an inheritance tax. By 2020, some $84 trillion—more than four-fifths of all U.S. household wealth—was consolidated in the baby boomer generation and those older than them. If passed on to family members as untaxed wealth "transfers," wrote Lily Batchelder for *The New York Times*, "this extraordinary transfer of resources will further cement the economic inequality that plagues the United States because this wealth is tightly concentrated in the hands of a few." America ranks near the bottom among industrial nations in intergenerational economic mobility—the degree to which children can change their economic status from their parents. Forty percent of American household wealth now comes from inheritance (with white households experiencing a twenty-six times greater increase in family wealth from inheritance than Black households). In the same way that Occupy exploded the economic myth that you can make it if you just try, the data on inherited wealth "means that 40 percent of why some Americans are extraordinarily well off has nothing to do with smarts, hard work, frugality, lucky gambles or entrepreneurial ingenuity," wrote Batchelder. "It is simply because they were born to rich parents."

In 2013, the French economist Thomas Piketty published his seminal book, *Capital in the Twenty-First Century*, a defining historical analysis of the long-term financial policies and practices that led to our era of extreme wealth inequality. The economic fortunes of the 1 percent are continuing on an upward trajectory while stagnating for everyone else. At the same time, a U.S. taxation structure that unashamedly tilts the scale heavily in favor of the richest Americans has all but guaranteed a widening of the wealth gap. As Saez and Zucman noted, 2018 marked the first time in history that billionaires paid a lower effective tax rate than the poorest half of Americans.

By the time the coronavirus pandemic derailed the U.S. economy in 2020, the nation's wealth gap had seen its most explosive decade ever. In 2014, forty-three individuals owned more wealth than the bottom half of the population. At the start of 2020, that number shrank to just three men, Jeff Bezos, Bill Gates and Warren Buffett—the country's richest .00000001 percent—worth more than $300 billion combined. The rest of America's six hundred billionaires, otherwise known as the .00000182 percent, collectively grew nearly three-quarters of a trillion dollars richer during the first three years of the Trump presidency. In fact, more than one in ten American billionaires *became* billionaires during that period, thanks partly to Trump and the Republicans' signature trillion-and-a-half-dollar tax giveaway to corporations and the wealthy.

Overall, the 1 percent grew their wealth by 18 percent between 2017 and 2020, adding another $5 trillion to their $30 trillion in value. This was more than ten times what the bottom half of American households added, whose wealth increased during those years by barely half a trillion dollars to total $1.67 trillion. By 2020, the 1 percent took home 20 percent of all of America's pre-tax income, and owned more wealth than 90 percent of the population, making the United States the most unequal among industrialized nations. Covid-19 further exposed the gulf of inequities that divide Americans; between mid-March and mid-May of 2020, a time period in which forty million people lost their jobs and ninety thousand lost their lives, the country's by-then 657 billionaires saw their wealth increase an additional $430 billion, or 15 percent. By the end of 2020, American billionaires' collective wealth rose by $1 trillion to total more than $4 trillion, while the world's four richest men— the new so-called centibillionaires, worth at least $100 billion each, including Bezos, Gates, Elon Musk and Mark Zuckerberg—exceeded $550 billion in value. As Trump's four years of incompetent leadership reached an end, young people in particular had had enough. The system had failed them, and now they sought to lead. In the decade after Occupy Wall Street, they had prepared the ground for a new kind of politics.

ADDICTED TO LIBERTY

OCTOBER 1, 2011

AS SOON AS I MOVED IN I GOT ADDICTED TO LIFE AT LIBERTY
Square. The mornings began early as a gray crust of dawn lit the camp and
the sounds of cleaning men with their heavy power-brush machines woke us.
In those moments I caught a vague sense of what homelessness might feel like:
hips sore from the hard ground, cold, lying on a sheet of cardboard, lifting
myself up with a stagger because I felt light, almost transparent and with an
urgent need to put something in my belly, a warm drink, a piece of bread,
anything. I walked to the kitchen at the center of the park where a few people
talked in hushed voices around yellow coolers, smoking the day's first cigarettes. I pressed the spigot and filled a weak cup of coffee; usually there was
no milk or sugar so I drank it black and sat down on a concrete bench as the
sky lightened and morning emerged into clarity. Soon people on their way to
work began filtering through the camp: women in suits and heels, men with
briefcases and ties. They crossed the square in quick steps, their eyes darting

from side to side, their mouths twisted into a grimace as they stepped over sleeping bodies and navigated around bags and tarps, carving a narrow channel through the encampment that had become a part of their city's landscape.

I got addicted to Liberty because after the voices stirred and the blankets were folded, rested figures would rise to their feet and an excitement filled the camp. The media center would spring to life as people plugged in and began writing, streaming, connecting. Bagels arrived, the sun appeared, more coffee and cigarettes and greetings around a park that was now in full bustle, and after a time I would hear the staccato of a drum: the signal that it was time to march! I got the bug for marching at Occupy Wall Street. We marched in the mornings and in the afternoons and sometimes we marched in the nights because marching was our job. It was our recreation, and as disheveled as we looked in our unwashed shirts and trousers, as disruptive as we might have seemed to those stepping into another day of New York City finance, for us the march on Wall Street was the most sensible thing we could be doing, which is why hundreds of us each day were doing it: walking, dancing, singing the same sensible song, *All day, all week, Occupy Wall Street!* By a quarter to nine the drumbeat echoed across Broadway, reverberating off the tall stone-and-glass buildings that walled the camp; flags and painted signs filled the air as late sleepers continued to rise, stretch, dust themselves off and fold up their gear. We stood like a semi-woken army as the chants grew louder: *The banks got bailed out, we got sold out!* Finally someone would start the slow procession around the square as we scooped up more signs off the cement and rousted those who still lay asleep until, fifteen minutes before the opening bell, our ranks would descend on Wall Street and the barricaded stock exchange as the roar filled lower Manhattan: *We are the 99 percent!*

I got addicted to Liberty because time at the park didn't look like time outside the park. Inside the park—inside the movement—time expanded. It became elastic, something you could stretch and bend as the minutes grew elongated and the hours appeared endless: interminable, hopeful, expectant hours that seemed to contain a surplus of time because we had lost ourselves in the sea of encounters. If we weren't marching we were speaking to one another, we were discussing, proposing, sharing, planning, rehearsing and we weren't just talking, we were listening, above all listening because those who came to Occupy Wall Street had so much to say. Like a thousand militant orators they came armed with an arsenal of ideas, opinions, strategies and beliefs about how to make an unfair economy fairer and an unaccountable politics more accountable. The dialogue in the park was deliberate: it was constant and consuming and the more time you spent there talking and participating, the more clearly you saw yourself in others and saw others in yourself. Most of us agreed on the basic facts: that inequalities of wealth and opportunity had grown too great, executives too greedy, banks and corporations too powerful and the laws to restrain them too impotent in a democracy too corrupt, which was why we had come from far and wide to make our voices heard.

At Liberty no one knew or cared or asked where you were from or what you did before you came to Occupy—the question was "What do we do now that we are here?" We jumped feet first into the movement of our time and suddenly we were eating and sleeping alongside people we didn't know a week or a day or even an hour ago; people we were nonetheless ready to give to and sacrifice for and go to jail with, if necessary. Because something more powerful than ourselves—an idea, a resolve, the desire for justice—bonded us together. At Liberty we bartered in ideas, conversation became the currency and it didn't matter what work you did or didn't do, which school you had or had not attended, which family or lifestyle or age or language or religion or résumé or talents you possessed—not even your name, none of it meant a thing. No one knew how far the movement would carry; we couldn't tell if we were in a marathon or a sprint so we prepared for a marathon but ran it like a sprint. We weren't going through the motions any longer, we weren't deferring or preparing for some future point: the zen of Occupy Wall Street was its immediacy. What mattered was that you had showed up: you had come to *say* something and *do* something. Suddenly this single act—participation—became the most important act you had ever committed.

But finally I became addicted to Liberty because of the sublime intoxication of *being there*. During the explosive early weeks of Occupy Wall Street, Zuccotti Park wasn't just a place you wanted to be—it was the only place you *could* be. Every moment away from Liberty was a moment you were missing a piece of history being written. Occupier Josephine Ferorelli referred to "this kind of uncorked exuberance, this intoxicating feeling of possibility" that came with life at the park. As the journalist and Occupy activist J. A. Myerson said: "It was totally magical. In a really internal sense, in my nerves and joints, it just felt different to cross that threshold into Liberty Plaza. It felt like liberty." For those inside the park, life on the outside appeared frozen in time, stuck in some immovable past that hadn't yet caught up with the rapidly advancing future. That's why in those weeks friends stopped talking to friends outside the movement; conversations became empty, pointless almost, between people within the occupation and people without. A spirit of tribalism was taking over, it was primal and it was swallowing us whole, addicting us in some instinctual desire to never not *be there*. Call it obsession, call it provocation: the movement was a romance—a sweet elixir, a potent drug—because while the world beyond Occupy was resigned to being what it was, at Liberty we committed to building what wasn't. In the moments when I would leave the square I felt I carried the movement wherever I went. I glowed with it. We were all glowing, tramping around the city radiating the park's pulse. The spirit of Occupy was infectious, it was something you could feel and you could see in your neighbor's eyes, which burned with new intensity and focus: the uncontrollable pace of our democratic awakening.

IN FACT, THIS WASN'T THE FIRST TIME I HAD STEPPED INTO A POP-ular uprising. In April 2000, I was teaching English in Cochabamba, the fourth largest city in Bolivia, when the price of water suddenly tripled for people whose average monthly salary was $100. The Bolivian government had sold the city's state-run water company to Bechtel Corporation, headquartered at the time in San Francisco, and the economic impacts of the privatization set off what came to be known as la Guerra del Agua—the Cochabamba Water War. Reporting for the *Bolivian Times*, a weekly English-language newspaper published in the capital, La Paz, I watched as *campesinos* by the tens of thousands marched in from the countryside and set up road blockades around the city using logs, refrigerators, scrap heaps and tires set on fire. Day after day, police launched tear gas and engaged in cat-and-mouse street battles with the surging crowds of students, teachers, doctors, house cleaners, unionists and farmers who were pushing their way into the tree-lined central square where the rebellion's leaders delivered passionate speeches from the balcony tops. On three occasions I interviewed Evo Morales, the leader of a union federation of coca growers who, in 2005, would be elected Bolivia's first Indigenous president. During the weeklong revolt for control of Cochabamba's water, the country's former dictator turned president, Hugo Banzer, sent in paramilitary forces and declared a state of emergency; one teenager was shot dead and many more people injured. An eventual truce negotiated between the protesters and the government succeeded in expelling the foreign-owned water company from Bolivia—a rare win for the Global South in the era of globalization, and my first experience as a journalist telling people's story as they challenged corporate power.

More than a decade later, when I came to Occupy Wall Street, I quickly realized how my skills could serve the movement. I wasn't an organizer. I didn't lead meetings or plan actions or even communicate particularly well in the anarchist-style working groups. But I could write and edit and help shape the language of the 99 percent, articulating to the public what we were doing and why we were doing it. So on the late September night after the general assembly approved by consensus the final wording of the Declaration of the Occupation, I rode the 1 train to Fourteenth Street and hurried through the West Village to the Brecht Forum. Cars roared down the West Side Highway along the Hudson and a warm breeze was blowing as I knocked on the rusted iron door. A woman opened and ushered me inside to a book- and poster-filled office space where a half dozen activists sat cramped between desks and couches, busy putting together the inaugural issue of *The Occupied Wall Street Journal*. A Kickstarter campaign had raised $75,000 for the project and the deadline with the union printers was the next day. One of the editors handed me a stack of copy and told me each story needed to be cleaned up and shortened, so I took the pages and went to work.

I had no idea when I showed up at Zuccotti Park that the experience would reshape my trajectory as a journalist—forcing me to decide whether to report on the movement from the outside looking in or from the inside out. Several packs of cigarettes later, after uninterrupted hours of collectively reworking and reediting that carried past dawn and extended to noon the next day, my choice was an easy one: I was now a writer for, not about, the revolution on Wall Street. With the newspaper's maiden edition put to bed, I stumbled out of the Brecht Forum, bleary-eyed and euphoric. I wandered downtown through the midday light of Greenwich Village. I needed to bathe and I needed sleep. I phoned a woman named Arlene whom I'd met in the park and who invited me to her Lower East Side apartment. A homemade meal, my first shower in five days, my first rest in a bed—Arlene was a lifesaver. I closed my eyes and when I awoke it was the next morning, Saturday, October 1, the day that Occupy Wall Street announced itself to the world.

It happened out over the East River under a gray leaden sky. We marched by the thousands across the Brooklyn Bridge. The procession had started in Zuccotti Park, where that morning the first edition of the *Journal* had shown up in tall stacks bound in plastic ties, dumped from a van on the southwest corner of the square. Soon the sea of newsprint was everywhere along with signs and banners and musical instruments and an array of creative props that people carried as they made their way in wide, sprawling columns up Broadway toward the bridge. The air was festive, fearless: we felt like an unstoppable mass and everything seemed possible on the two-week anniversary of the movement. As we approached City Hall, the chants grew louder: "*We are the 99 percent!*" "*Whose streets? Our streets!*" We aimed to seize another borough—

the city's great southern flank, Brooklyn—but when we turned onto the bridge the march divided: half of us remained on the upper portion for pedestrians while the other half, tacitly steered by a squad of white-shirt police officers, flooded the roadway below. A steady rhythm of drums and cheers reverberated across the occupied bridge and it seemed in those liberated moments as though our jubilant, peaceful tide might flow on forever. Then we hit a roadblock.

Halfway across, a phalanx of police vans with flashing lights raced at us. They trapped the marchers on the lower half of the bridge; unable to proceed, people sat in the road and the arrests commenced. I climbed up onto an iron beam to gaze down on our fellow protesters who, one after another, had their hands zip-tied and were led away to the wagons. Many let their bodies go limp, forcing groups of cops to drag them away. "What's your name—say your name!" people shouted from the deck, recording the identities of those who were carted off. Jeers, screams, laughter, outrage, cameras flashing, video rolling, megaphones blaring. "*Let us march!*" the cry arose from the thousands stranded out above the dark water. "*The whole world is watching!*" And in fact, it was. The melee caused by more than seven hundred arrests that day on the Brooklyn Bridge dwarfed any previous altercation between protesters and police. Media coverage swept the planet. It was the defining moment that made Occupy a household name. American law and order had asserted itself in a new way—revealing to the world that in the city anchored by Wall Street capitalism, disruptive peaceful dissent would be suppressed. But as the journalist Chris Hedges wrote in our next Saturday's edition of the *Journal*:

Those who worship money believe their buckets of cash, like the $4.6 million J.P. Morgan Chase gave last week to the New York City Police Foundation, can buy them perpetual power and security ... What the elites fail to realize is that rebellion will not stop until the corporate state is extinguished. It will not stop until the corporate abuse of the poor, the working class, the elderly, the sick, children, those being slaughtered in our imperial wars and tortured in our black sites, stops. It will not stop until foreclosures and bank repossessions stop. It will not stop until students no longer have to go into massive debt to be educated, and families no longer have to plunge into bankruptcy to pay medical bills. It will not stop until the corporate destruction of the ecosystem stops, and our relationships with each other and the planet are radically reconfigured.

3

OCCUPY POLITICS

THE POLITICAL REVOLUTION

REWRITING THE PLAYBOOK: CHARLES LENCHNER

TWO YEARS BEFORE BERNIE SANDERS LAUNCHED A POLITICAL REVolution that would ignite the progressive movement and remake the Democratic Party, a crack digital organizer named Charles Lenchner and a handful of Occupy Wall Street activists were busy trying to draft Elizabeth Warren to run for president of the United States.

It was 2013, a few months into Barack Obama's second term in office, and Warren had just pulled off an upset victory against Republican incumbent Scott Brown, flipping back to the Democrats the Massachusetts Senate seat that had been held for nearly half a century by Edward Kennedy, who had died of a brain tumor in 2009. A former Harvard law professor and the architect of Obama's Consumer Financial Protection Bureau—the watchdog agency created to tackle abusive corporate practices after the financial meltdown—Warren rode to office on the wave of populist anger spurred by Occupy. She had publicly backed the movement during the height of the protests in October 2011, declaring, "I created much of the intellectual foundation for what they do. I support what they do." Indeed, Warren's campaign, which called for stricter regulations on Wall Street, higher taxes on the rich, and economic justice for underwater homeowners, read like bullet points taken from the Occupy playbook. Unlike the leadership of her party, Warren wasn't pulling any punches. As she said in her speech at the 2012 Democratic Convention: "People feel like the system is rigged against them. And here's the painful part: they're right. Billionaires pay lower tax rates than their secretaries. And Wall Street CEOs, the same ones who wrecked our economy and destroyed millions of jobs, still strut around Congress, no shame, demanding favors, and acting like we should thank them."

Occupy organizers like Lenchner recognized in Warren the movement's natural political heir: a true progressive, the closest thing to an "Occupy candidate" they believed they were going to get, and the best chance to run someone—and better yet, a woman—to the left of Hillary Clinton, the front-runner for the 2016 nomination. "Among many Occupiers there was a discussion, 'What are progressives going to do about the coronation of Hillary as the Democratic nominee?'" said Lenchner. The activists from Zuccotti Park wanted a champion, "someone who confronted the bankers and could be the candidate for people angry at Wall Street," so when he and a small crew started the group Ready for Warren, it was Occupy's way of saying: Bring it on, Liz, the people are with you.

But at this early stage of her career, Warren wasn't ready for a run at the presidency. Instead she channeled her energy in more productive ways and quickly became the most exciting, passionate and articulate Democratic senator the chamber had seen in years. Seizing the party's progressive mantle, Warren dispensed with niceties as she castigated Wall Street CEOs and ridiculed their federal regulatory buddies in Senate hearings. An expert in consumer debt and bankruptcy law, Warren spent her first year in Congress introducing a raft of bills aimed at reversing economic inequality. Significant was her Bank on Students Emergency Loan Refinancing Act, which would let students refinance their college loans at the same 3.86 percent federal rate that the banks paid, as opposed to the 6 or 7 percent rate students were being charged.

Warren's more sweeping plan—and the one that most clearly invoked Occupy's calls for systemic restructuring—was the 21st Century Glass-Steagall Act, which sought to separate investment banking from commercial banking in the way that had successfully been done from 1933 until 1999, when Bill Clinton at the behest of Citigroup and the banking lobby repealed the law. Warren inspired millions with her aggressive talk about closing the revolving door between Wall Street and Washington and imposing a lifetime ban on members of Congress becoming lobbyists. In the hopeful season of 2013, the freshman senator from Massachusetts gave fresh direction to the party as she became its new face.

To Lenchner and his post-Occupy team, it didn't matter that Warren ignored their efforts to draft her as a presidential candidate: they were determined to get out their message of economic justice any way they could. Lenchner managed the Ready for Warren Facebook page, and he recalled the night when Warren came to New York for a speaking engagement and their group got press attention for a huge banner they unfurled that read "Run, Liz, Run!" Warren still wasn't ready, but they persisted. "There were no other people doing this at the time," he said, so the next year the group launched Ready for Warren chapters across different states. They were about to create a tax-exempt super PAC to begin fundraising for Warren when her attorney released a public cease and desist letter, warning them that any PAC that used her name would be in violation of federal restrictions. The Occupy crowd took it as a slap in the face. "It's not as though Warren was flattered by us. Her people saw us as an irritant," Lenchner told me.

By late 2014, bigger liberal organizations like Move On and Democracy for America introduced a rival campaign to draft Warren, and Lenchner's squad saw it as the right time to start making new plans. They consulted with the sixty thousand people on their Occupy-generated email list, asking Warren supporters who they would choose as an alternative candidate. A resounding majority answered with the simple words: "Support Bernie." A perennial outsider, Vermont's independent senator Bernie Sanders had made no indication that he was considering a run, much less on the Democratic Party ticket. But Sanders was now the clear Occupy favorite, so in the winter of 2015, Lenchner and his cohort began to shift their digital organization to a new site. In a fateful pivot that would help resurrect progressive politics and rebuild one of America's two major parties, "we had to create a new identity, and that was the birth of People for Bernie."

FOR YEARS, LENCHNER HAD BEEN AN ACTIVIST ON THE LEFT, DO-ing online politics from the time online politics existed. Born in 1969 in Pittsburgh to a father of East European Jewish descent and a Presbyterian mother who converted to Judaism, Lenchner moved at the age of six to Israel, where he found his political compass. "I grew up in a country that actually had a left, a real left, which didn't have to hide itself behind something else," he said. In adolescence he started hanging out with radicals in Tel Aviv and by the eleventh grade had joined the Young Communist League, the official youth movement of the Israeli Communist Party. During high school, Lenchner organized a group of students who refused to do their military service in the occupied territories. He was drafted into the army in 1987, before the First Intifada, and became a refusenik who spent two months in jail and solitary confinement before the military kicked him out. "I had a really terrible year. I performed almost no useful labor in any place I was stationed or imprisoned. When you say no to the officer, there are consequences that are very well known and predictable. Israel was such a challenging place to exist as someone with my kind of politics."

Lenchner returned to the United States to attend the University of Massachusetts Amherst where he earned a degree in Middle Eastern studies. He married a German woman, had a child and later returned to Israel, working at the International Center for Peace in the Middle East. He then founded a Palestinian human rights organization and became the executive director of Green Action, which he likened to "a super militant Sierra Club" whose members carried out direct actions like chaining themselves to construction equipment, and mobilized "middle-class moms who were worried about pollution from a smokestack near their school." He also started a club called the Left Bank that combined theater, punk rock and activism to shine a light on Israeli's actions in the occupied territories. Meanwhile, Lenchner had his eye on the burgeoning anti-globalization movement, and during the protests against the World Trade Organization that culminated with the Battle in Seattle in 1999, he led solidarity demonstrations outside the U.S. embassy in Tel Aviv. The following summer he helped organize Israel's version of the international Carnival Against Capital, an event that drew inspiration from the Reclaim the Streets movement in England. Using the nascent email and internet technology that had become available, Lenchner built a formidable network of international organizers and activists, and he was soon hired by Friends of the Earth Middle East to open an office in Washington, D.C. There, he continued to work within the Jewish left—he helped start Jews for Peace in Palestine and Israel, which later merged with the non-profit J Street—and organized with the anti-globalization movement until it was disrupted and ultimately consumed by the anti–Iraq War movement starting in 2003.

Charles Lenchner made his entry into U.S. electoral politics in 2004 when he was hired first as an intern and then as the assistant campaign manager for progressive Ohio congressman Dennis Kucinich's long-shot presidential bid. "I had a window onto the whole campaign's operations," he said, and a few years later he moved to New York City to develop his expertise in fundraising, social media and digital politics. He wound up for a time selling organizing software created by Democracy in Action to help non-profits and political groups, and after being let go during the financial crisis, he worked for a year as the digital organizing director for the Working Families Party. Lenchner saw a need to digitally train and retool the labor movement, which hadn't figured out how to organize itself as a powerful collective voice. In 2009, he recruited partners to create Organizing 2.0, a conference that taught online skills and strategies to unions and community organizing groups. He became, as he said, "the digital labor guy."

Lenchner plugged into the beginnings of Occupy Wall Street six weeks before the movement began, showing up at meetings near the Wall Street Bull. There the activists who had organized that summer's Bloombergville encampment to protest New York City budget cuts were plotting their next steps forward. From the outset he had one goal in mind: "Can we use a database to send mass emails to organize people using all the tools we have access to?" At forty-two, Lenchner was older and had vastly more experience than most of the people at Zuccotti Park; a lot of them were feeling out the contours of a social movement for the first time, guided by an ethos that resisted calls for organized structure. As Occupy Wall Street progressed, his ideas gained little traction and Lenchner grew disillusioned by the unfocused direction of the movement. As Lenchner saw it, the Occupy activists wanted to address too many issues at once and overemphasized other people's struggles rather than addressing their own—such as high rents, low wages, burdensome student debt and other impacts from the financial crisis. "One campaign was to prevent the eviction of homeowners in Brooklyn, then it was helping the Teamsters fighting against an employer, then it was Trayvon Martin [the unarmed Black teen who was shot and killed in Florida in 2012]. There was always some more deserving group that needed our energy, our help." To Lenchner, this scattershot kind of activism dispersed the power of the movement and diminished its impact.

"Occupy never decided what *it* wanted: it never said, 'We're fighting for *us*. We're organizing to meet our *own* demands, to fight around our own rights, our own employment, our own student debt.' We kept fighting for other people, putting someone else's struggle as more important than our own," Lenchner added. "Imagine a meeting where everyone comes in broke, hungry, tired, and on the agenda is 'Which other group are we going to try to help today?' I don't believe successful organizing is a thing you do for other people—it's something you do for yourself and the people you're close to: to win things for your own lives. My goal was to build political power to represent the actual individuals that were involved at Occupy. I wanted Occupy to become an organizing group that organized for itself."

But Occupy did not organize for itself. Within less than a year, the movement had largely vanished from public view. And yet the ideas and the individuals that had inspired the movement did not vanish. By the spring of 2015, Lenchner, along with a skilled organizer named Winnie Wong and several other Occupiers, was busy fine-tuning the website that would help launch the Sanders political revolution. Most important, they created hundreds of People for Bernie Facebook accounts that would serve as ready-made landing pages for the diverse constituencies they believed would join the Sanders campaign once he announced his run: Georgia for Bernie, Idaho for Bernie, African Americans for Bernie, Muslims for Bernie, and so on. "We understood how to mobilize the internet," said Lenchner, and "we understood that the internet was the first thing that Bernie had in his favor, the second thing he had in his favor and the third thing he had in his favor: the internet *was* his campaign. We knew that Bernie would catch fire. We were not testing whether what we did would work—we *knew* it would work."

Bernie Sanders hadn't even floated his presidential bid yet, but Lenchner and other progressive insiders had a strong hunch that it was about to happen. For months, People for Bernie tried and failed to communicate with the Sanders team, hoping to share their social media tools and movement know-how to give his candidacy a running start. But "his campaign would not work with us, period," said Lenchner. "They were not responsive, so instead of just not doing it, we said, 'Well, fuck 'em, we're going to do it anyway.'" Working as a guerilla outfit for zero pay, with no donors or any type of "member" structure, the Occupy organizers at People for Bernie contacted their networks of activists around the country to prepare them for Sanders's expected announcement. These were the same people who had spent years in the trenches of digital activism: social media pioneers who helped make Occupy Wall Street a viral movement, who knew how fast a meme traveled, and knew that the moment Sanders declared his candidacy, "there would be a massive pickup of his campaign by many people around the country who wanted to engage. So instead of waiting for the campaign to create house parties, we organized them on our own; instead of waiting for Bernie messaging, we did it on our own. We knew there was dry tinder on the bed of social media and as soon as Bernie lit a fire, it would spread a wildfire. We were like forestry managers who knew exactly how it was supposed to work."

When the seventy-three-year-old senator finally appeared on a lawn outside the Capitol building to announce his presidential candidacy on April 30, 2015, he laid out the themes that would drive his campaign: "Ninety-nine percent of all new income generated in this country is going to the top one percent. How does it happen that the top one percent owns almost as much wealth as the bottom ninety percent? That type of economics is not only immoral, it's not only wrong: it is unsustainable." Sanders told the reporters assembled there, "We can't continue having a nation in which we have the highest rate of childhood poverty of any major nation on Earth at the same time as we're seeing a proliferation of millionaires and billionaires." Calling out the Supreme Court's decision on *Citizens United* that allowed the Koch brothers to spend hundreds of millions of dollars to "buy the candidates of their choice," he said, "the major issue is: How do we create an economy that works for all of our people rather than a small number of billionaires?"

Lenchner felt the tidal wave breaking. On the day Sanders announced his run, somewhat unbelievably, his campaign "didn't have an events tool on their website, they hadn't finished building the website, the entire infrastructure by which a campaign can communicate with supporters was nonexistent—they didn't have staff to send people emails or return phone calls or even answer press calls, so the thing we knew was going to happen, happened," Lenchner said. "Bernie doesn't trust people easily. He wanted to work with the people he's known a very long time and they're the wrong age to be part of any social movement, so by default he had already restricted himself to white people in and around Vermont and D.C. These were not movement people—they definitely weren't from Zuccotti Park—and we knew his campaign would fail when [supporters] showed up. We also knew from our experience at Occupy that there was a way to build a horizontal effort that would engage those people immediately with no delay. In 2015, not a single entity in the U.S. would have known what to do: the only people who would have known what to do were Occupy veterans because we had just come through a massive, grassroots, social media–based movement, so all the tools and experience we had with the growth of Occupy was the set of solutions that we had for the Bernie campaign."

On the very next day—International Workers' Day, May 1, 2015—People for Bernie launched a shiny website and sent out a press release to announce its first action: organizing ninety-nine house parties for Bernie and the 99 percent. "It was about finding a way for people who wanted to make a difference to plug in. People wanted to do something, they wanted to experience being a Bernie supporter through their actions, not their wallets," Lenchner said. People for Bernie instantly started receiving phone calls and emails. In the absence of a nimble Sanders campaign that could respond to the flood of public and press inquiries, Lenchner and his crew filled the void. People for Bernie became the de facto messaging page for hundreds of thousands of volunteers who tuned in and sought to get involved. Their guiding principle was simple and ingenious: access to participation. "The [Sanders] campaign wasn't telling people what to do. On the other hand, we were a wall-less garden and everyone was responded to, because we didn't have to do it ourselves—we just created volunteers."

In a novel exhibit of Occupy-style tactics for the decentralized age, People for Bernie rewrote the playbook of digital electoral politics. Four weeks later when Sanders formally launched his campaign in Burlington, Vermont, on May 26, People for Bernie had populated hundreds of social media accounts and recruited thousands of volunteers who organized two hundred house parties reaching every state—even a house party in Antarctica. This compared with Sanders's own campaign, which didn't list a single house party. "People for Bernie created a decentralized online meme base for Sanders long before he had any real volunteers," said Occupy Wall Street organizer Nicole Carty. Working at the speed that was required for the viral social media campaign to succeed, the group rapidly connected volunteers and became a trusted intermediary between the public and the candidate. According to Lenchner, by the early months of the primary, "if you supported Bernie and wanted to hear from someone about it, you were more likely to hear from us because we were accessible. We trusted the people and told them to do what they thought was right. Someone would write from Tacoma, Washington, and say, 'Do you think we should do this thing?' and we'd say, 'That sounds great! Want to help on that page?' and we'd assign people to be in charge. Then multiply that by ten thousand. All the normal, typical behavior of campaigns wasn't what we were doing. We gave away the keys."

That year, as the national fervor grew for the grandfatherly anti-corporate candidate who stood up to Wall Street greed and Washington corruption, People for Bernie generated billions of engagements by email and social media channels, blowing away all prior presidential campaigns—even Barack Obama's historic run in 2008—with its volunteer numbers both on- and offline. The passion was primarily driven by young people who were "Feeling the Bern," who had endured the disappointments of the Obama era and were galvanized because Sanders spoke directly to them on the issues that mattered most: healthcare for all, debt-free college, solving the climate crisis, raising the minimum wage. Millennial voters mobilized by the internet became the unforeseen X factor of his candidacy. Lenchner said he later learned that Sanders's own people hadn't expected to compete to the end. "Senior staffers and consultants on his campaign thought they would be home by March, that they'd go through a few primaries then call it quits." But it wasn't to be. The more people sought ways to join Sanders's political revolution, the more the organizing power of People for Bernie fueled his rise. "If you were running a Facebook campaign and you could reach a million people, that would be awesome. But we reached tens of millions. If you were Latino and you wanted to organize for Bernie, it was our messaging page that existed."

Ascending from its origins in the Occupy movement, People for Bernie topped one and a half million fans on its Facebook page and generated the early groundswell of support and excitement that helped transform Sanders's candidacy into a populist movement unique in the country's history. The journalist J. A. Myerson called People for Bernie's distributed organizing model the "magical ingredient" of the Sanders campaign because it acted as a sort of funnel capturing the diverse strains of support for Bernie and channeling them into the collective movement. The key, Myerson said, was that the group offered "many different front doors: you can be a yoga teacher for Bernie, a labor activist for Bernie, an undocumented immigrant for Bernie," and it wasn't only on the front end where they provided people an entry point. More crucial was the manner in which People for Bernie handed over the wheel, enabling people everywhere to steer the movement as they saw fit. "As volunteers came in, they would just turn over the passwords to those people, creating a distributed sort of movement driven by these new digital modes of coordination and mutual inspiration."

The Sanders campaign, according to Lenchner, never formally thanked or even acknowledged the organizers of People for Bernie for their role boosting his campaign into the political stratosphere—though gratitude was never what they were looking for. What they wanted were results. "It's like someone saying, 'I'd really like to water your garden,' and you ignore them, then one day you realize that the garden is being watered," he said. People for Bernie transformed U.S. politics by showing that grassroots organizing didn't depend on a top-down structure with gatekeepers and communications directors and messaging specialists. Rather, their strategy was to open the floodgates: to make every potential Sanders supporter a stakeholder and empower millions of people to become personally invested in his campaign. And unlike Occupy Wall Street, Lenchner noted, Bernie knew how to deliver.

"Sanders said, 'Fight for your own interests: *you* need Medicare for All, not *they*, *you* need free college, *you* need debt forgiveness. And as a result he was able to mobilize tens of millions of people, correcting a very basic political mistake by Occupy Wall Street—and making it happen because this old politician was doing politician work." As of 2020, Lenchner was working as the digital director for The Real News Network in Baltimore; his twenty-seven-year-old daughter, amid the coronavirus pandemic and monthslong racial justice protests, was serving as a Sanders delegate at the virtually held Democratic National Convention. Lenchner didn't kid himself about Occupy's influence on Sanders as a person. "There's nothing that Occupy said or did that Bernie needed. He was perfectly formed forty years ago and was doing the exact same stuff since. He knew that to mobilize large numbers of people to change this country they had to be fighting for themselves, not only for others who are more deserving. The evolution of the left in this country was from these self-centered, performative, incoherent politics of Occupy toward an actual, power-building machine doing electoral politics, which was the Bernie campaign."

REBIRTH OF THE AMERICAN LEFT

BY PROVIDING THE POPULIST MESSAGE THAT THRUST ANTI-corporate senators like Elizabeth Warren and Bernie Sanders into the electoral spotlight, Occupy Wall Street arguably did more in six months to move American politics to the left than the Democratic Party was able to do in six decades. Following the New Deal and World War II, America's love affair with capitalism was reborn. Economic growth and prosperity, unimpeded by ideological differences between the two major political parties, flourished under the Eisenhower and Kennedy administrations. It wasn't until President Lyndon Johnson passed the Civil Rights and Voting Rights Acts in the midsixties that Southern Democrats, feeling betrayed and pushed out by the party's pluralist appeal, fled to the Republican Party.

Fueled by rising tensions over the Vietnam War, the conflicts initiated an era of polarization that has intensified ever since. In the decades that followed,

Republicans became the party of white grievance that unified around social and economic issues while Democrats became the party of coalition: African Americans, Latinos, minorities, union workers, the "party of the rest." The party's traditional commitment to "look out for the little guy" hit stumbling blocks in the sixties and seventies as it sought to negotiate a complex, diverse array of interests and voter constituencies. Along the way, both Democrats and Republicans embraced the neoliberal Chicago school–style economics of small government modeled on spending cuts, lower taxes, deregulation and Wall Street–centric policies. The corporate duopoly consolidated its hold during the Reagan years, and by the time Bill Clinton left the White House, Democrats' fealty to unrestrained free-market globalization revealed how far the party had strayed from the moral economic argument and New Deal populism of FDR.

Then, at the dawn of the millennium, cracks in the system began to appear that eroded people's basic trust in the legitimacy of American institutions. As the UC Berkeley historian Adam Hochschild tells it, the "cumulative force" of public anger started with "the way the 2000 election came out—an election basically decided by the Supreme Court—which I think awakened a lot of people to the fact that the court was really not something that was above the law, but was a very political instrument, which in this case decided to hand the election to George W. Bush." A few years later, the launch of the Iraq War, based on false intelligence peddled by the Bush administration and embraced by majorities in both parties, further added to the sense that deception was integral to the workings of the political class in Washington—particularly since "some of the greatest demonstrations in American history preceded that war and protested that war, [yet] we weren't able to stop it and I think that was something that made people angry." Next came the housing crisis and 2008 economic crash, "where it was so evident that the banking and finance industry had sold a terribly destructive bill of goods to the American people. That it had been eased by deregulation under a Democratic administration in the nineties also fed the belief that there was something wrong with the system," Hochschild said.

Obama brought so many young people into the political process, raising a generation's hopes that change was on the way, then failed to deliver on those bold promises. "I would give him credit for inspiring a lot of people to get involved politically. Paradoxically I think it was not dissimilar to the 1960 election of John F. Kennedy, who in many ways was a Cold War liberal—who raised the military budget, who got us deeper into Vietnam—yet nonetheless unleashed a wave of youthful idealism even though there was this disjuncture. And of course Occupy was a manifestation of some of the anger and some of the hope under Obama," Hochschild added. "If I were, fifty years from now, writing a history of the United States in the early part of the century, Occupy would certainly be one of a number of events that signaled a real reawakening of the left in this country. And I think it's very good for people to be reminded of these landmarks, because if there's a way in which we know people have fought these battles of justice in the past, we can be inspired by them, we can take heart in them—we can realize that we've made some steps forward, and we've got to take a lot of steps forward." In political terms, however, economic inequality poses a crisis on a different, more abstract scale than other clearly defined struggles in America's past. "In a way it's an even harder battle than abolition," he told me, "because the abolition of slavery could finally be done by the stroke of a pen: the Emancipation Proclamation. Congress can pass a law and do it. But Congress can't pass a law that suddenly gives everybody equal opportunity economically. That's a much tougher battle."

After decades of failed neoliberalism, the party was finally returning to its liberal populist roots. In the words of Justin Wedes, an early organizer and social media creator at Occupy Wall Street, "Occupy said, 'Actually there is a value set behind the American left and it's rooted in working-class solidarity, in common values of inclusion, of economic equality and fairness'—a value set that had been pandered to by the Democratic Party but not really implemented, so it exposed that real failing." In its place, Occupy "rewrote the rules for how a political party or social movement navigates politics today. In the Obama movement it was clear there was a rising young, multicultural, racially diverse electorate, but it wasn't clear what the ideological leanings were of the movement. But I think Occupy made that clear." As for the progressive voices in Congress, it's not as if they didn't exist prior to Occupy; some people had been saying the right things, the problem was that no one was listening or took them seriously. Radio host Egberto Willies told me, "They had always shut Bernie down. Bernie was a comedy; he was a joke before Occupy. Dennis Kucinich was a joke. Elizabeth Warren would have been a joke. They were right, but they were jokes, because we had the Powell Memo, the CATO Institute, the Heritage Foundation, which had all moved the country to the right. But no longer, because people saw what Occupy was saying made sense. Occupy saved the country, period. Obama was getting rolled. The media was in cahoots with the right wing to give people the impression that Obama was doing full-fledged socialism. Then Occupy defined and showed the problem to the masses: it brought it to the fold, right there up in front of your face. If I look at someone and say, 'Fuck you!' you remember that. Occupy gave you that shock value so that you absorbed the reality. It brought an awareness that stuck."

People often compared the Occupy movement to the Tea Party. It wasn't exactly a fair comparison, but it was an understandable one: the Tea Party was the only recent populist rebellion people had to refer to. The similarity between the movements was clear on one basic point: like Occupy, Tea Party activists were spurred to protest by their outrage over the bank bailouts. But where the Tea Party people called the system corrupt, and big government the source of its corruption, Occupy Wall Street said no, it's the banks and corporations and financial institutions that are the problem, because they're the true source of the corruption. Wall Street is the culprit, not Washington: it's the corporate CEOs and the 1 percent who are systematically paying to elect and control lawmakers and regulators to enforce their interests—not the other way around. Within months of raising a ruckus in the streets, the Tea Party morphed into an electoral movement messaged, fueled and funded by the Koch brothers and their libertarian allies. By the 2010 midterms, a rabble of angry right-wing protesters had been transformed into one of America's biggest voting blocs. The Tea Party rocked the GOP establishment, taking the Republican anti-government stance to its reactionary extreme. They seemed to want to do away with government altogether.

Occupy's solution to the problem was not less government but more effective government: enforceable law without loopholes and revolving doors, robust rules and regulations in the people's interest, an end to the corporate stranglehold on Washington. Occupy Wall Street had no ambition for politics. It very deliberately eschewed the idea of leaders, of designated spokespeople. It was deeply skeptical of the efficacy of electoral politics, asserting that government had been so corrupted by Wall Street banks, corporations and the 1 percent that the system was beyond being fixed simply by voting new candidates into office.

After the Occupy encampments were cleared in November 2011 and the noise and attention died down, media and mainstream culture moved on. The movement had provoked the powers that be, and protesters had paid a price—subject to more than seven thousand arrests over the course of several months. But in its failure to draft demands, promote candidates or create any sort of political organization, Occupy faded from the public eye. "I think for a long time people didn't want to recognize Occupy's impact, and we were seeing it being written out of history," said Ronan McNern, a media organizer at Occupy London. Yet as we can see today, looking back a decade, the movement had a more long-term impact on the nation's politics than was readily apparent. As Sam Pizzigati, labor journalist and founder of Inequality.org, said, "Occupy essentially put the spotlight on the 1 percent, and on the top one-tenth of the 1 percent, and when Americans looked at what they saw—that the three richest Americans owned as much wealth as the bottom fifty percent of the population—they didn't like it, and it changed American politics. It made it possible for Bernie Sanders and Elizabeth Warren and other politicians to emerge."

Ro Khanna, a Democratic congressman representing California's Seventeenth District around Silicon Valley and a surrogate for the 2020 Sanders campaign, told me that before Occupy, "the Clinton vision and the Democratic vision was that we're going through an economic transition due to globalization, and we need to invest in human capital to help people prepare for the digital economy. There's a value to that perspective, but the Occupy movement came in and said, 'That's not enough: the reason the working and middle class isn't doing well isn't because of the right tools or preparation, but because the rules of the economy have been rigged to help a governing elite, and we need to change the rules.'"

Khanna, who is a member of Justice Democrats, the grassroots organization that helped get Alexandria Ocasio-Cortez and a new generation of anti-corporate candidates elected to office, saw a clear through line from the Occupy movement to the transformative, populist agendas laid out by the country's leading progressive senators, Elizabeth Warren and Bernie Sanders. Following Occupy, "Warren comes in and provides an intellectual framework to show why some of these financial rules—stock buybacks, allowing banks to speculate, having tax deductions for depreciations but not for investments—and structural inequities in our economic system have led to the decline of the middle class. Next, Bernie comes in and says it's ridiculous that so much wealth is controlled by so few and we need a shift in economic policy to tackle this. Sanders's and Warren's life's work was happening well before the Occupy movement, but I'm not sure the country would have been ready to listen to their voices—and I don't think they would have emerged as national figures—if it weren't for Occupy putting the issues of wealth and income inequality front and center. Occupy created the conditions for the emergence of a progressive wing of the Democratic Party, and in the long run the progressive wing is ascendant and is likely to succeed."

ECONOMIC INEQUALITY RESHAPES THE POLITICAL ARENA

LONG BEFORE ELIZABETH WARREN TORE INTO THE DISGRACED Wells Fargo CEO John Stumpf in a Capitol Hill hearing, or Bernie Sanders made his stunning first run for the White House, Occupy had already reshaped the American political landscape by providing President Obama the theme that would secure his 2012 reelection: economic inequality. Obama's Republican challenger, the former Massachusetts governor and multimillionaire venture capitalist Mitt Romney, had already staked out his ground when he declared at the 2011 Iowa State Fair: "Corporations are people, my friend." Obama saw his cue. Eleven weeks after Occupy Wall Street began, the president spoke in Osawatomie, Kansas, where he refashioned his message as the country's uniter-in-chief, calling inequality "the defining issue of our time" and striking a decidedly populist tone. In recent decades, Obama told the crowd, "the average income of the top 1 percent has gone up by more than 250 percent to $1.2 million per year, [while] for the top one-hundredth of 1 percent, the average income is now $27 million per year. Those at the very top grew wealthier from their incomes, their investments, wealthier than ever before, but everybody else struggled with costs that were growing and paychecks that weren't. This kind of inequality, a level that we haven't seen since the Great Depression, hurts us all . . . These aren't Democratic values or Republican values, these aren't 1 percent values or 99 percent values: they're American values, and we have to reclaim them."

In the heat of the summer 2012 campaign, Obama's newfound rhetoric drew an especially stark contrast with Romney, who sank himself as an unelectable 1 percenter when he uttered his famous "47 percent" line at a private fundraiser. In the speech, caught on film by David Corn of *Mother Jones*, Romney claimed that Obama relied on support from "forty-seven percent [of Americans] who are dependent upon government, who believe that they are victims, who believe the government has a responsibility to care for them, who believe that they are entitled to healthcare, to food, to housing, to you-name-it . . . these are people who pay no income tax." For all of his later heroism standing up to Donald Trump as the lone voice of dissent in the GOP Senate, Romney was widely derided in 2012, seen as out of touch and insensitive to the daily economic hardship of working people. His views on wealth paved the way for Obama's second term.

In 2013, a wave of Democratic lawmakers at the local level made wealth and income inequality a core talking point—and for some, the central plank of their platform. The most notable, New York City mayor Bill de Blasio romped to victory that year winning nearly three-quarters of the vote by styling his campaign on a 99 percent message to shrink the wealth gap, which he likened to "a tale of two cities." After a little over a year in office, de Blasio had expanded pre-kindergarten access to tens of thousands of New York families; created municipal ID cards for undocumented immigrants; reformed stop-and-frisk police policy; increased affordable housing; invested in the city's public parks; guaranteed paid sick leave for workers; and formed a national task force of mayors to address nationwide economic inequality at the municipal level. Other city executives followed suit, like Pittsburgh mayor Bill Peduto, who authored a responsible-banking law and pushed for affordable housing, clean energy projects and universal pre-K; mayors Betsy Hodges (Minneapolis), Marty Walsh (Boston), Ed Murray (Seattle) and Javier Gonzales (Santa Fe) all pushed populist agendas to reduce inequality, a policy trend scarcely imaginable before Occupy laid the groundwork. "We all ran on similar platforms," Peduto told *The American Prospect*. "It just emerged organically that way. We all faced the reality of growing disparities. The population beneath the poverty line is increasing everywhere. A lot of us were underdogs, populists, reformers, and the public was ready for us." (A former union president, Walsh would become labor secretary under President Joe Biden.)

A flurry of measures introduced in Congress that year solidified the sense that at least one of America's major political parties was now taking wealth and income inequality seriously. Illinois representative Jan Schakowsky reintroduced the Fairness in Taxation Act to raise taxes on millionaires and billionaires. Meanwhile, Minnesota congressman Keith Ellison introduced the Inclusive Prosperity Act, known as the Robin Hood Tax, which sought to impose a tiny financial transaction tax on all Wall Street trades to raise around $300 billion a year. In the Senate, along with Warren, Democrats like Tammy Baldwin, Jeff Merkley, Sheldon Whitehouse and Al Franken helped elevate policies on inequality, and Ohio's Sherrod Brown proposed legislation to end "too big to fail" institutions. The moment was ripe, the public sentiment was there. Though the encampments of Occupy had become a distant memory for many Americans, the movement's political legacy was beginning to assert itself.

Republicans flipped sixteen Democratic seats in the 2014 midterms to increase their hold on the House, but by the time the presidential primaries rolled around the next year, inequality and the growing wealth gap had become a defining campaign issue—one that even the staunchest GOP candidates could no longer ignore. Former Florida governor Jeb Bush acknowledged that "far too many Americans live on the edge of economic ruin, and many more feel like they're stuck in place, working longer and harder, even as they're losing ground," while Texas senator Ted Cruz came out and admitted at a Freedom Partners forum that "the top 1 percent earn a higher share of our income nationally than any year since 1928." Still, Republicans were falling back on old diagnoses and even older prescriptions, arguing that low regulations and taxes were the only way to fix the problem. Even as Florida senator Marco Rubio suggested turning earned income tax credits into a subsidy for low-wage earners, the GOP went about slashing government spending on food stamps, college grants, Medicaid and other programs for poor and middle-income Americans.

But by now the genie was out of the bottle. In poll after poll, two-thirds of Americans said they wanted to see corporations and the wealthy pay higher taxes and the government play an active role in reducing economic inequality. Simply ignoring the crisis the way politicians on both sides of the aisle had done for decades would no longer cut it. As the historian Jill Lepore wrote in 2015 in *The New Yorker*, "What's new about the chasm between the rich and the poor isn't that it's growing or that scholars are studying it. What's new is that American politicians of all spots and stripes are talking about it, if feebly: inequality this, inequality that," mainly, she added, because "it's no longer possible to deny that it exists." And the person who knew better than anyone how to communicate the crisis of extreme inequality—why it existed, who was causing it, and how to roll up our sleeves to solve the problem—was Bernie Sanders.

After People for Bernie launched the senator's popular grassroots movement that propelled his candidacy into the top tier of 2016 presidential contenders, Sanders still had to fight it out among a field of Democrats who were moving to the left of Clinton on economic issues. Former Maryland governor Martin O'Malley made regulating Wall Street a central tenet of his platform as he called to strengthen Dodd-Frank and reinstate Glass-Steagall. "If a bank is too big to fail without harming the common good of our nation, then it's too big and we must break it up before it breaks us," O'Malley said on the campaign trail in Iowa. Jim Webb, the decorated military veteran and former Virginia senator, pushed for a tax on Wall Street profits and stressed a mantra of "economic populism and fairness."

Afraid of upsetting her wealthy donor base, Clinton remained quiet about inequality for as long as she could, offering opaque observations, such as, "Extreme inequality has corrupted other societies," or when she told a Center for American Progress panel, "A lot of our cities truly are divided. They have a lot of inequality that has only gotten worse." Writing at the time, the president of the Institute for America's Future, Robert Borosage, asserted that Clinton would "champion pay equity and day-care and family-friendly policies as part of her lifelong commitment to working women. But on the big structural challenges—Wall Street, trade policies, empowering workers, curbing CEO excesses, expanding shared security, strategic investment and fair taxes—her views are still largely undefined."

For Bernie Sanders, of course, Clinton's corporate establishment views were already sharply defined and they provided a perfect foil for his insurgent campaign. In his Brooklyn-accented call for a political revolution, Sanders went where no presidential candidate running on a big party ticket dared to tread. In city after city, he lit up arenas with a growly, no-nonsense performance, declaring that "the business model of Wall Street is fraud and deception," and that "the most serious problem we face is the grotesque and growing level of wealth and income inequality." Sanders's grassroots fundraising machine was groundbreaking as he rejected funds from super PACs and corporations and relied instead on individual donations averaging $27 each. People across the political spectrum flocked to hear his message condemning "those at the very top who have continued to separate themselves from the rest of our society" by using "loopholes and exceptions [that] have made a mockery out of true economic fairness." In his campaign blueprint, "An Economic Agenda for America: 12 Steps Forward," Sanders laid out a program heavy on infrastructure spending and government investment to provide universal single-payer healthcare, paid leave for parents, tuition-free higher education, a higher minimum wage, tax reform to help working people, higher taxes on the wealthy and tighter regulation of Wall Street banks.

Sanders's words and the conviction with which he spoke them had struck a nerve. In a primary season that jolted the establishment he won twenty-two states, routing Clinton by double digits in New Hampshire, Colorado, Minnesota, Oklahoma, Kansas, Nebraska, Maine, Idaho, Utah, Alaska, Hawaii, Washington, Wisconsin, Wyoming, Rhode Island, West Virginia, Oregon, North Dakota, and his home state of Vermont. Sanders ran the most successful left populist campaign in U.S. history, but on June 6, 2016, news media reported that Clinton had reached the required number of delegates and was declared the Democratic nominee. Sanders supporters cried foul, convinced that the delegate votes had been skewed and back-room establishment deals had cut short Sanders's chances. Six weeks later those fears were confirmed when, on July 22, just three days shy of the Democratic National Convention in Philadelphia, WikiLeaks released a trove of Russia-hacked Democratic National Committee emails revealing party insiders had overtly favored Clinton and sought to undermine the Sanders campaign. A contingent of "Bernie or Bust" delegates staged a rebellion that threatened to derail the convention process, though Sanders managed to pull his people back from the brink, declaring in unequivocal terms to his supporters and the nation: "We must vote for Hillary Clinton." Three months later, Donald Trump received nearly three million fewer votes than Clinton but won the electoral college—defeating her by less than eighty thousand combined votes in the three Midwestern "Blue wall" states of Pennsylvania, Wisconsin and Michigan—making him the second Republican in a row to win the presidency while losing the popular vote, and exposing yet another deep structural flaw in the U.S. political system.

To say that America under Trump's reign took a turn for the worse is a painful understatement that historians will be reckoning with through the remainder of this century and beyond. But the fateful 2016 election did something arguably more important for the country's future: in the wake of a financial crash caused by Wall Street greed, and an Occupy movement that changed what the American electorate believed they had a right to demand from their government and their economy, people were finally ready to listen to and vote en masse for a leader who spoke truth to power, who put people over profits, and whose progressive vision signaled a new direction the country wanted to pursue. The political revolution had arrived.

THE OCCUPY CANDIDATE

SANDERS'S BACK-TO-BACK RUNS FOR THE PRESIDENCY IN 2016 AND 2020 didn't deliver the electoral results his backers had hoped for: putting a democratic socialist in the White House. But when the books about our tumultuous era are written they will tell a story of the profound ways his candidacies changed how Americans not only acknowledged but chose to act in response to class injustice and inequality. If there is a single person who came to embody the moral ethos of Occupy Wall Street—its commitment to fairness and equality under the law, its demand to hold the 1 percent accountable for its corruption—it was Bernie: the Occupy candidate.

Whereas the consensus-based movement at Zuccotti Park was incapable of making decisions and developing an organization that could reshape electoral politics, Sanders transformed the Democratic Party and reoriented American politics in a way that was scarcely imaginable before Occupy prepared the ground. "If you have a thousand people and you're going to decide things unanimously, you're not going to decide anything, so that's not a way to generate social change," said the economist Dean Baker. "On the other hand, Occupy advanced these ideas, which continue to gestate, then you get Bernie Sanders running in 2016 building on the Occupy sentiment, and now you've had the whole party move to the left." Adam Chadwick, a filmmaker who took part in Occupy Wall Street, said, "It was a marker that Occupy has gone into the highest realms of politics now—the idea that somebody like a Bernie Sanders is able to become a contender for the highest office in the United States is proof that the ideas are no longer fringe ideas."

Could Bernie Sanders and his political revolution have been possible before the Occupy movement reframed the discussion, shattering decades of silence on inequality? Likely not. "We don't talk about class much in this country," Peter Olney, the former organizing director of the International Longshore and Warehouse Union, told me. "We don't call the billionaires the enemy, and Bernie picked up on that [message] to his great credit." The former Occupy Wall Street activist Dana Balicki said that Sanders's platform "wouldn't have had the roots or ability to grow if Occupy hadn't done what it did. We brought that conversation of income inequality into the mainstream, and that conversation endured and developed and it never went away, and that was what Bernie organized around; it stayed in the cultural conversation and he brought it back and upped the ante." Another filmmaker, Dennis Trainor Jr., who produced the Occupy documentary *American Autumn*, agreed. "I don't think Bernie Sanders's viral appeal of 2016 could have existed without the Occupy movement," he said, calling issues like Medicare for All, free college tuition and a $15 minimum wage the new litmus tests for Democratic candidates. "There's a struggle over the soul of what the Democratic Party is going to represent, and a lot of millennials came to his campaign out of disappointment—either organizing or voting for Barack Obama, and not seeing the hope and change they thought they were going to get. Bernie speaks eloquently to the evils of wealth inequality that we're experiencing."

On March 7, 2020—four days after Joe Biden's dramatic Super Tuesday campaign comeback, and one week before the explosion of coronavirus shuttered the American economy—*New York Times* columnist Frank Bruni declared that, despite the election results,

> Sanders won the Democratic primary. He won it when his rivals talked more about whether Medicare for All could ever get through Congress than about whether such a huge expansion of the federal government was a good idea in the first place. He won it when they competed to throw many more trillions than the next candidate at climate change. He won it when the disagreement became not about free tuition at public colleges but about the eligibility of students from families above a certain income level. While Sanders's fellow candidates didn't parrot his vocabulary and denounce "oligarchs" and "oligarchy," they spoke expansively about gross income inequality and the need to tackle it.

In his victory speech on Super Tuesday, Biden hailed Sanders as the "most powerful voice for a fair and more just America." Bruni's colleague at the *Times*, Sydney Ember, concluded that Sanders had "moved the [Democratic] party to the left" by introducing progressive policies "that are now embroidered into the fabric of the party. Now Mr. Sanders is in the uniquely awkward position of being venerated by a party he has never joined but which he has shaped so much that it now can't push him away."

Part of Sanders's success was the strength of his populist organizing machine: he had raised a reported $96 million from 1.4 million individual donors in 2019—no billionaires included. For the Occupy Wall Street organizer and movement trainer Nicole Carty, Sanders's grassroots campaign fundraising model left a permanent imprint on the party and was another legacy of the Occupy movement. "Bernie Sanders is an Occupy candidate," she said, noting that his refusal to take any PAC money starting in 2016 sparked a sea change in the way progressives saw a path to elected office. In the years since, Carty said, a "mixture of many movements, partly Women's March, partly Occupy, partly Black Lives Matter," have lined up to elect a new generation of local, state and federal lawmakers, proving that the Sanders strategy is working. "Alexandria Ocasio-Cortez is a direct result of Occupy," she added. "Looking at the Democratic field, many are now refusing to take corporate PAC money, and that's because of Sanders and because of Occupy."

Also unlike any presidential candidate in modern memory, Sanders focused relentlessly on the needs of the working poor, the underinsured, the underemployed and even the homeless—a constituency that by 2020 exceeded half a million Americans and that politicians rarely even mentioned. "Occupy really focused on the problems with American democracy and the American economy," said Khanna, the congressman from California. "Bernie is much more about 'Here's what we're going to do for you: we're going to give you education and healthcare, we're going to make sure you've got childcare and a chance at going to college.' He's very concrete and simple about what we're going to do for folks, not tied to an ideology, and I think the simplicity of that messaging is helpful. We have a geographical divide in this country with communities totally left out of the digital and knowledge economy. A lot of Bernie's policies are actually preparing us for a twenty-first-century digital economy. He spends far more time talking about what he is going to do for people left out than he does critiquing the injustices in the system."

Occupy's utopian call for big structural change got people's attention— and once Sanders homed in on the policy specifics, the movement's idealism started to sound a lot more like commonsense reforms. Sanders "was really running against business as usual, saying that in another world people would have healthcare, it wouldn't cost a dime to go to public college—things that weren't just progressive points but actually clean breaks with the dominant, mainstream, bipartisan sweep of politics," said J. A. Myerson. Sanders crystallized the intangible demands that Occupy Wall Street had put forward but failed to structure in the litany of accusations against the 1 percent, and "now his platform is everybody's platform."

Sanders's greatest contribution to American politics was the ability to take what only a decade ago were considered fringe positions and meld them permanently into the mainstream—broadening the possibilities for the kind of socioeconomic transformation that had been articulated first by Occupy. "Whether it's environmental strategy or social strategy or Medicare for All, the Occupy movement helped push voices to aggregate. It unleashed the floodgates," said Nomi Prins, author of *All the Presidents' Bankers: The Hidden Alliances That Drive American Power.* "We weren't really talking about universal healthcare at all. Bernie was talking about it, and it gave him that ammunition and momentum going forward that allowed Medicare for All to become political discourse on Capitol Hill, and I think that wouldn't have happened had there not been a growing connection that came out of that movement." For Susan Griffin, author of *Woman and Nature: The Roaring Inside Her,* Sanders walked through the door that Occupy Wall Street had opened. "Occupy gave Bernie a platform and gave him permission to talk about these things. It gave him a national audience."

Filmmaker Adam Chadwick saw Sanders's relevance heightened even further in 2020 by the moral contrast he struck with Trump—a man who embodied the greed and unaccountable power of the 1 percent. "We have this guy in the White House who represents ground zero for everything, and it doesn't matter what side of the political spectrum you're on—you have to be engaged now, there's no turning back, so it allowed Bernie Sanders who was running with the Occupy narrative to step in and really bring that conversation to the mainstream even more. Maybe our demands are only coming forth now because we've had this conversation for a decade and that's what needed to happen," he said. Returning to the derivatives-analyst-turned-Wall-Street-watchdog Alexis Goldstein, Sanders's lasting impact not only validated the principles of economic justice voiced by Occupy, but also marked the movement's turning point of influence on American politics. "I was shocked at how popular he was at first, and the surge of people that he had. Bernie really motivated and inspired people talking about something that was so outside what was considered acceptable, normal politics," said Goldstein. It was the message: "We tried the nonpolitical way, so let's try the political way."

ALEXANDRIA OCASIO-CORTEZ AND THE NEW PROGRESSIVE ERA

ON JANUARY 21, 2017, THE DAY AFTER DONALD TRUMP WAS INAU-gurated into office, I joined tens of thousands of people filling the streets of downtown Oakland as part of the nationwide Women's March. More than four million protesters assembled that day across some seven hundred U.S. towns and cities to protest his hours-old presidency. From the coasts to the heartland, a bobbing pink sea of "pussy hats" colored the landscape in the country's largest single-day demonstration to date. The Women's March had used a distributed model of organizing that allowed activists in communities everywhere to launch their own sister marches; like a lot of the protest movements that have evolved over the past decade, it built on the digital tools and strategies first honed at Occupy. The march, exuberant and explosive, felt like a release valve for an outraged, unnerved public, but then it was over. That very day, Trump visited the Central Intelligence Agency, where he lied about his inauguration crowd size; the next day his handler Kellyanne Conway went on national television and introduced America to the regime's reliance on "alternative facts"; the day after that Trump lied to congressional leaders, saying three to five million illegally cast ballots had caused him to lose the popular vote to Hillary Clinton; the day after that Trump approved construction of the Keystone XL and Dakota Access pipelines that millions had protested and Obama had vetoed; the day after that he signed two executive orders to begin construction of the southern border wall that he claimed Mexico would pay for; the day after that he told Sean Hannity on Fox News that waterboarding works as a legitimate means of extracting information and he wanted to bring

it back, and on the seventh day he signed Executive Order 13769 banning trav-
elers from seven Muslim-majority countries from entering the United States,
which set off waves of protests that engulfed airports across the country and
internationally for weeks. Thus was the forty-fifth presidency underway.

In my hometown of Berkeley, I joined what was fast becoming the most
dynamic movement of the anti-Trump resistance, Indivisible, which went on
to help engineer nationwide protests that summer and fall to successfully block
Republicans from achieving their number one priority: abolishing Obamacare.
I wanted to move beyond protest so I sought out ways to get involved in the
insurgent electoral movement that was flourishing across the land. A friend
connected me to a little-known group called Brand New Congress, which
aimed to draft a new generation of progressive, anti-corporate candidates to
run for congressional seats in the 2018 midterms. Founded by a handful of
organizers from the Sanders movement, the group received a flood of interest
after Trump's victory. "There was this new feeling throughout the country of
'I need to do something more,'" said Caitlin Remmel, a former BNC deputy
communications director. I had volunteered to write press releases for several
of its candidates. Brand New Congress didn't succeed in getting a radical crop
of newcomers elected during the Blue Wave midterms of 2018. There was,
however, one exception: a twenty-nine-year-old New York City bartender,
struggling with student debt, named Alexandria Ocasio-Cortez.

Ocasio-Cortez was born in 1989 in the Bronx. Her father was a South
Bronx native who worked as an architect in the city and her mother, who came
from poverty in Puerto Rico, cleaned houses. Before Ocasio-Cortez entered
grade school the family moved to Yorktown Heights in Westchester County,
a half hour north of the city, to give her and her younger brother, Gabriel, a
better education. Raised in a Catholic household that valued strictness, respect
and strong moral ethos, Ocasio-Cortez excelled in science and math and from
an early age exhibited excellent debating skills. She got her first real sense of
economic inequality while helping her mother clean the homes of rich people.
Ocasio-Cortez didn't go on all the field trips at her almost all-white middle

school because her parents couldn't pay for them; at the same time, she had options that her extended family back in the Bronx did not have. "I grew up with this reality and understanding of income inequality as, 'When I'm in this zip code I have these opportunities, and when I'm in that zip code I don't have these opportunities,'" she told the news site *Mic* in 2018. "At a very young age I knew it was wrong. The fact that my cousins didn't have adequate resources or public services and good schools, and I did, was something that just didn't strike me as right."

Ocasio-Cortez took out student loans to attend Boston University, where she majored in international relations and economics. During a college internship with Massachusetts senator Ted Kennedy, she found herself the only Spanish speaker in an office that often received calls from spouses and family members of people who had been rounded up by Immigration and Customs Enforcement; her job was to help them navigate the labyrinthine federal system. In 2011, a few months before Wall Street protesters took over Zuccotti Park, Ocasio-Cortez graduated cum laude with $30,000 in college debt and moved back to the Bronx. She worked as a bartender and waitress in Manhattan while trying to help her mother stave off foreclosure. She also started a publishing company, Brook Avenue Press, committed to increasing literacy in underprivileged communities, and worked for the National Hispanic Institute helping Latino students develop leadership skills. It wasn't until the 2015 presidential primary season, when she started hearing speeches by Bernie Sanders addressing the issues that mattered to her most—Medicare for All, a $15 minimum wage, free college, the transition to clean energy—that Ocasio-Cortez knew where she wanted to apply herself: to politics.

During off-hours from the Coffee Shop bar and restaurant on Union Square where she worked, she volunteered at Sanders's field office in the Bronx. "She had done grassroots organizing before, but it had always been for a cause, never for an election," wrote Charlotte Alter in *The Ones We've Been Waiting For: How a New Generation of Leaders Will Transform America*. "This was the first time she had ever put in the work for a candidate, because this was the first time a candidate had ever talked about systemic inequality in a way that made sense in her life." Ocasio-Cortez labored with the campaign until the New York state primary, in April 2016, when Clinton dealt Sanders a nearly sixteen-point defeat. On the November night that the electoral college handed Donald Trump the election, despite his losing by almost three million votes to Clinton, Ocasio-Cortez wrote presciently on Facebook: "Like it or not, you will have to listen to the clear message working Americans sent last night. If you truly love others, you will go beyond the fight against racism—for that is an effort to change a man's attitude. By fighting for economic justice, you seek to change his life. That is the path forward."

THE BLUE WAVE OF 2018, WHEN DEMOCRATS GAINED FORTY-ONE seats to retake the House of Representatives, was a harbinger of the Second Progressive Era that continues to gain momentum. At that time, an array of well-organized grassroots groups rose to meet the moment—Swing Left, Sister District, Flippable, Run for Something and others—each geared toward unseating the GOP House majority and installing a new generation of politicians in city, state and nationwide office. To a large degree, they succeeded. Run for Something recruited seventy-two millennials on ballots across fourteen states, and nearly half of them won—most resoundingly in Virginia, where Flippable and Sister District helped Democratic candidates take eight out of fifteen seats to turn the House of Delegates blue, the party's biggest victory in the state since the nineteenth century. But progressives didn't prevail everywhere: the Georgia and Florida governors' races featuring powerhouse Black candidates Stacey Abrams and Andrew Gillum—who lost by a combined eighty-seven thousand votes in elections marred by voter suppression—ended in stinging defeats.

Seven years after Occupy Wall Street, the 2018 election results seemed to validate the long transition that progressives had initiated at Zuccotti Park: from insurgent social protest to populist organizing power. Donald Trump provided the perfect catalyst. As Representative Khanna told me, speaking a year and a half before the 2020 presidential election: "The organizing we did in communities across the country translated into so many progressives being elected to Congress, and my instinct is the post-Trump era will usher in a progressive era like we saw in the 1890s. There's going to be a reaction to Trump that will make the pendulum swing in the other direction and we may see this new progressive era emerge as almost an antidote to Trump." Optimism was in short supply during the four years of Trump's authoritarian assault on democracy, and apart from recapturing the White House—and by the slimmest margin of 50–50, using a vice-presidential tie break, the Senate—Democrats came up shorter than they had hoped in the 2020 elections. As Khanna said, "If we believe that with Trump in some sense there was a correct diagnosis of a problem—communities were left behind, and a large part of the country felt frustrated and taken advantage of—the next leaders will hear the discontent but will offer a progressive prescription."

Ocasio-Cortez's meteoric rise to progressive standard bearer of the Democratic Party started with an epic road trip that she and a few friends took the month after Trump's election in 2016. They drove west to join the water protectors occupying the Standing Rock Indian Reservation in North Dakota, a camp established eight months earlier by young members of the Lakota Sioux tribe seeking to halt construction of the Dakota Access Pipeline. Fresh off their six-year-long, hard-won victory over the Keystone XL pipeline—a plan President Obama had rejected in November 2015 under enormous pressure, but which was revived by President Trump in his first week in office—thousands of activists from around the country poured into Standing Rock throughout the summer and fall of 2016. Defying police who used water cannons and attack dogs in their attempt to disperse the peaceful protests, young people stood en masse with the Indigenous-led movement and lit a new fire of national resistance. Ocasio-Cortez wanted to be part of it, so she launched a GoFundMe campaign to buy sleeping bags, cots, stoves and firewood for the water protectors, then embarked on a trip that would crystallize her political and economic beliefs.

While on America's highways in late autumn, Ocasio-Cortez first experimented with Facebook Live, streaming what she and her travel companions called "The Road to Standing Rock." She talked about the combination of media bias, racism, misogyny and elitism that had contributed to Clinton's loss to Trump, and speculated on whether Sanders could have won. As her audience grew into the hundreds, she asked pointed questions about how to secure people's jobs amid growing automation, and how politicians in Flint, Michigan, could have deceived their own people by allowing them to drink lead-poisoned water, and what ought to be done about the influence of money in politics. She also meditated aloud on the critical role played by public protests in shaping policy and driving legislative change. "The whole trip had the feel of a college bull session," wrote Alter, but more importantly, "Alexandria was beginning to learn how to think on camera, how to have conversations with people in the comments, how to bring her viewers along for the ride and deliver her opinions in stream-of-consciousness lectures that were at once natural and informative. It was the birth of a social media persona that would define her later political career."

During the several days she spent at Standing Rock, Ocasio-Cortez was drawn to the moneyless, communal spirit of the camp, where people offered what they had to others and committed themselves in solidarity with the Sioux whose water the pipeline threatened. The journey connected "a lot of different dots" and was "the tipping point" for her, she later told *New York* magazine, because she "saw how all the people there—particularly the native people and the Lakota Sioux—were putting their whole lives and everything on the line for the protection of their community. I saw how a corporation had literally militarized itself against the American people, and I just felt like we were at a point where we couldn't afford to ignore politics anymore." Her realization came at the right moment: on the day she left the reservation, Ocasio-Cortez received a phone call that would change her life and alter the trajectory of progressive politics in America. The voice on the other end was from Brand New Congress and they wanted her to run for New York's Fourteenth Congressional District seat.

Caitlin Remmel, who attended law school at American University while directing communications for BNC, recalled that at the group's candidate boot-camp training held in Knoxville the next summer, Ocasio-Cortez stood out from the crowd. "We would always say, 'If only one person is going to make it, it's going to be AOC,'" said Remmel, who took weekend trips in 2017 from D.C. to the Bronx where she would crash on Ocasio-Cortez's couch and work on her campaign. At one point Remmel's communications team sought to lend a hand and took over AOC's social media accounts. "We were doing tweets for her and it was so bad—no one does social media better than her, her fingers were just magic, so after about forty-eight hours she was like, 'No, it's okay guys, I can take it from here.'" As funds dwindled and the 2018 primaries drew near, Brand New Congress chose to funnel its remaining resources to the candidate with the best chance of winning. "A lot of energy was put into AOC's campaign because everyone could see the momentum—she had knocked on so many doors, and raised a total of $300,000. There was just this combination of fire and passion and relatability, and this ability to be so articulate." And also humble, Remmel added, like the weekend when she told Ocasio-Cortez she no longer worked with any of the other candidates. "She said, 'But Caitlin, why me, why my campaign?' and her question surprised me because in my mind it was just so obvious, but she didn't see it because she had a certain humility—she cared so much about all the candidates. She's always going to use her platform to bring up other voices."

In the New York state primary held in June 2018, Ocasio-Cortez crushed her incumbent rival, Democratic Caucus chair Joe Crowley—a man who had served ten terms in the district, stood fourth in line in the House Democratic leadership, and outspent her eighteen to one. Her victory stunned the party and sent shock waves through the establishment, signaling a sea change in liberal American politics. Ocasio-Cortez proudly wore the democratic socialist mantle popularized by Sanders two years earlier, and her win—which *The New York Times* called "the most significant loss for a Democratic incumbent in more than a decade"—invoked comparisons to the ground-shaking upset that Tea

Partier Dave Brat pulled off four years prior when he unseated Republican House majority leader Eric Cantor in Virginia's Seventh Congressional District. Still just twenty-eight and as yet unelected, Ocasio-Cortez became the party's new rock star, and she wasted no time endorsing fellow populist progressives running in tight races nationwide; that summer she traveled to Kansas, Missouri and Michigan in her bid to, as she put it, "advance the front lines for economic and social justice everywhere." Since the inspired trek to Standing Rock, Ocasio-Cortez had mastered her social media presence and matured as a charismatic and authentic voice demanding systemic change. Red-baiting quickly got underway as far-right media personalities like Rush Limbaugh warned of "a Marxist communist running for election [as] a Democrat," and Sean Hannity called her candidacy "downright scary" for freedom-loving Americans. But her battle cry that "the status quo is not an option" had caught fire: it was the message her generation had been waiting to hear, and when she captured the general election that fall, a new progressive movement's time had come.

WHEN RADIO HOST EGBERTO WILLIES INTERVIEWED OCASIO-Cortez shortly after she announced her run for Congress, he recognized instantly that she had a political persona "different from anybody else. I was so impressed with her. I could see she had the *it* factor." For Willies, who had participated in Occupy Houston, Ocasio-Cortez's ability to go to the heart of issues of economic injustice, in language incisive and inspiring, marked a clear evolution in the years since Occupy Wall Street first confronted corporate power. "AOC isn't there without Occupy. And now AOC is doing it correctly: all the middle Democrats, they need to fear being primaried because the country has already stated that it is a liberal country economically. Ask them about the policies they want: Medicare for All, pay it forward education, [childcare] aid for parents—they're all over sixty percent support. They killed the physical Occupy movement, but they didn't kill what Occupy stood for," he said. Now Ocasio-Cortez stood in its place.

From a technology perspective—specifically the ability to harness social media as a way to project progressive goals into the mainstream—Ocasio-Cortez also built on a precedent set at Occupy. "I think that Occupy, the idea, lives on and the lessons learned about how to have serious impact using social media are still just getting started. Look how quickly Alexandria Ocasio-Cortez has become one of the country's most influential voices—having the temerity to run for office herself, and then using social media to get the message out," said Harry Waisbren, a media organizer at Zuccotti Park who went on to work with Lenchner to create People for Bernie. "AOC is one of the best public figures leveraging social media who has existed to this point, and her main advice about how to build up these channels is to get right on the issues: her popularity is part and parcel with her advocating Medicare for All and the Green New Deal and abolishing Immigration and Customs Enforcement—movement efforts that also got their start at Occupy Wall Street. The Occupy idea that we need a democracy and a government that works for all of us, not only the 1 percent, is central to all of these extending issues." Ocasio-Cortez helped "make it a moral argument" for voters, he added, and "that's what's shifted so much right now."

In the long arc of things, wrote Alter in *The Ones We've Been Waiting For*, "Occupy Wall Street didn't directly dismantle the financial system, but it did sow the seeds that would flower into the revived progressive movement of the next decade. The movement told a story of American politics that would become the defining narrative for the next generation of progressives: Occupy identified a central problem (income inequality), pointed at the culprits (big corporations), and described how those culprits had controlled the political system (with campaign donations legalized through Citizens United)." The fact is, and something most people informed about the movement readily admit, "without Occupy, Bernie Sanders would have stayed a fringe senator from Vermont, Elizabeth Warren probably would not be running for president, and Alexandria Ocasio-Cortez likely wouldn't be in Congress. Many of the people who ended up working for progressive candidates five years later had camped out in Zuccotti Park that fall." The political environment—confronting the presidential crisis of our lifetime—also played a role accelerating the pace of the transition. "Trump's election had suddenly changed the moral calculus for a generation of young progressives, and apathy was no longer cool," wrote Alter, so that when the 2018 midterms rolled around, "for the first time in their careers, many young activists began thinking about elections, and many of the D.C. political creatures started engaging in activism. Five years earlier, the bedraggled tent-dwellers at Occupy and the frenzied workaholics in Washington, D.C., had almost nothing in common: they spoke different languages and existed in different universes. In the beginning of the Trump era, they would start to sing the same song."

Notably, Bernie Sanders's most fervent level of support came from millennials—people who could have been his grandkids. It only follows that as his democratic socialist successor, Ocasio-Cortez would build on Sanders's campaign to develop an even deeper and more compelling message for her generation: inheriting the foundation of economic justice principles he established, then advancing the debate to those who had the greatest stake in building a sustainable future. "Occupy absolutely paved the way for Bernie, and Bernie absolutely paved the way for the new batch of congresspeople like Ocasio-Cortez—I would draw a straight line from Occupy to them," said Martin Kirk, co-founder of The Rules. But "AOC sees a system change—the cultural terms, the ecological terms—in a broader way than Bernie ever did. It's no surprise she came in and went straight to a Green New Deal: she's broadening what it means to fight climate change. It wasn't that Bernie's economic message was bad or not radical, but the new generation has racial justice baked into their worldview. It's just evolution: Occupy set the scene for Bernie, who came on the stage with a very clear economic message and it resonated way more than anyone could have expected, but this new crowd is deeper radicals—they know the climate is wedded to the economy and that it's nonsensical to talk about the economy without talking about the environment."

During her first week in elected office in January 2019—and a month before she rocked the political world with her proposal for a Green New Deal—AOC went on social media and television to discuss the possibility of raising the top marginal tax rate for the highest income earners to 70 percent, returning us closer to the standard set in the post–World War II era. It was a gutsy way to kick off a congressional career and it might have backfired on any other barely sworn-in freshman. But AOC understood meme culture better than anyone and knew exactly what she was doing: floating an aggressive if undefined plan to start a national conversation. According to Kirk, "Ocasio-Cortez has this very instinctive, systemic understanding and can separate narrative and memetic action from policy action. The two big early ideas she dropped in—a seventy percent marginal tax rate and the Green New Deal—she did it with tweets, without a big policy agenda, and was smart about the narrative aspect in ways that even Bernie wasn't. She was born into it, raised on social media." As a result, he added, "she's genuinely shifting the narrative and the terms of the debate. AOC is not a leader in the traditional sense—she doesn't use the language of leadership—but she has a distinct understanding of leaderless revolutionary language and is re-scripting the whole economic logic. It's not hierarchy leadership, but position leadership."

When the coronavirus pandemic swept through New York City in the spring of 2020, Ocasio-Cortez found her district at the epicenter of the crisis. Queens was hit hardest in sheer numbers of infections and deaths early on; during an April interview on *The New York Times* podcast *The Daily*, she said, "Out of the top ten zip codes in the United States that are impacted by Covid casualties, the top five are in my district." But Ocasio-Cortez wasn't so much focused on the alarming numbers as she was on the socioeconomic dimensions of the crisis. Pointing out the huge imbalance of suffering in Black and Brown communities, she said, "In New York City, about sixty-five percent of all frontline workers are people of color, so the folks who are stocking our grocery stores, acting as our home health aides, visiting our parents and the disabled, the people working in our hospitals, are disproportionately impacted . . . This pandemic is not happening in a vacuum. It's happening in a social and economic context and there are people that are saying we're going to transition to working from home, but working from home is an enormous privilege—and to be able to do your job remotely, it cleaves along class lines."

In extended comments with *The Daily* host Michael Barbaro, Ocasio-Cortez spoke about bigger trends she was observing in her party and among progressives. "On one hand I feel that we are winning the larger conversation around the issues. In exit poll after exit poll, we have had stunning support for progressive policies—for Medicare for All, for a living wage, for tuition-free public colleges and universities—so it's not a rejection of the agenda. I think what we're seeing right now is an emerging progressive movement that just exploded in a real way four years ago. Bernie Sanders really unleashed that. I remember in 2016 I was a waitress and it was literally the first time I had ever heard in my life a political candidate running for president that was actually articulating my material reality—actually telling me and telling people in this country that being underinsured is a norm for working people, and it is an unacceptable norm. Demanding a fifteen-dollar-an-hour wage in 2016 was insane, and then last year the House just passed it on the floor. I feel like we're really winning in terms of movement, but electorally there are unique challenges. Winning on issues is not the same thing, obviously, as winning an election."

"LIBERALS HAVE BEEN RADICALIZED; RADICALS HAVE BEEN ELECTORALIZED"

BY THE WINTER OF 2020, AS ELIZABETH WARREN AND BERNIE Sanders challenged Joe Biden in the final debates of the pre-pandemic primary season, issues like Medicare for All, the Green New Deal, debt-free college, universal childcare and raising taxes on the rich formed the crux of the Democratic Party conversation—along with the overriding need to defeat Donald Trump. The candidates' tax policy proposals differed slightly: Warren sought a

2 percent tax on wealth over $50 million and a 3 percent tax on more than $1 billion, while Sanders pushed a 1 percent tax on wealth between $32 million and $50 million, with a progressive tax on richer Americans. But their goal was the same: to begin to move the wealth back down the economic ladder. It was the same discussion the younger generation had started at Occupy and now, a decade later, a more progressive electorate was ready to make it happen. "Occupy shifted the political culture of the U.S.," where the time had come to finally turn activism into policy, Maurice Mitchell of the Working Families Party told me. An important part of that shift was a new "appetite for individuals as leaders"—a phenomenon embodied in the talents of Ocasio-Cortez, who in 2018 became the youngest woman ever elected to Congress. "AOC, before she was AOC, was an individual who was not tied to any institution and who was like, 'I'm gonna do this,'" he said. Ultimately, the leaderless movement that challenged Wall Street greed and the 1 percent has "emboldened people to take leadership, to take action and not ask for permission," and as a result, "now we're in a moment when liberals have been radicalized, and radicals have been electoralized."

So much of this, perhaps, was foreseeable given the decades of moral and tactical failures by Democrats to present an alternative to Wall Street–sponsored rule by the 1 percent. In rhetoric and in policy, the new wave of AOC-style progressives are "occupying the Democratic Party, because the Democrats had just capitulated" to corporate interests, said Sara Burke, a policy analyst at Friedrich-Ebert-Stiftung, a think tank in New York. "Bernie was the first to do it—he came from outside the party and said, 'I'm going to run for president as a Democrat.' Occupy couldn't build a political party, but it's because of Occupy that we have Bernie and AOC and a shift in the Democratic Party. Occupy was a catalyst and it is maybe not because of Occupy but because of this whole shift—the refusal to listen to experts, the refusal to listen to finger-wagging politicians like Hillary Clinton who wanted to tell us what to do—that we had Trump. Occupy uncorked everything, and now the right and the left have to wrangle things out."

To assess the role that progressives are now playing in the redesign of the Democratic Party, journalist J. A. Myerson posed an intriguing frontier analogy comparing the relationship between social uprisings and formal politics—and why the one must build upon the other. "A social movement opens up and conquers terrain, it takes over ground in the political arena—it creates a new field. What formal politics can do is then step into that new terrain and build a town," he said. And the vital point is this: in order for one to truly succeed, they both must. "If you just open up the new conceptual, rhetorical world of the 99 percent, 'another world is possible,' etc., and then don't elect people to office to inhabit that new space, it'll get taken over again. Say you're a revolutionary army that liberates a certain land from an authoritarian government and you don't have people tending to it, the authoritarian government will come back in and occupy it. There's a reinforcing dynamic between popular movements and the politicians who are responsive to them."

The Tea Party anti-government protests of 2010 serve as an example on the right: the grassroots demonstrations lasted briefly before powerful special interests, led by billionaire businessmen like the Kochs, harnessed the anger and channeled the movement to elect dozens of anti-government zealots who hijacked the Grand Old Party. On the state level that year, Republicans added six governorships and a record-breaking 675 legislative seats, which resulted in a decade of gerrymandered districts that ensured the party's legislative control—even as it consistently found itself in the minority on big issues from healthcare to gun control to climate change. In Congress especially, the Tea Party played a consequential role in reshaping U.S. politics: from obstructing progress throughout both terms of the Obama administration to fueling the anti-liberal hatred that led to the rise of Trump. Never mind that the new right-wing extremists drove the Republican Party into a cul-de-sac of backward beliefs deeply unpopular with the American majority. By the grotesque standards of "winning," they achieved some of their aims.

Occupy, by contrast, was "a slower burn, but deeper," Myerson said. It produced no immediate candidates or legislative victories, but by awakening

America to indefensible levels of economic inequality, injustice and unfairness, it inspired the belief that a radical break was needed—and left a far more lasting impact. Occupy "took hold generationally, whereas the Tea Party was more of a momentary expression," Myerson said, and as a result, "single-payer healthcare and free college and taxing the wealthy and all the things that Hillary Clinton laughed at Bernie for proposing—all those things are now mainstream Democratic principles that viable Democrats are running on. The question for Bernie and AOC is: Now what? For Sanders, he has been promoting these things relentlessly from the very margins of politics for forty years, shouting into this gaping swamp of corruption and failure, and now because of Occupy, and the five years leading up to his campaign, and now Ocasio-Cortez, they're basically setting the agenda for the Democratic Party. So now, if that's mainstream, what do they do to push it farther, and what do we do to push it farther than even they do?"

The comedian Lee Camp concurred that while the Occupy movement didn't necessarily "change the makeup of the Congress" in the short term, "it changed the ideology and widened the debate to the point that saying socialism is acceptable, healthcare for all is acceptable, a seventy percent tax rate on the highest earners is acceptable. These debates weren't even being held, so it moved the conversation in this country and showed how ideas are more important than just winning a certain number of seats in the House." As a movement that lacked its own electoral ambitions, Occupy staked out a different place in history—one that will become clearer depending on which side wins the ideological and political battle in the years ahead. "People don't often remember where certain ideas came from that change society. No one will give Occupy credit one day when we have a seventy percent top tax rate or criminal bankers go to jail, but that doesn't mean the effect didn't happen," Camp added. "The dissidents will remember Occupy, the protesters will remember Occupy, those on the edges of society fighting for a better future will remember Occupy, but I don't know that the mainstream will read about Occupy in their corporatized history books."

Often what's hardest to see is what's right in front of you. This has been true of Occupy and efforts to measure its long-term impact. "The enduring value of Occupy Wall Street are the ripples that emanated from its center, even if people don't recognize that they're now for Medicare for All, a fifteen-dollar minimum wage, a Green New Deal or guaranteed income for all," said the filmmaker Dennis Trainor Jr. The lasting power of the movement, more than anything, may be that it forced people to realize if they want a stake in their own future, they have to demand it—both in the streets and at the ballot box. "I think there's a one-two punch in terms of movements and electoral formations, and if we can start to think of voting not as a virtue but as a tactic for movement-building, we'll be far ahead of the game. History will view Occupy differently based not necessarily on how Sanders fared in 2020 but how his platform fares going forward. If someone else can carry that through and win, history is going to have to make Occupy more than a footnote in that narrative."

Extending the idea further, Micah White, the former editor of *Adbusters* magazine, who generated the concept and meme of #OccupyWallStreet, wrote that the very future of free democratic society may hinge on its ability to transform protest movements like Occupy into new party movements that emerge out of them: what he called "hybrid movement-parties." Spain did something like this after the 15-M protests swept the country in May 2011, and leaders like Pablo Iglesias transformed an army of young Indignados from the Spanish squares into the base of the left-populist Podemos party—which launched in 2014 and, by the following year, had won 21 percent of the vote to become the country's third-largest party in parliament. Italy and Greece saw similar achievements with the Five Star Movement and Syriza, respectively. Now, "watching the sudden growth of hybrid movement-parties, activists are rightly wondering how long will it take for a new people's party to sweep Canada, Brazil, the United States or the United Kingdom," wrote White in his 2016 book, *The End of Protest: A New Playbook for Revolution.*

In White's view, the protests-turned-politics dynamic won't be limited to any one country. On the contrary, democratic power ultimately will manifest as a planetary movement. "The true realization of the merger between social movement and political parties will be a global force capable of winning elections in multiple countries in order to carry out a unified geopolitical agenda," he wrote. He acknowledged that organizers may still lack access to the kinds of tools they need, because "making complex decisions within a planetary social movement will require developing techniques of collective thinking that do not currently exist." But what White referred to as "the slow future of protest"—drawn out on a timescale not of months or years or even decades, but generations and centuries—foretells a supranational politics to come. Some have "estimated that every revolution takes three generations. Revolution is akin to building a cathedral in medieval Europe. The architects who designed it and the masons who built it did not live to see their work completed."

Envisioning a more pragmatic timetable, the heirs of Occupy may reflect on our current moment—amid climate ruin and a virus pandemic that have upended the status quo—as the best opportunity to get the world-movement project started. In some arenas, like the pan-European Democracy in Europe Movement 2025, or DiEM25, it already has. Because among the other gaping flaws the coronavirus exposed in America, we discovered that our country didn't learn as much as we thought from the 2008 financial crisis: of the trillions of dollars that Congress doled out as part of the Covid-19 relief legislation known as the CARES Act, a one-time payment of $1,200 along with four months of added unemployment benefits went to individual Americans in 2020 while hundreds of billions were earmarked as tax breaks for corporations and the wealthy—not to mention multi-billion-dollar bailouts for airline companies that had been profitably gouging customers for years. Clearly the lessons of the housing bubble, economic crash and bank bailouts that inspired the Occupy movement hadn't really sunk in. Growing numbers in our restive population feel there's still plenty of unfinished business.

"You look at Bernie, you look at AOC, many of their supporters were part of the Occupy movement and they're seeing their message continue to be put forth in their politics, their rallies, their organizers, their voters," the author Nomi Prins told me. "A lot of the points that were brought up at Occupy are things that haven't been changed—student loans, consumer debt, the fact that the population is living paycheck to paycheck. If anything they've gotten worse. We still have a situation where not only did bankers not go to jail for actual fraud—real crime on a seismic level—but instead of being even indicted, let alone jailed, their institutions were subsidized." A reckoning is yet to come. For those on the right, Donald Trump personified the backlash to decades of corruption in the Washington political duopoly of special-interest lobbyists and big-money donors. Millions of angry working- and middle-class voters, still feeling victimized by the financial crash that was never properly resolved, saw him as a hero for taking on the establishment. Aside from his nationalist and racist appeals, Trump's message worked because "there was still an economic undercurrent of uncertainty lingering from the financial crisis—because so many people came to the conclusion that they weren't being represented by their government to the same extent that the bankers were being represented," Prins added. "Financial unfairness is something that can resonate among all kinds of people: no one likes to feel they were the odd person out in a money grab, that they just didn't get it and other people did." Rather than "drain the swamp," Trump's administration only deepened it, ushering in a more perverse style of influence peddling and corruption.

Yet in gauging the long-term impacts of Occupy Wall Street, Trump's legacy can be seen as a by-product of the populist outrage the movement unleashed. "There wouldn't be a Trump without Occupy. Trump's assessment was an Occupy assessment—the elites are laughing at us, the system is rigged—even down to the focus on the villains: the corporations, organized capital, folks who support neoliberal trade policies," said Maurice Mitchell. "Trump's solution was right-wing racist fundamentalism and economic nationalism, but the assessment rang true because it's a legitimate assessment." At the same time, Trump magnified the intense social and political polarization that Occupy already helped provoke in its response to the Tea Party. "It might be difficult to assess the impact of Occupy because it's not a linear, trace-the-dots connection from Zuccotti Park to President Trump," said Justin Wedes, the Occupy Wall Street social media creator, "but there's definitely been a political realignment of large swaths of the population toward a more ideologically intense leftism as well as a more ideologically intense conservatism, and I think Occupy catalyzed and accelerated that process."

Wedes added, "It's not an exact analog, but what the Tea Party did to mainstream conservatism in many ways Occupy did to mainstream liberalism: it forced the Democratic Party, which for so long has been able to claim hegemony over left and center-left and even center-right politics in the United States, to have to accommodate a more radical left, communitarian, anti-neoliberal politics. You see some of that reflected in the rise of Trump and Sanders, because both ran largely on platforms against elements of neoliberalism, against free trade, against the elite. For Trump it was liberal elite in Hollywood and media, but in reality, that and the corporate Wall Street elite that Sanders campaigned against are overlapping concepts." For the economist Lawrence Mishel, the "class struggle" for the Democratic Party is on the elemental question of whether "to make low-income people and workers a priority," and "you don't have to look any further than Trump as well as the Democrats in the election campaign of 2016 to see that the whole notion of income inequality and wage stagnation were now a basic fact that everybody understood. I think that Occupy put this into mainstream culture, into the bloodstream of America."

In the winter of 2019, at the age of twenty-eight, Caitlin Remmel graduated from law school in Washington, D.C. By that time she had already managed a San Francisco Bay Area field office for Bernie Sanders's 2016 presidential run, helped launch Alexandria Ocasio-Cortez's political career through Brand New Congress, and served as deputy policy director for Andrew Yang during the 2020 presidential primaries. If there's a millennial who understands the systemic crises and political challenges facing her generation—and the progress that has been made in the decade since Occupy—it's Remmel. "Occupy got the values right, talking about the systemic problem. What was missing at Occupy was the ability to organize—to take hold of what is happening in the movement and translate it into positive policy," she said. For those who came after, the lessons learned at Occupy informed their approach to political action, their views on strategy and structure. And on the most important issue facing their generation and future ones—climate change—a new era of activists would improve on Occupy to build an environmental movement that will not be stopped.

PIZZA AND CIGARETTES

OCTOBER 8, 2011

AFTER SLEEPING AT ZUCCOTTI AND BOUNCING AROUND COUCHES for several weeks, I rented a room for $800 out in Brooklyn's Sunset Park. I shared the apartment with a small, wiry Dutchman named Cruso whose buzz cut, salt-and-pepper goatee and taut frame told you one thing: he was a New York City survivor. Cruso worked brutal hours in the entertainment industry coordinating rides and doing gofer tasks for stars like Bono and Miley Cyrus when they came to town. For weeks he'd be on a job that pushed him out the door at six and deposited him back home at midnight. That fall he was tasked with picking up Madonna's dancers every morning from a Midtown hotel and driving them to a stadium where they rehearsed her halftime show for the Super Bowl. Cruso loathed Madonna like he loathed pretty much everyone whose unending needs and demands consumed him. Deafened, desensitized, fueled by alternating habits of weed and cocaine, Cruso would come home late and sit glued to the giant TV screen in the living room where slowly, hourly, a part of him expired. I remember when he was between jobs he would take a full week to just camp out on the couch and stare. It didn't matter what he was watching because Cruso wasn't seeing the images any longer; freed momentarily from stress and hustle, by nine in the morning he'd crack his first Bud, prepare a pipe, light a Marlboro and turn on the TV where series and game shows occupied the rest of the day. Cruso was a model of working-class frustration and unhappiness, toiling without an escape hatch in service to the 1 percent. He hated the rich, but he didn't think much of Occupy either. "A bunch of losers and anarchists," he told me, "just messing up traffic for the rest of us."

Partly because I shared space with Cruso and his unhealthy lifestyle, but mostly because of my own bad habits, my health declined precipitously. Within weeks at the park, I shed ten pounds. I wasn't the only one getting thinner on the low-rest, high-nicotine, fast-metabolism diet of rebellion. We were all on our feet most of the day, marching a lot and eating a little, keeping up with the frenetic pace at Liberty Square and, as Todd Gitlin described in *Occupy Nation*, living "pell-mell in the grip of what sociologist Barrie Thorne, writing about the sixties, once called *event time*, hurtling from action to action with high fervor and much jubilation." I knew adrenalin alone wouldn't keep me alive but I survived on it anyway. We all survived on it: wired from unending conversations and round-the-clock organizing where it seemed the less food and rest we took in, the sharper and clearer-focused we became. The drug of revolution is a powerful one, and its mad energy fed us.

Not that we were starving; far from it. There was enough food spilling out of Liberty to feed an army, and it did. Thousands lined up throughout the day to receive plates of salad, pasta, rice, vegetables, chicken, fish, fruit, soup, sandwiches and whatever else they were preparing in the kitchen. The kitchen anchored Liberty and the people who ran it formed a bulwark at Occupy, as laid-off chefs joined the scene and "Feed the movement!" became a rallying cry answered by mountains of fresh produce trucked in daily from upstate. When they weren't dialing in donations from restaurants, many New Yorkers cooked food in their apartments that they then hand-delivered on large aluminum trays to the square. The tabloids mocked Occupy protesters for their bounty of edibles. Sure, the people who hadn't changed their clothes in a week, who slept outdoors on cement and used the McDonald's across the street as their public latrine, *they* were the snobs. Occupy Wall Street even modeled best practices in recycling, as bicyclists with the "compost bucket brigades" left Liberty at regular intervals pedaling hundreds of pounds of organic waste in wagons to deliver to urban farms across the city.

Ultimately, though, what our survival at Zuccotti hinged on more than anything was pizza. Pizza was the movement's identity. Without pizza, the argument could be made, Occupy would not have existed at all. Much of the pizza came from the restaurant Liberatos, which took orders from people calling in from around the country and places as far away as Germany, France and Greece. Some of the earliest pizzas, in fact, were donations from Egypt, where the same people who overthrew Mubarak were now trying to help us overthrow Wall Street. The pizza arrived sporadically at first, but once it began to show up, it didn't stop. Box after donated box of hot pies appeared at all hours in the square, sometimes delivered as late as four or five in the morning so that the endlessly replenishing pizzas came to resemble a sort of fifth column: a chest-high cardboard fortress whose cloudlike aroma of hot cheese and dough permeated the park.

The other smell that filled the air at Liberty was tobacco, which I, like so many others, consumed in unwholesome quantities. I had never chain-smoked before, but the moment I joined Occupy I started puffing like crazy and suddenly I found myself at all times with a cigarette between the lips; either it was lit or it was waiting to be lit or I felt myself anxiously unwrapping the pouch of tobacco in my hands to roll another. It didn't even feel like a choice: nicotine was in the breeze, we were all smoking, exalted on fumes, running around Zuccotti with endlessly burning cigarettes trailing a haze around our endless conversations. There was comfort entering the park through that gray-blue fog, like the busy plumes that rise from factories signaling a new day of work. The smoke enveloped our settlement and fueled our dialogue. Listen, inhale.

Talk, exhale. We didn't question the madness of our habit: so long as you had something to smoke and something to say there wasn't a thing you could better imagine yourself doing. Smoke was our breathing space and we absorbed tobacco like oxygen, mowing down cigarettes morning, day, and night like soldiers trapped in battle: the will to consume and be consumed.

Soon enough I picked up a dry, persistent cough—we called it Zuccotti Lung—and hints of strep developed in those long autumn nights spent chattering in the cold. The cough became part of us—we treated it like company, just another character in the conversation, but we weren't about to banish the tobacco because the tobacco was fueling our revolt: strengthening nerves, cutting tensions, stoking courage. There was even a special table they had set up in the southwest corner of the park called Nic at Night, where piles of damp, loose shag were available to roll at all hours. Nonetheless, many at Liberty didn't do that and they didn't carry their own cigarettes either, they just poked around for handouts and when you pulled a pouch from your pocket it was like an invitation to gather. At any time, midday or midnight, someone at the park was asking you for a smoke and if you had one you gave it away. Never mind that Bloomberg's tax had lifted the cost of a New York City pack to $14, the most expensive cigarettes on the planet. We weren't only ruining our bodies, we were emptying our wallets, too. But giving what you had was the spirit of Occupy. Pizza and tobacco: the diet of revolution. We were inhaling and exhaling Liberty together.

Yet finally my body recoiled because of one elemental deprivation: sleep. Sleep was the hardest thing to do at Occupy. Even if you weren't camped out in the park any longer, even if you were exhausted and came home to an apartment and a bed, there was still too much commotion banging around inside to turn it off and rest. My mind operated in a semipermanent state of urgency as I would return to my room in Sunset Park and open up a screen to flying unending emails, messages, tweets, texts, plans, proposals, all taking shape through the dark October night. Like the city that it inhabited, Occupy Wall Street never slept. It was a twenty-four-hour movement and I rarely dozed for a quarter of them, starting in the last pre-dawn hour when I managed to finally close my eyes and stop my mind running, only to start again later that morning, heading back out into the justice encampment, the madness and the euphoric unsustainable energy of it all that couldn't possibly last, though in our heart of hearts, we wished it would.

4
_____

OCCUPY CLIMATE

A GENERATION TO SAVE THE EARTH

FROM OCCUPY TO SUNRISE: EVAN WEBER

AS A BOY GROWING UP IN THE HAWAIIAN BEACH TOWN OF KAILUA, on the southeastern shore of Oʻahu, Evan Weber gained an early respect for the environment, appreciating the ways humans both impacted and depended on it. "I had mountains in my backyard, ocean in my front yard," he said. Though his parents came from the continent—his father was a doctor, his mother worked as a nurse at a local hospital—Weber grew up learning the "Indigenous wisdom of the land. It was instilled in me at a young age." Born in 1991, he studied at the prestigious Punahou School in Honolulu, the same high school Barack Obama attended in the late 1970s. When Weber graduated in 2009, America was floundering in the Great Recession and it wasn't hard to draw some basic connections, "learning about how messed up our economy was, how it was only working for a few people at the top, and at the same time learning about our climate crisis. And here was this president who went to my high school, who said he was going to fix all of it: slow the tides of the ocean, fix the economy, end the tyranny of oil."

It was enough to get Weber fired up to confront the high challenges facing his generation, and when he left that fall to begin studies at Wesleyan University in Connecticut, he felt somehow optimistic about his and the country's future.

Weber—who has thick black hair, scruff around the chin and cheeks, and a round boyish face with an earnest expression—decided to double major in economics and environmental studies. He got involved his initial years in student organizing around labor issues and socially responsible investing through endowment activism. Then, in the summer of 2011, Weber was back home working at an internship for a Hawaiian electric utility when he started to see Twitter chatter about "this thing called Occupy Wall Street." He returned to campus that fall to begin his junior year and learned that all of his activist friends were heading to New York for the movement's kickoff. So Weber joined three dozen students from Wesleyan who boarded a train on the morning of September 17 and showed up at Battery Park in lower Manhattan. The day started slow but eventually a couple of thousand people assembled, and Weber ended up toward the front helping lead the first march on Wall Street, all the way to the Trump Building. That afternoon, and the sustained Occupy uprising that continued through autumn, would recast Weber's life and transform the American climate movement in the process. "I was not a leader by any means," he told me when we met for beer in downtown Oakland in the summer of 2019. "But that experience, just coming back a couple of weeks later and having there be nine hundred other occupations around the globe, awoke in me this idea that ordinary people are capable of doing extraordinary things that can change the dialogue and the course of history in this country. I think really since that moment of seeing Occupy explode in the way that it did, I knew that we had to do something like that on climate change if we were ever going to break through and make it a political priority."

THE ROBUST CLIMATE RESPONSE WE SEE TODAY—MORE THAN $15 trillion in funds divested from fossil fuels; cities and states racing to transition to zero-carbon economies; a Green New Deal with majority support from Congress and the American public—bears little resemblance to the politics of climate change before Occupy came along. Through its language, its tactics and its youthful, militant sense of urgency, Occupy rebooted the U.S. environmental movement just at the moment when the country perceived the climate crisis beginning to spin out of control. As the new regularity of devastating heat waves, droughts, floods and superstorms started to enter the public consciousness, and with little being done at the federal level to tackle the problem, it fell to a generation radicalized by the Occupy movement to articulate solutions and demand transformational change. By redirecting the unfocused energy of Occupy into a clear, strategic narrative around saving the climate, some of the young activists who first cut their teeth at the Wall Street protests would evolve to become leaders spiriting this new era of action.

By way of context, it helps to remember back before Occupy to the moment when Americans' hopes for a muscular approach to combat climate change were crushed—the moment the U.S. Supreme Court handed the contested 2000 presidential election to the country's first climate denier-in-chief, George W. Bush, dealing a fatal blow to Vice President Al Gore's planetary crusade. Josephine Ferorelli, another Occupy Wall Street activist who would later take part in forging the country's modern climate movement, summed it up: "I think that election did more to bury climate as an issue than anything else that happened that decade." A flurry of anti-globalization protests at the century's start signaled the chance for a growing environmental influence on U.S. politics. But activist opposition to the Iraq War soon sucked up all the oxygen in the room, and forceful climate resistance stalled in the 2000s. The era of the non-profit industrial complex flourished, as a landscape of lobby- and donor-based advocacy organizations—Greenpeace, World Wildlife Fund, Natural Resources Defense Council, and on down the line—grew more entrenched and grassroots activism waned. "The environmental movement as a whole lost its militancy as these major organizations went from being radical upstarts in the 1970s that created twenty million people in the streets on

Earth Day, to calcified institutions that we see like Sierra Club and the rest," Weber told me, "and that was largely what the environmental movement was: older white liberals who grew up in the Civil Rights Movement." As the planet warmed and fossil fuel corporations deepened the politics of climate denial in Washington, the Sierra Clubs of the world stood incapable of energizing, much less mobilizing, a new generation that demanded action.

Author Bill McKibben provided the spark in 2007 when he and a handful of his students from Middlebury College in Vermont founded 350.org, the country's first explicitly youth-led climate movement. The group drew its wonky name from the atmospheric threshold of 350 parts per million of carbon dioxide, after which science told us the effects of climate change would be catastrophic (by 2020, the Earth had passed 415 PPM, a level climatologists believe had not been reached in the past three million years). The perils posed by a changing climate were recognized twenty years prior, during the presidency of George H. W. Bush, but no one in power had the courage to confront its enormous implications. By 2007, the World Meteorological Organization had labeled the previous decade the hottest on record, and that is when a handful of college students leveraged their new organization to inspire the first mass marches and demonstrations calling for an end to fossil fuel subsidies and the transition to a renewable energy infrastructure. The events were successful and built a growing legion of young people who participated in "global days of action" to promote energy solutions: weatherizing homes, planting trees, painting bike lanes.

But, as Weber recalled, 350.org offered "less of a militant rebel energy and more of a mass action type of [organizing] that could appeal to as many people as possible." It was joined by another group, Energy Action Coalition, which began to turn out tens of thousands of young people in demonstrations that were part of a movement known as Power Shift, demanding a stronger response to climate change. At the same time, in 2009, a high-stakes round of United Nations climate talks, which I covered in Copenhagen, foundered as world leaders failed to reach any plan or agreement on cutting global emissions—

mainly due to competing United States and Chinese economic interests. Despite his bold campaign promises, and amid a financial crisis and recession that had altered the American landscape, President Obama refused to tackle climate policies in his first term, leaving the Hope and Change generation all but hopeless about any substantive changes to the global carbon economy. Sporadic demonstrations targeted the U.S. Chamber of Commerce, revealing the connections between fossil fuel industry money and the obstruction of climate legislation in Congress. Hundreds of young people came out at one point to stage a brief occupation of the Department of Interior. But the outcry fell on deaf ears. Nothing was moving the needle.

Then, in the late summer of 2011, days before Weber joined Occupy Wall Street's inaugural march through lower Manhattan, the dam broke and a new American climate movement surged into view. During the course of several weeks that August and September, more than twelve hundred people got arrested protesting in front of the White House as they called on President Obama to veto the Keystone XL pipeline. Washington's agreement with the oil giant TransCanada seemed to be a done deal at that point: Obama and Secretary of State Hillary Clinton had all but signed off on the $8 billion project to pump eight hundred thousand barrels a day of tar sands crude through a seventeen-hundred-mile-long pipeline stretching from Alberta, Canada, across the American heartland to the Gulf of Mexico. The mass arrests marked the largest civil disobedience campaign since the anti-nuclear protests of the 1980s, and the country's biggest show of environmental resistance ever. From Native Americans to ranchers, cowboys, Texas grandparents and college kids nationwide, opposition to the Keystone "carbon bomb" grew loud. But the money was louder. Obama appeared poised to ignore public pressure and put oil interests over his stated concerns for the climate. Then, Occupy appeared on the scene, the two nascent movements converged, and suddenly, faster than anyone could have predicted, the old fossil fuel playbook was redrawn.

I remember taking a bus from New York to D.C. on the bright morning of November 7, 2011, while Occupy was in full swing, to be part of the most spectacular of the Keystone XL protests. Thousands of people bussed in from around the country that day to stand against the pipeline. After assembling to hear speeches by McKibben, Indigenous leaders and others, the crowd divided and organized itself over the course of several hours into a vast, uninterrupted, twelve-thousand-person human chain—linking arms around the White House. Visually stunning, politically brilliant, this single act reshuffled the deck as the energy and dynamism of the Occupy protests infused what was becoming a new, strategic direct action movement to save the climate. The fit wasn't immediate, Weber said. "The climate movement wasn't speaking a populist language, and I think it didn't know [at first] how to relate to Occupy." But in the months that followed, he noticed a clear change of tone: climate activists had been radicalized. The environmental movement "gained so much energy that you can directly trace back to Occupy and the momentum it generated. People really saw the power and ability of direct action to capture the public's imagination—to help guide and shift the conversation and tell a story—and I think the climate movement latched on to that."

Most important, Occupy Wall Street pointed a finger at those responsible for the planetary meltdown. For years, environmentalists tried in vain to address climate change by emphasizing individual actions: recycling, driving lower-emitting cars, consuming less meat, boosting civic engagement through voting. "But people hadn't leaned into naming villains in the story of what was happening with the climate crisis." Now, the generation had discovered its narrative. "I think it wasn't just a tactic but also the message and story of Occupy itself: this idea that there's a 99 percent and a 1 percent and the problems we're all facing can be traced back to a handful of individuals," said Weber. "Those things are extremely true in the climate crisis as well, where we have a small handful of fossil fuel executives and politicians and lobbyists who have colluded to co-opt action and deceive and mislead the public in order to serve their own power and profit for decades, while the rest of us are increasingly bearing the burden and cost. The climate movement did not have that story before Occupy. I think for a lot of people, Occupy was a formative social movement experience that really shaped everything we did afterward."

OCCUPY SANDY

THE FIRST MAJOR CLIMATE DISRUPTION OF THE POST-OCCUPY ERA happened the following autumn, in late October and early November of 2012, a few days before Obama's reelection, when Superstorm Sandy flooded New York City and New Jersey while hammering the Eastern Seaboard from Florida to Maine. The largest Atlantic hurricane then on record killed 285 people, caused nearly $70 billion in damages and wrecked communities. But in what became an unexpected first test of the movement's handling of a crisis in real time, activists from Zuccotti Park launched Occupy Sandy within hours of the storm's devastation. In the days that followed, the group delivered an effective grassroots relief effort that put slower, more lumbering organizations like the Red Cross and Federal Emergency Management Agency to shame. With New York City in darkness, the subway underwater and destroyed cars littering streets from the Rockaways to Red Hook to Coney Island, volunteers with Occupy Sandy set up distribution sites at two Brooklyn churches that provided clothing, blankets, food and other crucial supplies to the city's neediest. The movement improvised construction crews, medical clinics, full kitchens with food delivery, mold removal teams and ride shares that helped residents get back into their ruined neighborhoods. As a *New York Times* headline put it: "Where FEMA Fell Short, Occupy Sandy Was There." Comprised of tens of thousands of volunteers, the group acted more nimbly and with greater competence in the crucial first weeks following the storm than any of the federal or non-profit agencies sent to address the crisis, charting a new model for mutual aid and disaster relief in the era of climate upheaval.

One of the first people on the scene at Occupy Sandy was Tamara Shapiro. Shapiro had worked with the tech operations team at Occupy Wall Street to build InterOccupy, an online network that connected the movement's hundreds of national groups; she also helped Occupy incorporate a new conference calling system known as Maestro, which later became a useful tool deployed for Black Lives Matter. In late October 2012, Shapiro and some fellow activists were at an organizers' retreat upstate when they heard about the hurricane, so they rushed back to the city. "The next day, after the storm, we drove some batteries to Red Hook and people started talking about different places to drop off supplies. We came for an hour or two," she said, "and we ended up staying for a month." Occupy Sandy not only set a new benchmark for the way community-driven mutual aid can impact victims of a natural disaster; it also showcased some of the tech innovations from Occupy that future social movements would build upon. The InterOccupy network, for example, became a key tool activists used to coordinate assistance and maintain reliable lines of communication during New York City's blackout. Occupy Sandy set up a database of volunteers, a transit dispatch system and even a wedding registry, through Amazon, which collected donated supplies that volunteers hurried to desperate families and communities.

"It proved the decentralized organizing model—one that worked better than FEMA, better than the Red Cross, because centralized structures don't work well in moments with a lot of confusion. If you're in a big bureaucracy, you see a need and you have to go up the chain and down the chain to start filling that need," Shapiro told me, but "the idea of decentralization is that you see a need and you start filling it." While reviving Occupy networks that had gone dormant, activists at Occupy Sandy demonstrated a movement that not only stood *against* corporate greed but *for* helping people in critical need. "I think, a year after Occupy, the network [of Zuccotti Park activists] would have died in New York but Sandy, as terrible as it was, brought it back together." Occupy Sandy was also, in retrospect, a crucial event that drove the Occupy movement in the direction of climate activism as organizers drew explicit links between a broken economic system ruled by the 1 percent, and a broken climate system where the same 1 percent were fueling denial, corrupting politics and obstructing progress. "After Sandy, many Occupy activists became a lot more environmental," journalist and Zuccotti veteran Peter Rugh told me. As people "linked the financial crisis and its aftermath—the fact that the bankers never went to jail and got a payday after they ruined the economy—they took that analysis and applied it to climate change, which became a much more central issue for them," he said. Journalist J. A. Myerson called Occupy Sandy "the movement's redemptive second act," one that set the stage for a generation that was done camping out in tents and parks and was ready to occupy the climate front lines.

THE DIVESTMENT MOVEMENT

IN THE FALL OF 2011, THE MESSAGE OF OCCUPY WALL STREET RES-onated across university campuses. Protesting sky-high student debt, cuts to public schools and a low-wage job market, a group calling itself Occupy Colleges inspired thousands of students at more than one hundred U.S. campuses to stage coordinated walkouts in solidarity with the movement. Meanwhile, a series of high-profile protests—like the one famously caught on film at the University of California, Davis, where a cop blasted bright orange pepper spray into the faces of a dozen nonviolent students seated cross-legged on the ground—boosted national support for Occupy. Then, in 2012, mobilized by their concerns around climate change, students repurposed that energy into a clean, fresh demand: igniting a call for divestment, they told their academic institutions to stop bankrolling the companies responsible for climate change and immediately dump fossil fuel companies from their stock portfolios.

Modeled on the successful global divestment campaign that transformed apartheid South Africa in the 1980s, the student fossil fuel divestment movement started small, sprouting forth at first at only a handful of colleges. But by the spring of 2012, in the wake of Occupy, the movement swelled as more than fifty universities committed to selling off their coal and oil stocks. From there, divestment started to go mainstream. "The dominant political narrative in the country was shifting thanks to the work of Occupy Wall Street," Katie McChesney, a former 350.org divestment campaign manager who helped build the movement on campuses nationwide, told me. "The 99 percent and the 1 percent resonated with young people who were facing the mounting challenges of a climate-unstable future, student debt and inheriting an economy that isn't designed to work for all of us."

That July, Bill McKibben published a seminal essay in *Rolling Stone* entitled "Global Warming's Terrifying New Math," which revealed in stark new terms the depth and speed of the growing climate threat. And later that summer, McKibben's twenty-two-city "Do the Math Tour" galvanized the climate movement as students embraced divestment as the natural, and more pragmatic, successor to Occupy. "Occupy was definitely a part of shaping the political moment and the energy in young people to want to organize. At the same time, [McKibben's] article laid out the math of the climate crisis and fossil fuel investments, which piqued everyone's interest because people were feeling this deep sense of economic stress and trying to digest that in the context of the climate crisis," added McChesney. "Occupy provided a useful model for what a different style of campaigning and power-building could look like, and divestment gave students a more specific campaign to latch on to next."

The following year, the divestment movement migrated off campus as Seattle and San Francisco became the first big U.S. cities to strip fossil fuel assets from their public funds. Their moves set in motion a snowball effect, and the movement took off nationally. In 2014, conservative institutions like Stanford University dropped coal investments from their multi-billion-dollar endowment, the British Medical Association closed its doors to fossil fuels, and the Rockefeller Brothers Fund—whose vast fortune had been built on oil—cleansed its portfolio of dirty emitters. Heightening the public's outrage over inequality, news reports that year revealed one hundred corporations were responsible for more than 70 percent of global emissions—further connecting the economic crisis to the climate crisis, and helping push the number of divesting institutions to one hundred and eighty-one with a total portfolio value of more than $50 billion. By 2015, the campaign was considered the fastest growing divestment movement in history, as public and private institutions globally—in the U.K., Ireland, Sweden, Denmark, Germany, Holland, Norway, Australia, New Zealand and elsewhere—lined up to remove oil, gas and coal from their ledgers.

A few years later, with oil and gas investments in free fall due to the lowered costs of renewable energy, New York State declared it was divesting its $189 billion pension fund from fossil fuels. Analysts at Goldman Sachs admitted the "divestment movement has been a key driver of the coal sector's 60 percent de-rating over the past five years." And in 2019, the European Investment Bank, the world's biggest public lender, announced an end to its investments in carbon-emitting fuels, cutting billions in funding to projects worldwide. By that time, more than $11 trillion had been committed to divestment by more than eleven hundred institutions, including banks, governments, universities, pension funds, sovereign wealth funds, global insurers, philanthropies, healthcare providers and faith-based organizations.

Then, in January 2020, a few months before the coronavirus pandemic tilted civilization off its axis, BlackRock, the global investment firm and largest money manager on Earth, which oversaw some $7 trillion in assets, committed to stop investing in companies that failed to meet strong sustainability and climate goals. The company's ban on fossil fuel stocks sent shock waves through the financial sector, not least because BlackRock owned significant portions of Exxon, Chevron and other big emitters. In a letter to company executives, titled "A Fundamental Reshaping of Finance," CEO Larry Fink wrote: "Awareness is rapidly changing, and I believe we are on the edge of a fundamental reshaping of finance. The evidence on climate change is compelling investors to reassess core assumptions about modern finance." As unlikely as it might have seemed a decade ago, what began on a few college campuses, where Occupy's message inspired students to try and wrest power from the 1 percent in the fossil fuel industry, had developed into a worldwide economic movement to save the climate.

IGNITING THE FOSSIL FUEL RESISTANCE

PARALLEL TO THEIR EFFORTS TO RESHAPE FOSSIL FUEL FINANCING, many more young people were beginning to realize that in order to stop the expansion of carbon-emitting projects, they would need to occupy them, literally putting their bodies in front of the machinery. It's important to remember that up until the Keystone XL protests at the start of the last decade, there wasn't much of an American "climate movement" to speak of. Years before anyone had heard of a Green New Deal—or of the Swedish teenager Greta Thunberg, who would launch a worldwide movement that drew millions of students into the streets for the Global Climate Strikes in September 2019—vocal opposition to fossil fuels was still occurring largely on the fringe. But then something happened that directly connected the climate crisis with people's health in a way that had never occurred before: the fracking revolution.

The United States wasn't always the world's largest oil producer, a distinction it reached only in 2018, and the technology that got it there—a sand-and-water-intensive horizontal drilling process known as hydraulic fracturing—remained a new vocabulary term to most Americans until just a decade ago. The gas boom that started in the late nineties in the Barnett Shale of north Texas, and peaked in the rush to frack North Dakota's Bakken formation in the late 2000s, made little impact on most people's lives or on their pocket books, though it disrupted the fossil fuel industry completely. By the second decade of the century, cheap natural gas and affordable wind and solar energy had flooded the market, pushing the coal industry toward bankruptcy. For a time the public bought the argument that natural gas was a cleaner, healthier "bridge fuel"—a crucial piece of President Obama's "all of the above" energy strategy. But the anti-fracking movement, which was sparked and in many ways shaped by the organizing that emerged from Occupy Wall Street, changed that narrative, igniting a nationwide resistance to fossil fuels and paving the way for the climate generation to emerge.

Perhaps nothing did more to jumpstart the anti-fracking rebellion than

Josh Fox's 2010 Oscar-nominated documentary *Gasland*, which followed the
New York filmmaker on a grim, personal road trip to expose the poisonous
effects of fracking on people's lands and wells. Fox's film, in the words of *The
New York Times*, had "brought 'hydraulic fracturing' into the nation's living
rooms." But there was a difference between raising awareness and raising a
ruckus, and in 2012, insurgents from Occupy Wall Street organized a series of
well-choreographed protests against the Spectra Pipeline, a gas project being
built under the West Side Highway in Manhattan. The "fracktivist" demonstrations began locally, but they lit a fire under what was becoming a growing conversation across the state and the Northeast region about the risks of
fracking. From there, the movement never looked back. "So many people went
from Occupy right into the anti-fracking movement," said the journalist Peter
Rugh, who closely followed the pivot toward climate activism. "They went on
to form groups in upstate New York and Pennsylvania, they became leaders,
they disrupted drilling and pipeline sites, they went to Washington and got
arrested in front of the Federal Energy Regulatory Commission. Occupy really
gave people a mission to put their bodies on the line and to use radical tactics
a lot more often—to be more insistent in calling out the economic greed that
underlay this environmental destruction." He added, "When Occupy ended,
people kept organizing and forged alliances in these different communities,
and that became the radical grassroots wing of the environmental movement."

A militant brand of anti-fracking protests soon galvanized towns and cities across the country, and remarkable results followed. After sustained public pressure, statewide fracking bans were instituted in New York, Maryland
and Vermont while dozens of city councils and county seats in heavy fracking
states like California, Texas, Colorado, Ohio and Pennsylvania voted to set
indefinite moratoriums or halt the process altogether. Building on the digital
strategic success of Occupy, anti-fracking protesters harnessed social media
and online organizing tools to quickly spread information, grow their support base and mobilize opposition to drilling projects nationwide. As victories
spread, the resistance also grew beyond opposing regional hydraulic fracturing

to addressing larger carbon conflicts. This happened especially in the Pacific Northwest, which became the new battleground over fossil fuel expansion as a young, organized climate movement took on an array of oil pipeline, coal train, and gas and coal export terminal projects—and in case after case, defeated them.

One person who made the shift into climate activism was Occupy Wall Street protester Josephine Ferorelli, who in 2012 relocated with her partner from New York City to Olympia, Washington. That summer she attended one of McKibben's "Do the Math" town halls in Seattle, a city that was quickly turning into ground zero of the Occupy-turned-climate movement. Ferorelli learned about a number of projects in development to ship carbon-intense fuels through British Columbia, Washington and Oregon to Asian markets, and became part of the burgeoning grassroots resistance that employed not only direct action but legal arguments to combat the port and pipeline expansions. "Everybody had recently been together at Occupy encampments in Olympia and they were figuring out how to use environmental impact statements, necessity defense and other tools to address climate change, because the threats were popping up everywhere," she said. "For a lot of people at Occupy, it was a feeling of coming together—cross-movement building, sharing values, sharing goals, sharing skills—and it inspired a lot of people to keep on working. We were like, 'No fossil fuels are going to leave this part of the country. We are going to be the Thin Green Line that prevents them from going,' and we tried to build scalable, legal environmental wins."

The double-pressure strategy turned out to be the right one. Over the next several years, an army of activists backed by court decisions managed to shut down oil train transports, block pipeline constructions and put an end to a dizzying array of coal and gas export terminals. One after another, in a domino effect, defeats for the fossil fuel industry swept the Cascadia region as the list of billions of dollars in doomed coal export projects mounted: SSA Marine's Gateway Pacific Terminal at Cherry Point, Washington; Ambre Energy's Millennium Bulk Terminals at Longview, Washington, and Morrow

Pacific Project at Coos Bay, Oregon; Shell Oil's East Gate Rail Project at Ana-
cortes, Washington; RailAmerica's Coal Terminal at Hoquiam, Washington;
Kinder Morgan's Port Westward Terminal on the Columbia River in Washington; and Prince Rupert Port Authority's Ridley Coal Terminal Expansion
in British Columbia. High-profile oil pipelines in British Columbia, including
Enbridge's Northern Gateway Pipeline and Kinder Morgan's Trans Mountain Pipeline Expansion, got the axe; a half dozen oil-by-rail projects were also
quashed in the courts. While Occupy didn't lead in name, organizers' skillful
and aggressive tactics borrowing from the movement helped galvanize community groups, non-profits and everyday citizens to demand a stop to fossil
fuel development on their lands and waters. The Pacific Northwest became the
place, in the words of renewable energy executive Lou Soumas, "where energy
projects go to die."

For Ferorelli, who worked to halt construction of the Gateway Pacific Terminal in Cherry Point, Occupy Wall Street gave environmentalists the shot
in the arm that set the modern climate movement on course. "Most climate
activists I met [in Washington] had been at Occupy in their town or city. It
wasn't that Occupy *became* a climate movement," she said, "it was that climate
people were part of Occupy, and had been heartened and radicalized by the
experience. It spurred a lot of us to make climate the priority, reorganizing our
activist vision so that climate justice is the first and last thing that we think of
when we go to work." In 2015, Ferorelli co-founded Conceivable Future, an
organization connecting people at house parties and events across the country
to discuss the perils and confront the fears of bringing children into a world of
climate instability. As more extreme storms, heat waves, fires and floods have
battered the country in recent years, Americans are not only tuning into the
climate emergency but connecting the dots to the reckless policies and profits
of the 1 percent—and realizing that a dramatic collective response is needed.

"The personal stakes are that we're terrified of losing who and what we love,
and this has a particular resonance for millennials: people whose reproductive
windows line up with these last ten years that we have to make substantive

change," Ferorelli said. "We're trying to push people out of this analysis that 'not having a kid is my solution to the climate crisis,' or 'my reduction of one [person] is a major political action.' We're saying, no, that's not political, that's personal: you live the life you need to live and then you fight like hell to make the world livable. Stop with the small, incremental, concessionary stuff and just make the absolute demand. We're asking people to radicalize."

FROM THE PEOPLE'S CLIMATE MARCH TO STANDING ROCK

AFTER HE GRADUATED FROM WESLEYAN, EVAN WEBER MOVED TO Washington, D.C., where he co-founded and directed the advocacy organization U.S. Climate Plan. Then, on September 21, 2014, he joined half a million people in the streets of New York City for what was at the time the country's largest-ever climate mobilization: the People's Climate March. "It was probably the biggest thing the climate movement has ever done in the U.S.," Weber recalled, and what excited him even more was the follow-up action that occurred the next morning when thousands of protesters, mostly dressed in blue, convened in the financial district for a more militant action known as Flood Wall Street. Thought up by many of the same activists who had organized at Zuccotti Park three years earlier, Flood Wall Street targeted the banks, the corporations and the 1 percent for their financial and political role exacerbating the climate crisis. The day's message was clear in the three-hundred-foot-long banner that marchers carried through the city, which read: "Capitalism = Climate Chaos. Flood Wall Street." The event shut down Broadway and resulted in more than one hundred arrests as the sea of bodies spread across lower Manhattan—a forerunner of climate civil disobedience campaigns that would erupt worldwide a few years later. As Occupy Wall Street organizer Michael Premo said that day: "Just like the financial crisis, the climate crisis is a product of an underlying political crisis. It's the result of policies that serve the shortsighted interests of the few over the survival and well-being of everyone."

Finally, it seemed the Occupy movement had reached its most consequential juncture: the fight to save the planet. For Weber, "that moment of Flood Wall Street was part of my journey coming full circle—from Occupy to being an actor pushing the climate movement."

As the fossil fuel divestment and resistance movements continued to notch victories, President Obama delivered a high moment for environmentalists in February 2015 when he vetoed the Keystone XL bill passed by Congress, citing its unfavorable carbon and economic impacts. Vindicating four years of work by climate activists, the decision energized the broader climate movement, and suddenly it was no longer only in the Pacific Northwest or the heartland but all across the nation where pipelines seemed up for grabs. "The Keystone fight was kind of the beginning of them all," McKibben later recalled, speaking with Dorothy Wickenden on *The New Yorker*'s podcast *Politics and More*. "At the time no one thought that it was really possible to stand up to the fossil fuel industry ... because Big Oil had never lost a fight like this. But we managed to rally enough protest, between Native American groups and farmers and ranchers and climate scientists and everybody else, that we were able to eventually get the Obama administration to put the kibosh on the thing. And I think as people saw that it was possible to stand up to these guys, that sentiment spread. Everything gets fought now: every pipeline, every frack well, every new coal port." Projects like the Bayou Bridge Pipeline in the fragile Atchafalaya Basin of Louisiana, and Enbridge's Line 5 pipeline crossing Michigan and Wisconsin, received growing scrutiny as protesters dug in to prevent their construction. But the showdown over oil, the "black snake" of Native American lore, which most captured the country's imagination was the drama that unfolded over ten months at Standing Rock: the battle over the Dakota Access Pipeline.

Led by young members of the Standing Rock Sioux reservation, who initially started their campaign under the banner "ReZpect our water," the #NoDAPL movement gathered momentum in the spring of 2016 when thousands of protesters from across the country descended on the rolling fields of North Dakota to stand in solidarity with the Indigenous "water protectors" defending their sacred grounds. There had been occupations by Native Americans before, most famously the nineteen-month-long Occupation of Alcatraz in the early seventies. But this time was different because suddenly Indigenous people weren't out there fighting alone. The popular nonviolent movement drew together a diverse range of allies, including many activists from Occupy Wall Street, and marked the most radicalized stage yet of the climate movement—one whose demands embodied the meaning of climate justice in an escalating challenge to the 1 percent. "Standing Rock took Occupy and truly innovated on it—they took it to the next level and did something better," said Martin Kirk, co-founder of The Rules. Indigenous leaders and their supporters "took the 99 percent and deepened the system's language: from being protesters to 'We are protectors, and we're not only protecting nature, we are nature fighting back!' It's a profound statement, a concept of deep ecology filtering into mainstream progressive spaces, and it's one of the ways that Standing Rock picked up the lessons of Occupy and deepened it." Marc Armstrong, co-founder of the Public Banking Institute, agreed that Standing Rock represented "an extension of Occupy in that it was fine-tuning it—saying that we not only have to talk about the economic injustices, but about the importance of water: that it is life, and it is being polluted and degraded in any number of ways. Native Americans enhanced people's understanding of the economic regime that we're fighting, and enhanced our perspective that it is yet another important thing the 1 percent are destroying before our very eyes."

As Standing Rock and the presidential election campaigns accelerated through 2016, Evan Weber underwent a period of personal reckoning with the climate movement, which he didn't feel was moving fast enough. The previous year, President Obama had instituted a Clean Power Plan to curb pollution at the nation's existing power plants, while still touting a multipronged energy strategy that did little to reign in the influence of fossil fuels. "A lot of people were so happy that the Obama administration was doing anything on climate change, they were cheering him on. The environmental movement was really afraid to go up against him because they were desperate for something to happen," Weber recalled. But as his organization, U.S. Climate Plan, began to take a riskier and more confrontational approach to the administration's policies, he began to see a shift. "We were one of the few voices saying, 'This isn't enough, we need to be doing more,' and we found our message taking off with young people in particular. It was similar to what happened at Occupy: they were hungry to have someone telling them the truth."

More deeply, Weber understood that the institutional work being done by advocacy organizations like his wasn't having the transformative effect on politics, or the public, that he believed was necessary to confront the climate emergency. "We needed to spark a moral crisis in this country around climate change," he said. So Weber did something simple but effective: he wrote a ten-page memo, which he shared with friends and colleagues, laying out his concerns and vision for the movement. Many agreed with him that it was time to take the climate fight to the next level. "I found out that there were other people who were thinking a lot of the same things and asking a lot of the same questions that I was." Organizers from 350.org, the divestment movement and U.S. Climate Plan "basically found each other, and we were like, 'What are the ingredients to create a social movement that this country needs to confront the climate crisis?'" The answer he and others came up with, it turned out, would reshape the Democratic Party platform and set America on a new course to addressing humanity's greatest crisis.

MOMENTUM TOWARD A GREEN NEW DEAL

THE NEW ALLIANCE OF CLIMATE ACTIVISTS TURNED TO HISTORY for guidance. Their idea was straightforward: by studying both the successful and failed organizing strategies employed in past social movements—ranging from the Civil Rights era and the Color Revolutions of Eastern Europe, to the Arab Spring, Occupy Wall Street and Black Lives Matter—they would build an effective hybrid capable of driving institutional change in climate policy.

"We were looking to a lot of different places for inspiration," said Weber, and one of those places was a group itself born from Occupy Wall Street, called Momentum. Part training institute, part "movement incubator," Momentum was co-founded in 2013 by Max Berger, one of the early organizers at Zuccotti Park, and was modeled upon the experiences of Otpor (Resistance), the grassroots pro-democracy movement in the former Yugoslavia that overthrew the dictator Slobodan Milosevic in 2000. Momentum's goal was to push more American activists and organizations out of their online setting—where they tended to mobilize around signing petitions and soliciting donations—into an offline setting of decentralized organizing to escalate people's numbers in the streets. Taking lessons and best practices from prior civil disobedience movements, Momentum sought to help the next generation "develop movements that would be stronger and more resilient and strategic," said Nicole Carty, an Occupy Wall Street organizer who, like Berger, transitioned into training activists with Momentum.

By correcting some of the basic mistakes made at Occupy—a movement broadly acknowledged to have suffered from a lack of leadership, structure, direction and goals—Momentum explicitly taught young activists to "plan your strategy, plan what you're going to do, plan how you're going to bring people into your movement, plan the intervention or change that you're going to make in society—then move into a yearlong action process," said Carty. Quickly, the difference in organizing tactics between the movements became notable. Whereas "Occupy didn't have strategy, these movements have actual orientations and strategies, they know how to build power, and they know what they need to win." She added, "If you want to really shape the debate, that's how you do it: build a movement that politicians can be pushed to embrace—like the Green New Deal."

In November 2016, during one of Weber's first training retreats with Momentum, Donald Trump was elected president. The event dramatically shifted the group's calculations; suddenly they were no longer just talking about protesting, but designing a movement that could enter the political arena—à la

Micah White's "hybrid movement-parties"—to shape policy from the inside. In the era of Trump, "we knew that an electoral, political component needed to be part of our strategy," Weber told me, because "that was where the energy of our base was going to be: seeing politics as a vehicle for struggle and change. The election helped to crystallize a lot of things for us."

In 2017, after completing the training with Momentum, Weber along with seven of his climate activist peers, including Sara Blazevic and Varshini Prakash, launched their generation's response: the Sunrise Movement. Of the many lessons and experiences that contributed to Sunrise's "theory of change," Weber said, none perhaps shaped the youth climate movement as much as Occupy—both what it got right and what it got wrong. "When we were creating the plan for Sunrise, Occupy was one of the most potent examples of what both success and failure can look like in social movements: the value of a powerful story that people can see themselves in, the need to have a broad *us* and a narrow *them*, the opportunities around decentralization, the perils of structurelessness. Occupy is what happens when there's no clear structure and hierarchy and ability to make decisions," he added, but Sunrise tried to show that "you can have decentralization and autonomy, which is what movements need to grow and scale, while also having structure."

The movement struck a balance as it embarked on its initial goal: to get candidates who aggressively backed a renewable energy transition elected in the 2018 midterms, and to defeat those who explicitly refused to reject campaign funding from the fossil fuel industry. On a state level, the group saw some initial success, contributing to the victories of Maine state representative Chloe Maxmin, who would author and pass the first statewide Green New Deal bill; Greta Neubauer, who would champion the Green New Deal from the Wisconsin State Assembly; and a handful of other state representatives with strong climate plans, from Florida to Pennsylvania to New York. In the Blue Wave that saw Democrats pick up forty-one seats in the House, Sunrise helped mobilize voters to elect a diverse slate of progressives that included representatives Alexandria Ocasio-Cortez of New York, Rashida Tlaib of Michigan, and Ilhan Omar of Minnesota. Another climate ally that Sunrise helped elect to the House was Representative Deb Haaland of New Mexico, whom President Joe Biden would appoint in 2021 to be the country's first Native American secretary of the interior.

But it wasn't until the week after the midterm elections that the Sunrise Movement really got on the map by occupying the Washington office of House Speaker-elect Nancy Pelosi. In an event designed to maximize media coverage, hundreds of young people carried signs and wore matching black T-shirts that read, "We have a right to good jobs and a livable future," as they marched down the congressional halls to Pelosi's office and staged a sit-in. They demanded that she create a select committee on a Green New Deal, and that all Democratic congress members reject donations from the fossil fuel industry. Newly elected Congresswoman Ocasio-Cortez put in a surprise appearance at the protest, standing in solidarity with the generation of activists who were even younger than her. Praising their leadership, she said the introduction of Green New Deal legislation would be her priority upon entering Congress, and announced: "We need to tell [Pelosi] that we've got her back in showing and pursuing the most progressive energy agenda that this country has ever seen." Fifty-one nonviolent climate protesters were arrested that day. All of a sudden, Sunrise was on the nation's radar.

Weber's organization sensed the moment was ripe so they continued using the tactic of occupying to draw further attention to their cause—then once people were listening, issuing clear demands so that people understood exactly what they wanted. The next month, activists again occupied the offices of Pelosi as well as Democratic representatives Steny Hoyer and Jim McGovern, except this time more than one thousand protesters showed up, packing the congressional hallways with signs that read: "Back the Deal." "Do Your Job." "No More Excuses." Nearly 150 people were arrested that day as Sunrise activists highlighted a bleak October 2019 report, issued by the UN Intergovernmental Panel on Climate Change, which warned of catastrophic results if humans failed to act quickly to reduce carbon in the atmosphere. The deal from Sunrise was clear: "If the Democrats want the youth vote in 2020, they need to get to work on a Green New Deal in 2019," said co-founder Varshini Prakash.

Momentum was building. By the next week, forty members of Congress were on board supporting a select committee on a Green New Deal. Then, on February 7, 2019, five weeks after being sworn into office, the twenty-nine-year-old lawmaker Ocasio-Cortez went prime time, standing outside the Capitol alongside Massachusetts senator Ed Markey to unveil the fourteen-page resolution known as the Green New Deal. Invoking the urgency of Franklin Delano Roosevelt's Depression-era New Deal, the sweeping ten-year plan called on the United States to move to 100 percent renewable energy by 2030 through massive investments in zero-emission electric vehicles, high-speed rail, building retrofits, reduced agricultural emissions and other strategies—at the same time tackling inequality by creating millions of high-paid jobs to provide a "just transition" to the renewable energy economy. The Green New Deal overnight redefined the terms of the climate debate, forcing the Democratic Party—and its dozens of candidates running in the 2020 presidential primaries—to take a stand on the issue.

The policy earned immediate majority support from the public, as more than 80 percent of registered voters said they liked the plan, including, incredibly, around two-thirds of Republicans. By July 2019, an NPR/PBS NewsHour/Marist poll showed overwhelming numbers still backing the proposal, with 77 percent support from people between the ages of 18 and 38, regardless of party; nearly two-thirds support from Midwesterners overall; nearly 70 percent support from self-identified moderates, and close to two-thirds support from independents. For context, the comprehensive climate and jobs plan had a higher approval rating than a wealth tax, a semiautomatic assault gun ban, or free college tuition—and about the same approval rating as legalizing marijuana. "It enjoys wide popularity among almost all demographics: people with and without college degrees, whites and people of color, urban and rural Americans, and people who earn less than and more than $50,000," reported *Grist* magazine at the time. Though none of this, of course, was inevitable. It took the methodical and patient planning of Sunrise Movement organizers who pushed the Green New Deal to the top of the fold. "Sunrise had been building and growing their movement for a year and a half before it happened," said Carty. "They had a solid foundation of people and a plan of escalation, they were already going to be in Nancy Pelosi's office, and it definitely helped that they were able to say to AOC, 'We're pushing this thing—do you want to collaborate?' and then they worked together to build it. Now Democrats have it as a central piece of their platform, which is what Sunrise planned all along." It also revealed the power of organized social movements, in the post-Occupy era, to influence politics. "AOC and a lot of the younger people in Congress understand that if they really want to do something, they need a movement behind them."

Yet perhaps what stood out most about the Green New Deal, connecting it unmistakably to Occupy, was its social promise to take on inequality at the same time that it advanced a clean energy and jobs agenda. To many pundits and mainstream observers, the plan came off as overly ambitious and naive. But to Weber and his generation, solving the climate and inequality crises together made perfect sense because they understood that the one was inextricably bound to the other—and their vision shifted the way Americans thought about both issues. "The Green New Deal is about more than addressing climate change: it's addressing economic injustice as well, and that comes directly from Occupy Wall Street," said Marc Armstrong. "Some people are having a hard time digesting the idea that we have to address climate change as well as economic inequality; they want to separate the two. But the folks who went through Occupy say, 'No, they go together, you cannot separate them because we know what's going to happen: workers are going to get the shaft.' The plan is directly tied to Occupy because you have this additional focus on inequality: they recognize the importance of it, they're folding that into addressing climate change, and they're building on what Occupy started."

BROADENING THE CLIMATE REBELLION

AT THE SAME TIME THAT THE SUNRISE MOVEMENT VAULTED INTO the public spotlight at home, an even more radical civil disobedience campaign was taking shape on the global stage. In the fall of 2018, an army of British climate activists calling themselves Extinction Rebellion made their inaugural appearance in London, blockading five bridges across the Thames River in what *The Guardian* called "one of the biggest acts of peaceful civil disobedience in the U.K. in decades." The decentralized nonviolent movement—which took inspiration from Occupy among more historic social justice causes led by Gandhi, the suffragettes and Martin Luther King Jr.—gained an immediate following across Great Britain and quickly spread to hundreds of cities worldwide, where groups used an array of direct-action tactics, from flash-mob swarms to body glue-downs, fixing themselves in place by gluing themselves to the pavement so as not to be easily moved. Like Sunrise, Extinction Rebellion, or XR, sought to disrupt business as usual as part of its strategy to force leaders to declare a planetary emergency and begin making sweeping changes to the carbon economy. The movement's official coming out party, known as International Rebellion, took place on April 15, 2019, and launched weeks of climate protests that led to more than a thousand arrests as it paralyzed parts of the U.K. Satellite protests spread across the globe.

Adhering to the Occupy script, Extinction Rebellion focused its climate demands around the policy choices shaped by the 1 percent. Similar to Sunrise, some of the people who founded Extinction Rebellion had come out of the Occupy movement, and they acknowledged that the links between the two weren't all that subtle. "Here comes Occupy 2.0, who knows?" said Ronan McNern, an XR media organizer in London who was previously involved with Occupy London. "It's about economic disruption. People are learning from what we did at Occupy and what didn't work there. I remember years ago people saying, 'Occupy is dead.' It's clearly not. It's part of any disruption campaign."

The climate journalist Peter Rugh also tied Extinction Rebellion to its predecessor movement. "They are one hundred percent a direct descendant of Occupy. What XR is doing—occupying bridges and the arteries of major cities—is insisting that public policy be developed that benefits the majority of the people and not just wealthy bankers and oil executives," he said. "They're bringing the urgency of climate change to the public square in the same way that Occupy brought the urgency of the financial crisis to the public consciousness, using similar tactics."

At just the time that Extinction Rebellion was picking up steam, a fifteen-year-old Swedish student named Greta Thunberg took the global fight for the climate to the next level. Thunberg's personal protest began in 2018, when the teenager would leave school each week to go sit outside Swedish Parliament holding a sign that read, "Skolstrejk för klimatet," or "School strike for climate." Other students internationally soon picked up on her message and launched a series of weekly school strikes, called #FridaysForFuture, demanding that elected leaders confront the realities of climate change and start writing policies to change the energy economy. Thunberg quickly became the global face of the youth climate movement, moving people with her sharp, direct speaking style that condemned world leaders for their failure to address the crisis. A series of escalating student-led climate protests culminated in September 2019 when Thunberg arrived in New York to great fanfare—having crossed the Atlantic by sailboat to avoid putting any carbon into the atmosphere—and led weeklong protests known as the Global Climate Strikes. Coinciding with the United Nations Climate Action Summit—where Thunberg lashed out at world leaders for their inactive response on climate, accusing "How dare you!"—the strikes brought an estimated six to seven and a half million people into the streets in more than 4,500 cities across 163 countries, making them by far the largest environmental protests in world history.

In the decade since Occupy, global temperatures, extreme weather events and the long-term threats posed by climate change have all grown dramatically. But so, too, has the public's recognition of the crisis. Climate change didn't even make the top dozen list of priorities for the Democratic Progressive Caucus ten years ago. "It was seen as an unwinnable issue," the Occupy and climate activist Ferorelli told me, because "there wasn't a mass movement demanding climate action. We had work to do busting the taboo around climate change and getting people to take it seriously. In 2011, if you said something like, 'It looks like the world's gonna end,' it was a pretty fringy position to hold, even with all the science to back you up." Not fringy, apparently, any longer. For the comedian and news show host Lee Camp, the dynamism of today's global climate movement signals a natural evolution from the protests that began in 2011 in Zuccotti Park. "A good place to see Occupy is in the climate protests—movements like Extinction Rebellion, which are shutting things down and upsetting the day-to-day, and the Sunrise Movement, where people in their teens and twenties are sitting in lawmakers' offices," he said. What's different about mobilizations around the climate, he added, is that they speak to deep-seated fears in all of us—because no one, not even the most hyper-polarized, will be exempt from planetary catastrophe.

"You can be a white supremacist and you're still going to go through a drought. You can think America has never done anything wrong, with no inequality and no racism, and you're still going to get hit by that hurricane," Camp said. "I think the next protest movement that gains large-scale traction will have to be connected to the climate, because climate is on a timescale different from anything we've ever dealt with before—and it unites us all in a way that we've never been united before." He recalled once driving through Ohio after large floods, and "farmhouses were up to their windows in water—the water was so high the only thing that wasn't underwater was the highway— but I flipped on the radio to a right-wing station and the guy was yelling that climate change is a hoax: 'These environmentalists are beatable, we can beat 'em!' And I'm thinking, 'You're going to be in a rowboat and stop these environmentalists?'"

In late 2019, the worst fires in history ravaged Australia, and in the summer of 2020—the Earth's warmest recorded year to date—unprecedented fires scorched Siberia, and areas within the Arctic Circle saw temperatures top one hundred degrees for the first time. That June, America recorded its tenth billion-dollar weather disaster earlier than any previous year, and California hit temperatures exceeding 120 degrees as fires engulfed the state for the fourth year in a row. Nevertheless, in July 2020—during the long first wave of the coronavirus pandemic, which at that point had infected more than three million Americans and killed nearly 140,000—the climate movement caught a glimmer of hope. In a single week, the Supreme Court rejected the Trump administration's request to continue construction of the Keystone XL pipeline; a federal judge ruled that Energy Transfer Partners must drain out all the oil and shut down its Dakota Access Pipeline pending a more substantial environmental impact review; and two energy giants, Duke Energy and Dominion Energy, cancelled plans to build the Atlantic Coast pipeline. At the same time, a Biden-Sanders task force, led by former secretary of state John Kerry and Congresswoman Ocasio-Cortez, came out with strong recommendations for a Green New Deal.

McKibben told *The New Yorker* in that July week, "Sometimes it takes a while to build the kind of momentum you need to prevail over forces this big and powerful. But that momentum is here now, and we need to keep harnessing it, keep pushing hard—we've got to continue to just organize, organize, organize, because that's what works. I think that we've spent the last ten years like Sisyphus, rolling this boulder of fossil fuel political power up the hill, and I think now it's going to change from a Sisyphean task of rolling it up, to a Newtonian one of trying to guide its trajectory down the other side—and make sure that we get the change we need, at the pace we need."

For Weber—who experienced Occupy Wall Street as a twenty-year-old college junior, and anchored the message of the 99 percent in the Sunrise Movement—the legacy of Zuccotti Park has only grown more relevant with time. "I've seen the ripples of Occupy in so many other movements—and the people that were involved in Occupy going to lead those movements, whether

Black Lives Matter or immigrants' rights or the Bernie Sanders campaign. AOC wouldn't have run if Bernie's campaign wasn't as successful as it was, and Bernie's campaign wouldn't have resonated and been successful if not for Occupy. Occupy helped create a mood and understanding in the country of the populist moment that we're in, where so few have so much at the expense of the rest of us," he said.

For a generation whose time to fix the problem is running out, Weber said, direct-action climate protests reflect the spirit, and tactics, of Occupy in a more perilous context. "We really believe that a lot more disruption is necessary to make people feel the scale of the urgency and emergency that we're experiencing with the crises of climate change, inequality and democracy. We talk about building an army of young people, and now it's about training our army to begin flexing its muscles, [because] we're going to need to see at least the scale of mobilization and disruption that led to the original New Deal in the 1930s: mass sustained shutdowns, occupations, general strikes. Bringing society to its heels is what we believe is necessary to achieve the scale of change that is needed."

And to help bring about that change, the climate movement, like Occupy Wall Street before it, would turn to another powerful ally in the fight against the 1 percent: organized labor.

IN DEFENSE OF LIBERTY

OCTOBER 15, 2011

ON A BLUSTERY WEDNESDAY EVENING IN THE SECOND WEEK OF
October, Michael Bloomberg, then mayor of New York and the thirtieth richest person on the planet, showed up unannounced at Zuccotti Park. He seemed
to arrive out of nowhere, in darkness, sometime after seven, led by an entou-
rage of aides, security people and TV cameras that glided quickly ahead as
other assistants and bodyguards trailed behind, escorting the mayor down the
steps from Broadway into the heart of the Occupy Wall Street encampment.

At first no one seemed to give Bloomberg much notice. He was just another New Yorker passing through, getting his taste of our peaceful flavor of
dissent. But his presence seemed ominous. It was no secret Bloomberg wanted
Zuccotti emptied of the protesters. In a radio show that week, he addressed the
movement by defending the financial sector while accusing Occupy, somewhat
bizarrely, of seeking to hurt employment. "What they're trying to do is take
the jobs away from people working in this city," he said. Brookfield Properties,

the company that controlled the "privately owned public space" of Zuccotti, had just sent a letter to New York Police Department commissioner Ray Kelly saying that the "trespassing of the protesters" had created "a health and public safety issue that must be addressed immediately." In response, Bloomberg came to tell the protesters they had thirty-six hours to vacate the park for cleaning. His expression hovered somewhere between allergic and bemused as he surveyed the scene, and after his retinue rounded one of the flower beds near the middle of Zuccotti, the reporter in me couldn't resist so I approached.

"Mayor Bloomberg," I said, "what do you think about what you're seeing here?"

The mayor stopped and looked at me, then responded with the refrain he'd been repeating for weeks: "People have a right to say what they want to say. Nobody's a better defender of the First Amendment than I am."

With that, he continued past the kitchen where servers were dishing out steaming plates of food, past the medical center where a young man was applying a patch to a blister on his foot, but before he could make it through the diagonal length of the park, chants rang out behind him: "*You! Are! The 1 percent!*" Suddenly a crowd was surging around Bloomberg as his squad sped up, hurrying through the darkness under the trees, his royal bearing lost now amid the raucous uncensored voices who were hounding his walk, the beating drums, the encroaching bodies, and shouts bellowing the message: "*Our streets! Our money!*" Less than five minutes after he had arrived, Bloomberg was gone, vanished into the Manhattan night. The camp returned to its former rhythm with the carnival sounds of tambourines and horns, people dancing, the breeze blowing, a downpour threatening, and I couldn't help wondering what had passed through the mayor's mind—what, in fact, were his intentions—when he visited the camp. Had he sought some form of approval from the Occupiers? Was he paying his respects to a movement, a generational underclass, that he never imagined would appear on his doorstep in his twilight hours of office? Or was he simply getting a lay of the land, sizing up the youth battalion that had turned his city into the epicenter of a global storm? I wondered whether

Bloomberg, the most powerful man in New York, expected to gain something from Occupy. Had our movement intrigued him, frightened him, or only appalled him? Did it make him curious to know more, and did he even understand in the slightest what he was seeing?

WHEN THE CLOUDBURST OCCURRED THE NEXT NIGHT, OCCUPY Wall Street seized its opportunity to call the mayor's bluff. Hundreds had spent the day scrubbing and cleaning the park, wielding mops: the de facto symbol of resistance. The movement's sanitation working group had even applied turpentine to remove paint stains on the stone ground. The park owners wanted clean? The protesters would show them clean. By evening the rain started. It pounded the city for hours as flashes of lightening blanketed the sky. Then, sometime after midnight, the storm stopped and people crowded the square in commotion. They were drenched; many of them stripped off shirts as they washed, squeezing rags into buckets to make Zuccotti's wet floor and benches sparkle. The park was steaming with a fresh, sweet smell, as if the weather gods had heard our appeal and sent rain to assist the work. As one woman said, the rain literally "scraped the dirt off the ground." But in the giddy hours that preceded the historic dawn defense of Liberty Square, teeth were chattering, bodies trembling and it was more than the cold—it was the butterflies, perhaps, that made us shake. As we braced for Bloomberg's army, a terrific excitement filled the air and the bubbling tension rose as more people began to surge into the park—it was the middle of the night on the twenty-eighth day of occupation and now they were coming from all sides, from the boroughs, from uptown, upstate, out of state. They got the call that Liberty was about to be emptied, and they arrived to preserve it.

As the smell of burning sage wafted through the square, I spoke with a tall Black man named Hero who stood shivering in anticipation. In his early twenties, he had a broad handsome face and his long wet hair was pulled back in a ponytail. His eyes were shining. "I only thought I'd be here a week, I thought it would be over," he told me over the pandemonium of people cleaning and scrubbing around us. Hero had arrived by bus from Charlotte four weeks earlier, on the day that Occupy Wall Street began, and he recalled the early hours. "At first there was no one, only four or five of us, so I said, 'Hey guys, where's the Anonymous protest?' and we looked at each other and said, 'We're it!'" Then Hero saw people carrying signs, so he followed them to Battery Park and by later in the day several thousand had joined the march. Hero slept that night alongside a few hundred others beneath the canopy of honey locust trees, which now glittered with a golden aura of moisture. "I didn't know it would become a movement like this. It's not a protest: it's a movement," he said. "This is growing exponentially. It's uncontrollable. We're building history right now."

Some people, however, spoke with greater uncertainty about what might happen that night. They didn't want to repeat the mistake committed that spring by the 15-M movement, in Barcelona, where police told protesters they were closing Plaza Catalunya for cleaning then sealed off the square and never let anyone back in, confiscating all laptops, cameras and gear belonging to the Indignados. So the crowd at Liberty floated different strategies about how best to defend the space. One idea was to let police clean a portion of the park while protesters secured the other two-thirds. Another plan was to lock arms and form a multilayered human chain around the square, with women serving as the front line of defense. Jittery, on edge, apprehensive, eager: we felt the way a team feels before confronting a stronger opponent—outmatched, but un-daunted, and above all, prepared. Wandering through the park, I encountered others who had trained for the moment. "I went home and made love to my girlfriend," one man, Ryan, told me. "She wasn't happy. It was like I was going off to battle." Another man, Ted, said, "We're peaceful, we're compassionate, we're fighting for this country." A woman named Priya explained: "This is the people's park now. We want this park, we want a redistribution of wealth, we want a different society where we're not just commodities."

The hours passed, two in the morning, three in the morning, four in the morning, and all the while people kept streaming in, pouring out of student dorms and emerging from carpools that pulled up from Boston and Philadelphia and Washington. Some carried flags and banners and others wore costumes—Superman, Captain America, Benjamin Franklin in a three-cornered hat. They came with brooms and mops and they brought the spirit of revolt. Then, sometime before five, the reinforcements arrived: union members from the American Federation of Labor and Congress of Industrial Organizations (AFL-CIO), who marched down Broadway to Liberty hoisting flags and chanting, *"All day! All week! Occupy Wall Street!"* But as the number of protesters grew in the park, so did the number of police amassed in a perimeter around the square. They clustered especially near the northeastern corner, at One Liberty Plaza, where helmeted heads sat in rows waiting inside white elongated vans, lined up, lights on, engines running, a dozen cops huddled in each vehicle awaiting orders, nobody making a move. The cops probably had no more sense than we did how this contest was going to play out, sitting and standing in the hundreds, waiting, wondering whether it was worth all the law and order.

By five in the morning there were a thousand people crammed into the pre-dawn park and spilling onto its adjacent sidewalks as the roar grew louder, thundering off the buildings: *"We! Are! The 99 percent!"* A general assembly got underway and a man climbed atop one of the marble benches at the park's center to say: "The notice we received, we know it is a pretext to stop this movement, to silence your voices, to stop us from doing what we have been doing, which is to change the world! Bloomberg is afraid of beautiful people like you who have empowered each other against the economic and political elites, the 1 percent. We rise against them today!" Then, a short while later, the text came. A woman read it from her phone as the human microphone echoed her words across the square. It was from the city's deputy mayor announcing that Brookfield Properties had called off the cleaning. Our gazes froze, a momentary silence, then euphoria. Embraces, kisses, tears, song, exhilaration. The defense had held. We had won the battle without a fight.

I SAW HERO THE FOLLOWING DAY, WHEN COPS PULLED HIM VIOlently from the crowd marching up Sixth Avenue on its way to Times Square. The commanding officers in white shirts made a point of roughing him up; they pushed Hero against a police van and pinned him there as dozens of protesters rushed in with phones and cameras raised, shouting, *"Police brutality! The whole world is watching!"* Hero wore a proud, resigned expression, almost a look of boredom as he stood there with his chest pressed against the vehicle, long arms drooping while the officers cuffed him. His head was turned in my direction, his eyes gazing south at the sea of marchers that came surging in two giant columns up either side of the avenue—many thousands, the diverse faces of New York City, out to take over Manhattan on a warm Saturday—before he stepped into the paddy wagon and black-clad riot cops moved in on the crowd.

Coming on the five-month anniversary of the Indignados rebellion, the Global Day of Action on October 15 brought more than a million people onto the streets, from Nairobi to Johannesburg, from Bogotá to Buenos Aires. En masse they marched in Melbourne and Auckland and Hong Kong and Seoul, in Manila and Jakarta, Berlin and Rome—even in Zhengzhou, China, where people rallying for human rights supported the "Great Wall Street Revolution." By this time polls showed nine out of ten New Yorkers supported Occupy, and two-thirds of Americans agreed with the movement as well, which is why throughout the country that day, and across nearly a thousand cities in more than eighty nations, citizens united against inequality and greed and corruption were speaking one language: a language that said *Enough*. "What it is, the demand the 1 percent can't comprehend, is us. It is the individuals and villages, the cities and peoples across the world who are seeing each other on the far side of appeals and petition. It is the world we are becoming," wrote the editors of *The Occupied Wall Street Journal*, "and in our own backyard, in thousands of backyards, from Augusta and Jackson, Springfield and Sioux Falls, Vegas and Santa Rosa and Green Bay: Americans celebrated the occupation in its infancy. Jobs with dignity. Housing fit for families. Education. Healthcare. Pensions. The very air we breathe. What can those who want democracy demand from the king, except his crown? Regime change is in the air. America is looking at itself, its place in the world and who we are to be."

Where Broadway crossed Avenue of the Americas at Thirty-Fourth Street, the pace of the march quickened. Cops lined us on all sides; some sat on motorbikes but most stood forming an impenetrable wall of reflective shields. At one point the people broke through their lines and rushed toward Times Square, only to discover once they arrived that it was ringed in steel barricades and the police inside had traded mopeds for horses. Their towering frames stood mounted in rows, a ground infantry of hundreds guarding the vast cement plain with its gaudy flashing lights. As the sidewalks overflowed with protesters, people climbed up the scaffolding of restaurant awnings to witness the spectacle: steam rising from the grates of Gotham, the afternoon light turning to dusk as ten thousand voices cried, "*Let us in!*" "*We! Are! The 99 percent!*" Barricades scraped along the asphalt where crowds pressed into them. I spotted Michael Moore, standing fifty feet away from me, anxiously observing the popular challenge to the state. A restless pressure built until finally, at the corner of Broadway and Forty-Sixth Street, a small section of the crowd lunged forward. They pushed the linked barricades up and inward, standing them almost on end, and for a moment the steel barrier teetered there, at a diagonal, threatening to topple—a peak instant when the public was prepared to rush in and occupy the world's square. But just before the barricades fell, mounted police horses rushed forward, the animals reared on their hind legs, front hooves kicking the air as camera lights flashed and howls erupted from the crowd. The horses then spun, as if choreographed, and used their bodies as buffers to push back against the steel. They repelled the drive, and as the barricades resettled on the ground, Bloomberg's army stood inside the great square clutching batons they would no longer need. Gone was the sweet breath of Liberty's late defense, as salt replaced the taste of triumph. Darkness gathered, police lit flares, the steam from Manhattan's underground continued to billow up into the night sky. And in that season of hope, when we still believed that everything was possible, the defeat of our constitutional right to peacefully assemble was a crude reminder that power, when confronted, does not easily concede.

5

OCCUPY LABOR

WAGE REBELLION AND
THE NEW WORKERS MOVEMENT

A TIME FOR JUSTICE: PHIL CONNOLLY

IF YOU STUMBLED INTO ZUCCOTTI PARK IN THE WANING DAYS OF the encampment, it's possible you would have run into a Verizon employee camped out there named Phil Connolly. Standing five feet eleven inches and just shy of 220 pounds, Connolly carried the unmistakable traits of his forebears. "I've been told I've got the map of Ireland written all over my face," he liked to joke. Connolly didn't spend as long as many people living at the park—he lasted four nights. When he returned back home to his wife in Yonkers, on November 14, 2011, it was only hours before a legion of New York City police under the orders of Mayor Bloomberg showed up, in the middle of the night, to forcefully clear Liberty and bring the two-month occupation to a close. Connolly wasn't the political type. You'd hardly call him a leftist, much less an activist. But after three decades as a reliable union man working for the telecommunications giant, he joined the movement on Wall Street because, this time, he had a dog in the fight.

A month before Occupy got rolling, in August 2011, some forty-five thousand Verizon workers went on strike across the Eastern Seaboard, from Massachusetts to Virginia, demanding the company maintain employees' wages and preserve their pensions and healthcare benefits. Two weeks later, the employees—organized by Communication Workers of America and the International Brotherhood of Electrical Workers—returned to their jobs without a settlement, "hoping the company would bargain in good faith," as one Verizon shop steward, Stan, told me, "but nothing changed." So in October, riding the anti-corporate momentum fueled by Occupy, Verizon workers took to the streets. Phil was among them, and so was Stan, a tall man in his early forties with a muscular frame and steely blue eyes. I had met him as he was marching one afternoon on a picket line outside the company's downtown office, around the corner from the Freedom Tower and the 9/11 Memorial. Alongside him were hundreds of men and women dressed in bright red union T-shirts carrying signs that read, "CWA on Strike Against Verizon's Corporate Greed." For fourteen years, Stan had been installing networks for the company; he hoped to do another sixteen so he could retire. Working for Verizon used to provide good benefits and a solid middle-class life for him, his wife and three kids out in New Jersey, he told me. "But they lower the pensions, lower our contributions to 401(k), they're taking away my sick days and making us pay more for our healthcare, and at the same time they're making record profits. The rich want more and more and more."

By 2011, just 40 percent of Verizon's workforce was unionized—about half the number of employees who had enjoyed union representation thirty years before, when the company was Bell Atlantic. "It's like we're a dying breed for crying out loud," Stan said. The CWA had bargained with the company for years, agreeing to minuscule raises in exchange for decent health coverage. But what Stan really wanted to get across to me—and a point, he said, that the media often missed—was that their fight wasn't about salaries. "We're not asking for higher wages; wages are not the issue. Healthcare, sick days, benefits, job security, pensions: those are the issues. I came to a union job because I knew they provided good medical benefits and strong job security. Now they want us to start paying forty-five hundred dollars per family right off the top toward premiums, not counting co-pays and deductibles. They want to cut healthcare down to eighty percent coverage, they want to freeze our pensions, they want to contract out the work. At the same time they keep claiming surpluses and buying out other businesses. They make all that money off our backs—every line that I install makes the company money, and makes the business I installed more money—but they don't see the pain they're causing to the families of the workers who make Verizon run." His anger stemmed from a simple question that workers everywhere were asking: "Where's my share?"

Around the time of Occupy, Stan was taking evening classes in labor politics and history at City University of New York's Murphy Institute for Labor Education, where he was studying how unions could play a more defining role pushing for workers' rights. "That's how we're getting educated," he told me, because the battle that CWA workers were waging against Verizon was just the tip of the spear in corporate America. "We know we're the last bastion—Verizon is one of the last companies with full health coverage and no premiums—and we want to hold on to our benefits because if we lose them, no one will ever get them again. This type of job is what's held together the country for years—telephone jobs, regular jobs—and when you lose these jobs, that's a problem for society. Americans have bargained themselves down for nothing: now they need to bargain themselves back up. All I want is to be able to provide for my family."

Occupy Wall Street spoke to Stan the way it spoke to a lot of working people who, over the decades, had seen their living standards decline while corporate profits and shareholder wealth soared. When they heard the movement of the 99 percent attack income inequality, CEO pay and 1 percent greed, they knew exactly which side they were on. And in the case of Stan's co-worker, Phil Connolly, the call for economic justice was a long time coming.

Born in Astoria, Queens, in 1958, Connolly came from a union household. His father worked freight for American Airlines for forty-four years— "his first and only job"—pulling long shifts as a crew chief at LaGuardia and Idlewild, which later became JFK International Airport. The contract his father had with the Transport Workers Union of America made him the highest paid worker on their mostly Italian block, and Connolly was raised in a typical Irish home of that era, with parents who voted Democratic and kept "a picture of Kennedy and the Pope pretty much side by side. I was lucky I grew up with a union father who had a good job with good benefits," he said. "We weren't rich by any stretch of the imagination, but we were always well dressed and we never wanted for anything."

When Connolly was twelve, his father was transferred to Tucson so the family moved west. Connolly hated the Arizona heat and he didn't care much for the people, either. He played football and got into his share of fistfights, and his earliest memory of politics was the day he asked his father about the difference between Republicans and Democrats. "Republicans are for factories, Democrats are for the workers," he told him, and it was clear which end of the rope they held. Connolly studied art for a time at the University of Arizona before dropping out and hitchhiking back to New York. He moved in with some old buddies in Astoria and spent the next few years working odd jobs— movie usher, bank employee—while looking for work in commercial art. He applied to become a policeman, a garbage man, even a postman, then returned home one day in 1981 to find a telegram from New York Telephone sticking out of his mailbox, calling him in for an interview. The company at the time was part of AT&T, and would later become NYNEX, which changed to Bell Atlantic and, finally, Verizon. "That's a good pension job," his grandfather advised him, and Connolly took it.

That August, President Reagan crushed the air traffic controllers strike, firing more than eleven thousand workers and dealing a generational blow to the country's unions. Connolly's father was enraged; he knew some of the men who had been let go and felt contempt for the actor-turned-president, who "used to be in a union, and used to be a Democrat." Connolly joined CWA and started out making eight bucks an hour as a directory assistance operator. He handled hundreds of calls a day, stressful work with long hours. In 1983 he took part in his first strike, organized by the union, which was calling for higher wages, better conditions and the right of phone operators to keep their medical coverage. Connolly recalled the time his father had gone on strike with the Transport Workers Union, and "when it was over he was very happy. He said, 'We got what we asked for—we didn't lose things, we only gained,' so I knew back then that that was the way to make changes." The CWA strike lasted for three weeks and the workers won most of their demands.

The next time Connolly and his union went on strike was in 1989, again over medical coverage, but this time the walkout lasted many months. He drove a cab to pay the bills and helped coordinate the strike by ensuring that employees showed up at their assigned times to march. Connolly married in 1993, moved to Yonkers just north of the city, and soon became a central office technician—the highest paid "craft job" in the company, which increased his wage to $25 an hour. Then, on September 11, 2001, he found himself standing at his boss's window in Midtown Manhattan watching as clouds of black smoke billowed out of the first World Trade Center tower, and saw the second plane come in. Baffled by America's response to the attacks, Connolly joined hundreds of thousands of New Yorkers who marched in February 2003 to stop the United States from going to war. "I couldn't understand the Iraq War. Everybody who attacked America was from Saudi Arabia, so why were we going to Iraq?" he said. The more he learned about the companies involved there—like the security firm Blackwater, and especially the energy giant Halliburton, with its close financial ties to vice president Dick Cheney—the less trust he felt in a system where corporations were so openly corrupting politics. "It made me realize that's all it was about: oil. The whole thing really upset me. They never found weapons of mass destruction and I got the feeling that no matter what they said, we weren't being told the truth."

Connolly watched as America's epic folly in the Middle East was followed up a few years later by the housing crisis and the financial collapse—confirming his sense that the economic structure steered by Wall Street only worked for those at the very top. When Obama fever swept the nation in 2008, Connolly got engaged in politics for the first time, phone banking and even donating a few hundred dollars to try to get the first-term senator from Illinois elected to the White House. "I had never given a politician a buck before, but the only thing I wanted was to see this guy win. I was a big 'change' guy. I thought, here's someone who's got no ulterior motive, who would really speak to, and for, the people."

Soon enough, he saw those hopes dashed when Obama sat down with the heads of the country's largest financial institutions—the same ones that had gambled away millions of people's homes, pensions and life savings—and rewarded them with a generous bailout at no cost. Watching Bank of America, Goldman Sachs, Citigroup and others receive hundreds of billions of dollars without conditions, Connolly said, was the final straw. "The bailouts to the banks is what got me. Nobody's perfect, but this is like, 'Come on, people are losing their homes!' We're giving banks this money to help people, to get them lending and borrowing again, and it never happened because they just handed them the money without any stipulations."

Connolly, like so many others, viewed Obama's surrender of Main Street to Wall Street as the defining moment of his presidency, revealing the depths of America's corrupt political and economic system that only served the interests of the superrich at a time when people needed their government most. A few years later, the residual anger was enough to push a hard-working company man like Connolly into a plan of action he never imagined he might undertake: bringing a tent to live among the protesters at Zuccotti Park. Connolly had learned about Occupy Wall Street on the evening news, and was intrigued by the massive crowds of people holding signs and marching against the banks. The protests had been going on for weeks, and on the second Monday in November of 2011, he decided to head down to the financial district to see the movement for himself. What he experienced blew him away. "When

I got there I saw it wasn't a protest, more of a sit-in. I'd never seen people this dedicated, who were willing to camp out and stay there and make sacrifices to get their point across, and I thought, 'Wow, this is making a statement, I want to be part of this!' So I went and bought myself a tent and I said to my boss, 'I'm taking my vacation time this week.'"

After he showed up at the park with all his gear, Connolly spent a few hours walking around and talking to people as he looked for a place to settle in. What struck him most was the fact that no one was in charge: unlike organized labor actions, no spokesman or any person was giving directions or telling people what to say, and he liked that. He also liked that the financial industry employees heading to and from work had little choice but to pass the park, which stood a few yards from the uptown train, putting the movement square in the faces of Wall Street workers. Connolly finally found a spot that was barely big enough to fit into—"It was a tight squeeze, I pretty much slept at attention"—and at that point he stopped communicating with everyone but his wife, whom he texted daily just to let her know he was okay. One afternoon, Connolly was holding a sign behind police barricades when he got into an argument. "Out of nowhere this suit comes up to me and tells me to go get a job, and that pissed me off. I told him, 'Hey, I've got a fucking job. I don't know about you but I've been working for the same company now for twenty-nine years, and I'm here on my vacation,' and that shut him up."

The point a lot of people missed about Occupy, said Connolly, was that "these weren't all just homeless people getting together looking for a handout." They were workers like himself, and people without work, who felt the system had robbed them of dignity and opportunity and that the 1 percent must finally pay a price. For Connolly, the movement presented something he had never seen in unions or anyplace else: the clear and uncompromising demand for economic justice. "It was the first time in a long time that people got up and said, 'Enough!' This was a group of people—laborers, students paying off their out-of-control loans, older people, younger people, all saying, 'What about us?' The people who make everything—the people who work, who toil for a living—were saying, 'We deserve a piece of the pie. We deserve to be recognized. We deserve to have a voice.'"

ORGANIZED LABOR REENERGIZED

IN HIS ACCEPTANCE SPEECH AT THE 1936 DEMOCRATIC NATIONAL Convention in Philadelphia, FDR declared the working man's time had come. "For too many of us the political equality we once had won was meaningless in the face of economic inequality. A small group had concentrated into their own hands an almost complete control over other people's property, other people's money, other people's labor—other people's lives," he said. Unlike more recent presidents, Roosevelt didn't genuflect before the money men of Wall Street, and the laboring masses thrilled when he proclaimed "this generation of Americans has a rendezvous with destiny." He added, "These economic royalists complain that we seek to overthrow the institutions of America. What they really complain of is that we seek to take away their power."

Among the Roosevelt administration's numerous New Deal programs that helped struggling workers survive the Depression, the National Labor Relations Act stands out. The 1935 act legalized private sector unions, allowing workers to strike and collectively bargain for better pay and conditions. The Taft-Hartley Act of 1947 would weaken some labor rights, outlawing many kinds of strikes while enabling states to enact right-to-work laws, which prevented unions from requiring employees to pay dues. Yet organized labor enjoyed its greatest economic and political influence in the middle decades of the century, when unions were the backbone of a flourishing middle class comprised largely but not entirely of white workers. Between 1947 and 1980, more than two hundred strikes—each one exceeding a thousand workers—occurred annually. According to the U.S. Bureau of Labor Statistics, from the early fifties through the late sixties, when 35 percent of American workers belonged to a private sector union, between three hundred and eighty and four hundred and seventy such strikes took place annually.

The Immigration and Naturalization Act of 1965 replaced the restrictive quota system that favored immigrants from northwestern Europe with one founded on reuniting immigrant families and attracting skilled labor. With the exception of countries in the Western Hemisphere, immigration could no longer be based on race, ethnicity or country of origin. As a result, European immigration faded as African and Asian immigration expanded greatly, with several million people fleeing Vietnam and 4.1 million arriving from the Philippines over the ensuing decades. The browning of America had begun in earnest. But Mexican citizens and others from Latin America were blocked from immigrating legally. Consequently, from 1965 to 1995, 4.3 million Mexicans slipped across the border or overstayed their visas and settled in America. The longest wave of immigration in our history only peaked with the implosion of the economy and the Great Recession, by which time more than 11 million undocumented immigrants, the majority of them from Mexico, had made the U.S. their home. The racial and ethnic make-up of the country went from 85 percent white in 1965 to 66 percent white in 2009, and is projected to be white minority by 2042. The effect of this unprecedented influx of workers on organized labor, and on hourly wage workers in general, has been profound.

With a surplus of undocumented workers willing to work for less than native workers, the owners of capital enjoyed the advantage of a "split labor market," allowing them to set competing factions against one another to the detriment of organized labor in particular. In the 1970s the American Federation of Labor (AFL) was strongly critical of uncontrolled illegal immigration, demanding increased border enforcement and employer sanctions. Racial resentment was unavoidable and the shift of working-class whites toward the Republican Party—which began with the ten million who voted for segregationist George Wallace in 1968 and accelerated with the racist dog-whistle appeals of Ronald Reagan in 1980—culminated in the election of Donald Trump, a vulgar and outspoken bigot, in 2016. The AFL and organized labor have adjusted to this new demographic reality, embracing a rainbow coalition of workers fighting against a system of corporatized globalization that is profoundly anti-labor.

Even more damaging to the cause of labor and contributing to its resultant decline after 1970 were the upheavals and dislocations of the 1960s. Blue-collar workers remained consistently loyal to the Democrats as Kennedy restored a robust National Labor Relations Board, allowing collective bargaining and picketing, banning lockouts and guaranteeing union recognition if a majority of workers voted for unionization. Lyndon Johnson went further, passing a number of provisions that benefited the hourly wage earner, including a raise in the minimum wage, the application of labor standards to nine million more workers, laws against employment discrimination of any kind and, of course, the Voting Rights Act and Civil Rights Act. But those last two monumental achievements also carried within them the seeds of division. As Richard Trumka, president of the AFL-CIO, observed in 2014, "Racism is part of our inheritance as Americans. Every city, every state and every region of this country has its own deep history with racism. And so does the labor movement."

There was also a growing outrage at the anti–Vietnam War protests led largely by the college-educated class and students enjoying deferments from service. While union membership around the country was divided in support or opposition to the war, George Meany and the AFL leadership remained resolutely hawkish in backing Richard Nixon's prosecution of the war, even when Nixon announced the invasion of neutral Cambodia on April 30, 1970. When four students were murdered by the Ohio National Guard during a protest at Kent State, students in New York City called for an anti-war march. With the cooperation of labor leadership, the White House arranged for construction workers in New York City to mount a counterdemonstration. On May 8, one thousand college and high school students rallied at the intersection of Wall Street and Broad, a place familiar to Wall Street Occupiers. Hundreds of construction workers mobilized by the AFL-CIO broke through police lines and attacked the students viciously, seriously injuring seventy protesters as the police stood idly by.

The "Hardhat Riot" signaled a turning point in the blue-collar worker's traditional allegiance to the Democratic Party and the New Deal Coalition. Nixon was no friend to labor, but by tapping into racial, cultural and class resentment, he had found a message that resonated with the majority of white workers even as his economic policies favored business and the wealthy. Subsequent Republican presidents have refined Nixon's model, known as the Southern strategy, siding with business on a policy level while appealing to the so-called silent majority on the basis of thinly disguised racist tropes. None have mastered the technique better than Ronald Reagan, and it was no accident that he began his presidential campaign in Philadelphia, Mississippi, site of the 1964 Klan murder of Civil Rights activists James Chaney, Michael Schwerner and Andrew Goodman.

With Reagan's summary firing of air traffic controllers in 1981, labor power went into a precipitous decline. Globalization accelerated and manufacturing jobs disappeared, transforming the relationship between management and an increasingly expendable workforce. Executive compensation soared; stock buybacks enriched shareholders, and deregulation allowed corporate profits to skyrocket as workers' wages stagnated, job security diminished and health benefits were put on the chopping block. By the time Bill Clinton signed the North American Free Trade Agreement—NAFTA—into law in 1993, blue-collar workers who might have mobilized to protest were struggling to hold onto the jobs, benefits and working conditions they had. The labor blogger Dan Sisken wrote that what emerged from that era was a "non-militant, 'service' model of unions more closely associated with reformist advocacy groups as well as the centrist Democratic Party." The result was a weakened, conciliatory organized labor with fewer and fewer members and less and less clout.

Two terms under George W. Bush made the picture for workers that much clearer: after bankrolling and ensuring unconditional support from both major political parties, the corporations had won. The right to form or even join a union now became a battle, as Republicans across the Rust Belt states of Indiana, Michigan and Wisconsin inched closer to establishing right-to-work laws that degraded union power even further. When the financial crash finally hit, labor unions resembled a patient on life support—less influential than any time in the past eighty years, with national membership numbers nearing single digits. Contrasted with the regular work stoppages that unions carried out in the mid-twentieth century, in the three decades between 1981 and 2011, fewer than fifty strikes with a thousand or more workers occurred annually in all but five of those years. Beneath the surface, however, tensions were smoldering. "Fifty-eight million people want collective bargaining but aren't getting it," Lawrence Mishel, the former president of the Economic Policy Institute, told me, "and I've always considered our current situation like a tinderbox waiting for someone to light the fire."

The spark came seven months before Occupy Wall Street, in February 2011, when tens of thousands of workers and their allies launched what became a four-month occupation of the state capitol in Madison, Wisconsin. The uprising was in response to the so-called budget repair bill signed into law by the state's newly elected, Koch brothers–backed GOP governor, Scott Walker, which stripped public sector unions of their collective bargaining rights. Supported by the AFL-CIO and other unions, protesters took over the capitol rotunda and established a well-organized encampment outside it, replete with information, medical and food stations to help participants get through the harshest weeks of winter. The labor rebellion—which ignited three days after the Egyptians occupying Tahrir Square deposed Hosni Mubarak—jolted America awake. Andy Kroll reported for *Mother Jones* that the "raucous, sleepless, grizzled, energized protesters" of Madison comprised "the largest labor protest in my lifetime." Coming in the same progressive state that had birthed the nation's first collective bargaining rights for public employees, the first workers' compensation and unemployment insurance laws, and the American Federation of State, County and Municipal Employees, the message of working people fed up with austerity politics and economic unfairness resonated. The Wisconsin workers' revolt had important knock-on effects: the tent city in Madison known as Walkerville (in reference to Depression-era Hoovervilles) would later that summer inspire New York City activists angered by budget cuts to establish their own Bloombergville—a sidewalk encampment whose organizers, in turn, led the takeover that September of Zuccotti Park, launching Occupy Wall Street.

PHIL CONNOLLY'S RADICALIZATION PRESAGED A WORKERS' REBEL-lion that would spread across the American economy in the aftermath of Occupy, transforming employees into activists and heralding the birth of a new, reinvigorated labor movement. For working people, evidence of growing economic inequality in the workplace was an obvious and long-standing truth. But it was also in some ways an abstract one—hard to grapple with, and even harder to change. It was the nature of capitalism: bosses and shareholders took home more profits than they deserved, while the workers who produced those profits scrambled to get by. Just over a half century ago, the CEO-to-worker pay gap was an acceptable twenty to one; it became fifty-eight to one in 1989, and by the time of Occupy it had ballooned to 231 to one. In the four decades between 1978 and 2018, compensation for chief executives grew more than 1,000 percent, but grew less than 12 percent for workers over the same period. The trends were known, but it took Wall Street bankers destroying the economy in 2008 to lay bare the greed of the 1 percent. In the aftermath of a Great Recession that cost nine million jobs and stole $10 trillion in public wealth, working Americans like Connolly finally saw, in unmistakable terms, that the game was rigged.

In its call for systemic change, Occupy Wall Street inspired and energized organized labor, reawakening workers to the fact that nobody else out there was mobilizing for their interests. If the 99 percent wanted to rein in corporate power and reverse income inequality, they had to do it for themselves. With the class battle lines suddenly exposed, workers saw an opportunity to reassert basic demands with greater confidence and growing militancy, and their response shifted the country's balance of power. Prior to Occupy, the author Susan Griffin told me, "economic justice was a term that people weren't thinking about—it just wasn't there. It was there in the nineteen thirties and forties, but in the fifties, the corporate thinkers decided it would be healthy to have a prosperous middle class, and that's what we got. But it didn't translate into the strength of unions in the decades to come." Then, after the movement against Wall Street, the perspective of working people changed. "Occupy brought economic justice back into the public consciousness—focusing on the huge profit margins that a very small percentage of people are receiving while the rest of us are struggling—and that in order to meet the power of the corporations and the bosses, we need organizations to work together," Griffin said.

I remember the distinct moment when that sense of unity occurred, when labor unions in New York overcame their initial doubts about Occupy Wall Street and threw their weight behind the movement. It happened on a bright Wednesday afternoon, October 5, in the third week of the occupation, when tens of thousands of students and workers poured into Foley Square, a few minutes' walk from Zuccotti Park. The rally had been billed as a citywide student walkout to protest skyrocketing college debt, but it became about much more than that once the unions decided to lean in. Up to that point, city labor leaders were slow to publicly endorse the movement as union bosses debated the potential fallout of joining a protest some viewed as too radical. Steven Greenhouse and Cara Buckley reported in *The New York Times* that "in internal discussions, some union leaders voiced worries that if labor were perceived as trying to co-opt the movement, it might alienate the protesters and touch off a backlash, [while] others said they were wary of being embarrassed by the far-left activists in the group who had repeatedly denounced the United States government." But that afternoon, under a glaring autumn sun, workers by the thousands—representing the United Federation of Teachers, Service Employees International Union, United Auto Workers and others, with unanimous support from the AFL-CIO executive council—descended on the sprawling square in a show of force that signaled Occupy Wall Street's base had grown beyond young people, activists and the unemployed to include the working rank and file.

A few labor leaders had already stepped forward, like John Samuelsen, president of the Transport Workers Union, which, following mass Occupy arrests on the Brooklyn Bridge four days earlier, took the city to court to prevent New York police from forcing their members to drive protesters to jail. "TWU Local 100 supports the protesters on Wall Street and takes great offense that the mayor and NYPD have ordered operators to transport citizens who were exercising their constitutional right to protest—and shouldn't have been arrested in the first place," Samuelsen said. It was a start, but when a multitude of union members joined the rally that Wednesday, their collective voice lifted the protest tenor to a new pitch. And as I stood on the square's periphery, watching waves of workers in their matching colored T-shirts stream into the plaza holding signs and banners and shouting, "*We are the 99 percent!*," it became clear that this was no longer just about the unions supporting Occupy. It was about Occupy galvanizing the unions, reawakening a dormant American labor movement that hankered to spring into action.

After making my way through the crowd to the fountain at the center of the square, I spoke with a short, stocky man named Mike who told me the protest was labor's chance to "come in and really support this movement, bringing the issues of the working class back to the center stage of America's political system." Mike was the treasurer of the Recycling and General Industrial Union Local 108, and he called Occupy "a struggle I've been waiting to join for a long time—because the common people are doing it, because there's a lot of people being driven from their homes, and because corporate greed needs to be put in check. They say the top 1 percent is controlling the 99 percent through wealth. I'm one of the 99 percent," he said. "I'm living week to week, paycheck to paycheck, and I'm worried about the future for my kids. This is about us, the working-class people of America."

A decade on, we can look back at that afternoon in Foley Square as a critical juncture from which a more vigorous, mobilized, activist labor movement began to reemerge throughout the country. Unions traditionally looked out for their own, but suddenly employees across sectors were willing to fight not just for their personal paychecks and work conditions but for wage earners everywhere. Occupy Wall Street threw labor organizations a new lifeline: the chance to coalesce around a unifying message of economic justice in order to reignite the demands of a long neglected workforce.

For George Gresham, president of SEIU 1199 United Healthcare Workers East, the Occupy movement represented "a dream come true" for a national labor force that had been sitting too long on the sidelines. "It's outrageous what's happening to working people. Now, through the militant, the bottom, the youth, where revolutions always started, there's enough momentum to take this to another level." Likewise, Stuart Appelbaum, president of the Retail, Wholesale and Department Store Union, later told a meeting of assembled union leaders and Occupy activists: "The economic message resonating out of Occupy Wall Street is being heard in a way that it wasn't heard before. Labor has to tap into this energy, learn from Occupy and stand in solidarity with the movement. It's one struggle and we're in it together." But Appelbaum added that in order to win a broad base of support among working people, the movement must "talk about worker issues, and a living wage must be an essential issue for Occupy Wall Street."

It was a prescient message—one that would soon be manifested in a nationwide wage rebellion spurred by worker strikes and walkouts, altering the country's economic equilibrium.

FIGHT FOR $15: THE MINIMUM WAGE MOVEMENT TAKES OFF

THE OCCUPY MOVEMENT'S FIRST DIRECT AND LASTING IMPACT ON the lives of working Americans dates back to November 29, 2012, a full year after protesters were evicted from Zuccotti Park, when several hundred fast-food employees at dozens of franchise restaurants across New York City walked off their jobs. For months, organizers from Occupy Wall Street had been working in coalition with the SEIU, non-profits like New York Communities for Change, clergy members and the restaurant workers themselves helping to prepare the public launch of the nascent Fast Food Forward campaign. Low-wage employees' demands were specific: they wanted higher pay, better working conditions and the right to form a union without fear of retaliation from management. Occupy had already by this time largely disappeared from view, but the movement's activist energy had lit a fire. The message of economic fairness spurred the city's fast-food workers to introduce a singular, powerful, meme-like demand: a $15 minimum wage. The unprecedented strike—which included workers from dozens of McDonald's, Burger King, Wendy's, Pizza Hut, Kentucky Fried Chicken and other global restaurant chains—marked a breakthrough for organized labor, opening up a new workers' front that would become known as the Fight for $15.

The movement quickly spread. Four months later, on April 4, 2013, the forty-fifth anniversary of the assassination of Martin Luther King Jr., hundreds of fast-food workers in New York City again staged a coordinated walkout to demand higher wages and better conditions, but this time their action was also taken up by franchise restaurant employees striking in Chicago, Detroit, St. Louis, Milwaukee and Seattle. A mere six weeks later, on May 15, fast-food worker protests spread around the globe, from Brazil and India to Japan and the U.K. That same month, around one hundred McDonald's employees, church leaders and union members were arrested as several thousand protesters shut down the food giant's headquarters in Oak Brook, Illinois, to protest the company's chronic wage theft through off-the-clock work, illegal deductions and failure to pay overtime. A $15 minimum wage movement that was almost unthinkable a few months before was suddenly making daily headlines, and Americans tuned in to the next chapter in the inequality debate.

With the Fair Labor Standards Act of 1938, U.S. workers won guarantees of their first permanent minimum wage of twenty-five cents an hour. The federal minimum wage has grown incrementally ever since, although it has never exceeded the purchasing power it held at its peak, in 1968, when the base hourly pay of $1.60 was equivalent to $12.13 in 2020 wages. Under Reagan, the minimum wage froze at $3.35, and from 1997 through 2007 it remained stuck at $5.15. Between 2009 and 2020, minimum pay didn't budge from $7.25 an hour—the longest period without growth since the law came into existence.

By the time Occupy made wealth and income inequality a central part of the American conversation, the base wage was ripe for revisiting. Except now workers weren't just pressing for a raise: they demanded more than double the federal minimum, and public opinion by a wide majority swung in their favor. A wave of fast-food worker strikes, funded and organized by the SEIU, continued through the summer of 2013. On July 29, more than two thousand restaurant workers walked off the job in a dozen cities nationwide, and a month later another national strike broadened the movement to sixty cities. That fall, McDonald's provoked a backlash when its management suggested the company's employees should go on food stamps to make ends meet. By then, the Fight for $15 had become what the National Employment Law Project called "one of the first mass-scale labor actions in the United States in most adults' lifetimes," and the new show of worker militancy was starting to move the needle. As Josh Sanburn wrote about the movement in *Time*, "Instead of taking the traditional route of trying to reach some sort of collective bargaining agreement, they're betting that an Occupy-style public awareness campaign, based on the idea that their wages are inherently unfair, perpetuate inequality and fail to move them up the economic ladder, will lead to change at either the state or federal level." And as it turned out, the workers bet right.

At the end of that year, on December 5, 2013, fast-food employees staged their biggest protest to date as thousands stopped work in more than one hundred cities calling for a $15 wage and the right to form a union. The workers started to incorporate sit-ins in an escalating campaign of civil disobedience, and the movement reached a new level of global recognition the following spring, on May 15, 2014, when Fight for $15 protests swept 230 cities across thirty-three countries and six continents. Two months later, the first-ever fast-food workers convention in Chicago drew thirteen hundred restaurant employees who approved a resolution vowing to commit civil disobedience—as they put it, doing "whatever it takes"—to achieve their goal of a $15 wage. But the city that made even bigger noise, by translating the minimum wage protests into legislation, was Seattle.

Inspired by the steady drumbeat of strikes, Seattle's newly elected Democratic mayor, Ed Murray, declared in February 2014 during his first State of the City address, "We face the largest income disparity in our history, and this disparity strikes at the very cause and core of what it means to be a democratic society." By becoming the first major U.S. city to propose a $15 minimum wage, Murray said, "we have an opportunity to create a model that can be replicated across the country." Four months later, on June 2, Seattle's nine-member city council, led by the socialist Kshama Sawant, set a new national benchmark by unanimously passing an ordinance to raise the city's base wage to $15. "The City Council here went where no big-city lawmakers have gone before," wrote Kirk Johnson in *The New York Times*, "pushing Seattle to the forefront of urban efforts to address income inequality." As Sawant declared in her victory speech following the measure's passage: "Seattle is just a beginning. We have an entire world to win."

For Sawant—an economics professor who helped lead Occupy Seattle in the fall of 2011, and won city office in 2013 on a promise to support a $15 wage in the nearby town of SeaTac—the links between Occupy Wall Street and the minimum wage fight were unmistakable. "It was clear that there was so much momentum" coming off the Occupy movement, she told me, and "most important about the Fight for $15 was the acknowledgment that you need a concrete political demand around which to organize all these people who are angry and frustrated and want to do something. The story of Occupy is really the story of a period of social movements that opened in 2011, and a very important component is the labor movement. There was enormous openness among rank-and-file workers to engage in political struggle, and it's indisputable that because Seattle won fifteen dollars as a major city, it propelled the movement nationwide."

Seattle's first-of-a-kind legislation was quickly followed up by its progressive neighbor to the south, America's costliest city, San Francisco, where residents in the fall of 2014 voted by a wide margin to raise the minimum pay to $15 an hour. By that time, the low-wage protests had grown to include employees from other sectors, and in September 2014, the biggest nationally coordinated wage strike occurred when thousands of homecare workers allied with fast-food employees walked off the job in more than 150 cities, escalating their civil disobedience campaign with hundreds of arrests. Three months later, in December, thousands more fast-food workers went on strike in 190 cities, this time joined not only by caregivers but also airport workers, hospital workers, discount and convenience store employees, gas station clerks, and members of Black Lives Matter. Soon childcare workers and university adjunct professors would be on board the Fight for $15 as well. Within two years, riding the momentum from Occupy Wall Street, New York City's underpaid fast-food franchise employees had launched a global labor resistance across industries, forcing the political class—and most importantly, voters—to respond.

One person feeling the public pressure was President Obama, who in 2014 moved to raise the federal minimum wage to $10.10, an act the Congressional Budget Office estimated would lift earnings for sixteen and a half million workers. Republicans, using timeworn, big business scare tactics, claimed the higher wage would suppress job growth, but a study released that year by the Center for Economic and Policy Research found that states that raised their minimum wage enjoyed faster levels of job creation than those that did not. To boost the effort, more than six hundred economists signed a letter urging Congress to pass the federal minimum wage hike, arguing it would help, not harm, the post-recession economy. The bill had popular support: a Pew Center

poll showed nearly three-quarters of Americans endorsed raising the minimum wage to $10.10, with 90 percent of Democrats and more than half of Re-
publicans approving. When congressional Republicans blocked the measure,
cities and states took it upon themselves to raise workers' wages, and when they
did, they found it to be a winning campaign issue. During the 2014 midterms,
every place a ballot measure proposed increasing the minimum wage, the law
passed, leading to a wave of victories for workers. Even in red states like Alaska,
Arkansas, Nebraska and South Dakota, successful voter initiatives drove the
wage above the national average. By January 2015, twenty-nine states along
with the District of Columbia had enacted higher minimum wage laws, and
that same year, Los Angeles, New York and Washington, D.C., voted to make
$15 the new base pay in their cities. "For the first time in thirty years, salaries
are actually going up for most people because all these states have adopted a
fifteen-dollar minimum wage," said the late activist organizer Kevin Zeese,
"and that's a change-of-life impact from Occupy, which raised the issue of
inequality."

By 2016, the issue of $15 minimum pay had become a central plank of the
Democratic Party platform, and found its most ardent supporter in the presidential candidacy of Bernie Sanders. In 2018, Amazon bowed to the public's
demand by raising the minimum wage in its workforce to $15 an hour, the
movement's highest-profile win. The issue continued gaining traction as Sanders again made it one of his top policy issues heading into the 2020 presidential
primaries. At a Fight for $15 rally in 2019, he said: "There is no reason that Mc-
Donald's, a company that took in $1.4 billion in profit and paid its CEO $22
million, can't pay its workers a living wage." That same year, on July 18, 2019,
the U.S. House of Representatives voted to raise the federal minimum wage
to $15 by 2025, signaling that the employee activist movement had begun
reshaping policy at the highest levels of government. Over the course of the
decade, the National Employment Law Project estimated that state and local
wage laws contributed to a collective raise of $68 billion for around twenty-
two million workers.

During the national economic shutdown caused by the coronavirus pandemic, fast-food employees were thrust back into the spotlight along with millions of other high-risk, low-wage workers who could not afford to stop going to their jobs. In April 2020, as infection rates from Covid-19 soared and many fast-food workers tested positive for the virus, franchise restaurant employees organized by the Fight for $15 movement went on strike across the country, most comprehensively in California, where strikers converged at drive-in picket lines from Los Angeles to Oakland. Representing dozens of restaurants, including McDonald's, Burger King, Taco Bell, Domino's, Pizza Hut, Subway, Popeye's and El Pollo Loco, the employees were specifically protesting the lack of masks, gloves, sanitizer and soap available to them on the job, along with their employers' failure to provide $3 hourly extra in hazard pay and two weeks' paid sick leave for workers exposed to the virus. As one McDonald's cashier, forty-six-year-old San Jose resident Maria Ruiz, said, "Workers are scared of retaliation but we're not going to wait for one of us to die or get sick with the virus. We are tired of taking the risk: we are essential workers, but my life is essential, too."

WALMART WORKERS STEP INTO THE RING

WHAT THE FAST-FOOD WORKER STRIKES DID FOR THE RESTAURANT and service sectors, Walmart worker strikes did for retail. Even a few weeks before the first fast-food employees walked off the job in New York, in the fall of 2012, workers at the nation's largest private employer heard the message from Occupy Wall Street and decided that it was their moment to demand a bigger slice of the corporate pie. Known for its "always low prices," Walmart became the world's biggest retailer while paying its workers some of the lowest wages in the business, so low, in fact, that many of the company's one and a half million employees relied on $6 billion in annual federal assistance in the form of food stamps, housing aid, tax credits and Medicaid. A congressional study in 2013 revealed that Walmart was costing U.S. taxpayers between $3,000 and $6,000 a year per worker to compensate for their shortfall in wages. "That's money that we should understand as a subsidy to Walmart, not to the workers," wrote Sarah Jaffe in *Necessary Trouble*, because "it allows Walmart to save billions in wages and benefits by pushing those costs onto the rest of us."

In many ways, Walmart's phenomenal success as a corporation modeled the way cutthroat American capitalism was designed to work in the neoliberal era: sinking the prospects of working people in the service of ever-expanding profits at the executive level. It's also a case study in the way the country's wealth and income gap widened prodigiously over the last half century. Founded in 1962 in Bentonville, Arkansas, by the retail salesman Sam Walton—whose father made his money repossessing people's farms in Missouri after the Great Depression—the store's mission then was the same as it is today: sell the highest volume of goods at the lowest price possible. Within seven years, the independent discount business became a thirty-two-store franchise across four states. But Walmart's size and power truly exploded in the seventies, doubling its sales every two years, and by 1980 the company had 276 stores with sales topping $1 billion.

"Wal-Mart was spreading outward through the forgotten towns of middle America, laying waste to local hardware stores and pharmacies, saturating the regions it conquered so that no one else could compete," wrote George Packer in *The Unwinding: An Inner History of the New America*. Guided by a ruthlessly expansionist business philosophy that understood that "the hollowing out of the heartland was good for the company's bottom line," the retail giant became so successful that by 1985, Walton was America's richest man—worth just shy of $3 billion. The fortune would turn his family into America's wealthiest dynasty—one whose extreme anti-labor policies rivaled the nation's other big family empire, owned by the Koch brothers.

By the time Occupy rolled around, the six heirs to the Walton fortune were worth more than the bottom 30 to 40 percent of Americans, according to different estimates. In the tradition of so many of America's most profitable corporations, Walmart managed to avoid paying $1 billion a year in federal taxes by exploiting loopholes; according to Americans for Tax Fairness, the company paid a 29 percent as opposed to a 35 percent corporate tax rate while keeping more than $20 billion parked in offshore havens. Meanwhile, the company was merciless toward any of its drivers, clerks or other employees who dared to attempt to collectively organize. For years, labor unions including the AFL-CIO and SEIU failed in repeated efforts to organize Walmart's workforce. Then, in the boisterous afterglow of the Occupy movement, the tables turned.

The first Walmart worker protests ignited one month before the fast-food worker strikes, in October 2012, when about forty employees walked off the job at several stores in Southern California. Then, six days later, one hundred Walmart employees carrying grievances from thousands of their co-workers showed up at the company's headquarters in Arkansas to present corporate bosses with a "Declaration of Respect." Dressed union-style, in matching green T-shirts, workers used the call-and-repeat Occupy technique, known as the people's mic, to amplify their voices in a raucous display of worker unity that caught the company off guard. With support from the United Food and Commercial Workers, the employees had created the Organization United for Respect at Walmart, or OUR Walmart, which now issued its founding document of demands: freedom of association and freedom of speech; minimum pay of $13 an hour with full-time work available to all employees who wanted it; predictable work schedules; affordable healthcare, and a guarantee of benefits and wages adequate enough that no worker must rely on government assistance. Founded largely by women employees who were tired of being—or seeing their co-workers—intimidated by management while working longer hours under worsening conditions, OUR Walmart broke from the traditional union playbook. Rather, it was a kind of hybrid organization that centralized workers' demands but promoted a decentralized model of store worker activism. In other words: protest when and how you like, the organization will have your back.

Suddenly, low-paid workers at America's retail behemoth were operating with a new script, standing up, articulating needs, taking action. The next month, over Thanksgiving weekend—just days before the Fast Food Forward campaign would break national headlines in New York—OUR Walmart organizers staged their first signature Black Friday strike. Choosing the biggest shopping day of the year to make their point, employees walked off the job at thirteen hundred stores nationwide, demanding higher wages and better hours and conditions. Again, part of what helped them succeed was the support they received from Occupy.

Marianne Manilov, a grassroots organizer in San Francisco who founded The Engage Network and helped launch OUR Walmart, drew clear connections between members of the year-old Occupy movement and the retail workers' big initial strike. "The first year we did Black Friday protests, I was seeing all these volunteers pop up around the country," she told me, and among two hundred ally organizations that helped mobilize for the protests, one Occupy activist in particular became essential training Walmart employees in digital organizing skills that magnified the showdown. In some instances, regional Occupy groups—which had long since vanished from the streets but stayed organizing in their communities—carried out direct actions. "Occupy was outside of the parks—the Occupy tactic was over—but the leaders and the [movement] ecosystem grew roots to each other, so Occupy Ohio called me before Black Friday and said, 'We want to know if you want a lockdown, a kitchen, what?' and they said they could do it at twenty Walmarts. Around the country, the number of people from local Occupies that took on the Black Friday strikes was enormous," said Manilov. "The story that Occupy was dead was promoted over and over and over, but that wasn't what I was seeing from the ground."

In the months that followed, OUR Walmart broadened its influence within the company using an "online-to-offline" distributed organizing strategy pioneered at Occupy Wall Street. They built a robust online network that recruited and connected workers through social media, then migrated from the digital realm into actions in the workplace. Like Occupy, OUR Walmart took a decentralized approach to organizing that helped empower employees everywhere. "It was meant to spread horizontally across the country, to allow workers to take action in different ways, and to encourage them to act on their own without the supervision of an organizer," wrote Jaffe. The "strategy of minority unionism"—whereby workers didn't wait for a majority vote in order to strike, but could act independently at their own locations—allowed the organization to combine effective protest tactics developed at Occupy with clear demands. "Horizontalism allowed workers to feel as though the organization was theirs; it didn't mean the movement was leaderless or existed without professional, full-time organizing staff, but that anyone who wanted to be a leader could be one. Although only a few workers might strike at any given store, there was nearly always a willing crowd of supporters to accompany them in protest and to walk them back to work the next day," Jaffe wrote. "Walmart pits customer against worker; OUR Walmart wanted to pit customer and worker against a massive, global corporation squeezing both for its bottom line."

Along with former Occupy activists, fast-food workers in the Fight for $15 would later join OUR Walmart on the front lines of the annual Black Friday strikes, signaling the coalescence of a diverse and growing low-wage movement. Already the next autumn—in September 2013, as the fast-food worker walkouts were in full swing—thousands of workers joined OUR Walmart strikes across fifteen cities, and more than one hundred people were arrested for civil disobedience. On Black Friday in 2014, activist employees shut down Walmarts and staged protests at some two thousand two hundred stores nationwide. By then their demands had escalated to $15 an hour, access to consistent full-time work, and an end to gender discrimination in pay and promotions.

Finally, after three years of pressure, Walmart responded: in the spring of 2015, the company raised wages for half a million workers, setting a new base pay of $9 an hour, which became $10 an hour the next year. According to Emily Wells, a leading OUR Walmart organizer, the concessions—which included improved scheduling rules and a new policy for pregnant workers—amounted to a partial victory. "With $16 billion in [annual] profits and $150 billion in wealth for the owners, Walmart can afford to provide the good jobs that Americans need—and that means fifteen dollars an hour, full-time, consistent hours and respect for our hard work," she said. Paul Krugman wrote in *The New York Times* that the corporation's decision could have "spillovers," leading to raises for millions of other workers at other companies. By the time Black Friday rolled around the following year, OUR Walmart's coalition included such heavyweights as National People's Action, National Domestic Workers Alliance, Jobs with Justice, CREDO and Color of Change among other worker-aligned groups.

Aside from the organizational and strategic elements it contributed to help make OUR Walmart one of the great labor organizing successes of the decade, Occupy Wall Street did something even more fundamental: it discredited and delegitimized families like the Waltons, whose fortune was based on outrageous greed and excessive profiting off the backs of their poverty-wage workers. By calling the Walton family and other billionaires like them the root of the problem—the very topmost sliver of the 1 percent—Occupy laid the crucial groundwork that permitted OUR Walmart's message to resonate. "In many ways, the conversation that we can have about the Waltons really was much harder to have before Occupy," Dan Schlademan, co-director of OUR Walmart, told Jaffe. "Walmart would always position itself as the 'Protector of Customers,' and whatever we wanted was going to raise prices on their customers. It became impossible for them to make that argument when Walmart has created the single richest family on earth." For Manilov, the campaign's remarkable achievements were rooted in the new sense of collective power that grew from Zuccotti Park. "OUR Walmart won the largest victory in the history of the labor movement: $1 billion for half a million workers. They raised wages. They won a victory on part-time hours, they got their first family leave and a policy addressing [employee] pregnancy," she said. "I think the bravery to go and publicly speak out or organize at your store—when it means you might lose your job and not have food because Walmart will come after you—that courage comes from people connecting and seeing each other. It takes away the shame and fear when you see others participating; Occupy gave a name to that, the 99 percent. It's the sense that I am not alone, my story is connected, and I can have power with others."

A TEACHABLE MOMENT: THE RED STATE REVOLT

THE LABOR UPHEAVAL SPURRED BY THE FAST-FOOD AND WALMART worker strikes set the tone for the decade. In the years after Occupy Wall Street, protests by employees across the low-wage sector reverberated through the economy. The Service Employees International Union, the most reliably combative union advocating for working-class Americans, mobilized janitors and airport workers in a Raise America campaign that followed the demands of the Fight for $15. Thousands of domestic workers along with hotel employees from global chains like Hyatt, Marriott and Hilton entered the movement, hundreds getting arrested nationwide while calling for higher pay and improved working conditions. From nurses to healthcare and hospital employees, from construction workers to Stop & Shop supermarket clerks, people spanning industries from the coasts to the heartland joined the new era of labor activism, standing up en masse to affirm that the 99 percent had awakened, and that such levels of wealth inequality would no longer be accepted.

It wasn't only low-paid workers who joined the fight. In early 2018, hundreds of thousands of the working- and middle-class professionals who form the backbone of our society—America's teachers—decided that they too had had enough. Tensions over teacher pay and benefits had brewed for decades, as state budget cuts and reduced spending on public education led to increased class sizes, deteriorating facilities and a generation of educators consigned to using outdated textbooks and spending their own money, which they were often forced to earn from a second or even a third job, to supply basic classroom materials to students. Throughout the postwar period, and until the Clinton years, teacher pay remained on par with other middle-class jobs. But starting in the midnineties, teachers started to see their health benefits decline and watched their salaries notably decrease in comparison with other educated professionals. It was during this period that district investments declined, school infrastructure was neglected and class sizes exploded. At the same time, the joy and art of the profession was steadily eroding under relentless institutional pressure to "teach to the test." By 2017, teachers were being paid almost 20 percent less than workers in comparable fields, and it became an accepted fact that "the working conditions for teachers and the learning conditions for students had declined really radically," the historian Julie Greene told the *Washington Post*.

So, in a wholly unexpected, women-led, union-backed wave of strikes in 2018, the unity of demands captured the country's imagination as teachers walked out. In fact, the first visible sign that America's public school teachers were ready to revolt had occurred earlier, in September 2012, exactly a year after the launch of Occupy Wall Street, when the Chicago Teachers Union initiated a strike that put twenty-six thousand teachers on the picket lines for more than a week outside 580 Chicago-area schools. Led by CTU president Karen Lewis, the teachers denounced the rise in closures of city schools, the explosion in class sizes and Mayor Rahm Emanuel's proposal to pair teacher pay raises with layoffs. Their nine-day stoppage won them a 16 percent salary increase over four years. For many teachers, Occupy Wall Street's focus on unfair tax breaks for the wealthy had hit home because it revealed the source of underfunding of public education everywhere, and brought the discussion of inequality into a practical context. "Teachers, including the largest teachers' union, are now looking very diligently at the tax structure in various states and federally, because they understand that all these tax breaks for rich people have led to decreased funding for public education," the labor journalist Sam Pizzigati told me. In a direct echo of Occupy, "militant teachers are now linking teaching and learning to what's happening, and not happening, at the top of our economic order."

Chicago's teacher unrest was followed up in 2014 by sustained demonstrations in Oklahoma where some twenty-five thousand teachers swarmed the state capitol, protesting cuts to public schools and demanding that the state use a portion of its burgeoning oil and gas revenue to bolster education funding. In that movement, teacher groups, à la Occupy, took to social media to organize and mobilize their colleagues to get out in the streets. The popular Facebook page "Oklahoma Teachers—The Time Is Now" reached tens of thousands of followers, broadening the protests beyond unions to include ordinary people who stood up in solidarity with teachers. School funding in Oklahoma nonetheless continued to decrease, falling by more than 25 percent between 2008 and 2018, even as the state gained fifty-four thousand more students. The state's woes reflected trends teachers were experiencing all over the country, particularly in poorer, Republican-controlled states where anti-government legislators had slashed public spending. When the big revolt finally happened, in February 2018, almost as shocking as the sudden display of teacher militancy was perhaps the place where that militancy was exercised: in the former heart of coal country, a spot that more than any other had been hung out by the 1 percent to dry: West Virginia.

In the 2016 Democratic presidential primaries, Bernie Sanders gained a strong following in working-class West Virginia, where he ended up beating Hillary Clinton by more than fifteen points (Trump would go on to drub Clinton by nearly three times that margin in the general election). Sanders's populist candidacy sparked the creation of several chapters of Democratic Socialists of America, which some schoolteachers in the state joined. In 2017, they formed a study group to discuss labor activism, and, borrowing again from the Occupy playbook, West Virginia's teachers organized and strategized online through social media and chat platforms, especially a popular one run by a group called the Badass Teachers Association, or BAT. The organization of teacher activists stood opposed to standardized, high-stakes testing, and educated themselves on successful teacher organizing efforts in Chicago, Oklahoma and elsewhere. Through BAT, said one of the group's members who used only the name Scott, educators had created an "online forum where West Virginia teachers shared everything they could find on Chicago, educators in Arizona and Denver emailed with teachers in LA and Oakland, [and] a new kind of organizing was underway."

West Virginia's teachers weren't just focusing on wages but on a broader sense of economic injustice in the Mountain State—one of the poorest in the nation. "After years of relative passivity and accumulating grievances, it took a militant group of teachers in West Virginia with a 'class struggle orientation' to organize their colleagues and prepare to strike," wrote the labor blogger Dan Sisken. Things reached a tipping point when the government in Charleston announced an increase in dues for public employees' health insurance plans, and in February 2018, with 80 percent support from teachers across the state—and the backing of the American Federation of Teachers and the National Education Association—the walkouts began. Some thirty-five thousand teachers across all fifty-five counties brought the West Virginia school system to a halt, and after one week, teachers united in opposition to a weak agreement between state and union leaders forced a second week of closures. In reward for their holdout, the educators won a 5 percent raise. "When the West Virginia teachers went on strike, the question being asked was 'Can they possibly win anything, and will it be a sign of things to come?'" the Seattle city councilwoman Sawant told me, and "what we've seen is that the teachers strike was like Occupy: the opening lines of a completely new period, where public sector unions, led mostly by women rank-and-file members, started to reject what has been a status quo for decades and not only define the political establishments of the two parties—but in many cases, define the business unionism of their leadership."

Suddenly the attitude was that if it could be done in West Virginia, it could be done anywhere, and the state's rebellion inspired others to follow suit, igniting a national movement. The next place where teachers took charge was back in Oklahoma, where about one-third of educators belonged to a union, although unions alone didn't organize the 2018 strike. In April, some forty-five thousand teachers in the deep red, right-to-work state—where teachers hadn't engaged in a strike in close to three decades—staged a ten-day walkout. As a result, teachers received a $6,000 raise, while salaries for support staff went up by $1,250, and they also won an increase in school funding through a tobacco tax. That same month, the #RedforEd movement—also called the Red State Revolt, both because public schools were in the red and because the strikes were happening in predominantly GOP-governed red states—exploded as tens of thousands of teachers shuttered classrooms across Kentucky, Arizona and Colorado. Bus drivers carried out a strike in Georgia. In Arizona, the week-long statewide strike won teachers a 20 percent salary hike along with higher salaries for support staff, and in Colorado, two weeks of district-wide walkouts granted teachers a 2 percent raise and saw the state's education budget restored to prerecession levels. In Denver specifically, which had experienced a three-day strike in February, teachers won salary increases of 7 to 11 percent.

The next month, both North and South Carolina experienced one-day teachers' strikes totaling well over one hundred thousand people, which forced school districts throughout the states to close. Tennessee teachers from Nashville's public schools also staged a sick-out to demand increased funding. The rebellion was contagious: the more educators rose to their feet demanding long-overdue improvements to their lot, the more they saw that they could win. There was a lull in protests that summer and fall, as many of the same teachers poured their energy into defeating Republicans at the ballot box—a women-led effort that helped fuel the Blue Wave, which gave Democrats control of the House of Representatives and statehouses nationwide.

By the end of 2018, nearly half a million Americans had taken part in strikes, walkouts and other work stoppages—the highest worker turnout in more than three decades. And when the movement picked back up again in January 2019, momentum shifted westward, to California, where more than thirty thousand Los Angeles public school teachers representing the state's largest district went on strike to protest low pay, huge class sizes, lack of nurses and library staff, and an explosion of charter schools that were drawing away necessary funding. Around 98 percent of members in the United Teachers Los Angeles union approved of the weeklong action, the first strike in the district in thirty years. After all-night negotiations with the district, UTLA won teachers a 6 percent raise; reduced class sizes; an agreement to have a full-time nurse and librarian employed at every school; and even a nonbinding resolution calling for a cap on charter schools in the state. But the Los Angeles teachers didn't stop there: working with the California Teachers Association, they also got Governor Gavin Newsom to approve two bills that enforced more accountability for charter schools and gave districts a right to reject new charter authorizations.

Six days after Los Angeles teachers reached their agreement, a one-day walkout by teachers demanding higher pay in Virginia—another right-to-work state, like most of the others—resulted in a 5 percent across-the-board raise. The next month, thousands of teachers in Oakland, California, led by the Oakland Education Association, walked off the job for seven days and won an 11 percent raise over four years, along with a 3 percent bonus. In some blue states, but mostly in red ones, activist educators bolstered by unions had proved that they could unite to achieve fairer treatment. Most of the teachers, like the low-wage workers who mobilized before them, had not participated in the Occupy movement in 2011. But they represented the same underpaid, underfunded and undervalued generation that had matured in the Bush and Obama years, a period when economic security in their profession disappeared.

Dylan Scott, writing in *Vox*, explained: "The resurgence of America's teachers' unions is the story of austerity, as many states cut education budgets over the past decade and with them teacher pay and benefits. It is also a parable of millennial economic angst. The latest generation of teachers entered their classrooms with student debt, mediocre health care, and diminished job prospects. They found themselves open to aggressive political activism. But it is most fundamentally the story of the renewed American labor protest movement." A movement that, in all fairness, did not exist before Occupy Wall

Street stood up for the 99 percent and gave working people the jolt they needed to step forward and begin to reclaim their future.

GROWING LABOR MILITANCY: PLANES, CARS AND THE CORONAVIRUS STRIKES OF 2020

IN JANUARY 2019, THE AFL-CIO INVITED SARA NELSON, PRESIDENT of the Association of Flight Attendants, the country's largest air flight union, representing fifty thousand members from twenty airlines, to speak at its annually hosted Martin Luther King Jr. dinner, honoring her with the 2019 AFL-CIO MLK Drum Major for Justice Award. At the time, some eight hundred thousand federal workers were either furloughed or working without pay because Donald Trump and Republicans refused to back down on an appropriations bill seeking billions of dollars to fund construction of a border wall with Mexico. It was the longest U.S. government shutdown in history, and at the dinner, Nelson, a rising star in the labor movement, urged union leaders to seize the tremendous opportunity by carrying out a nationwide industrial action on behalf of the federal employees.

The moment was ripe, she said, for labor to regain its historic leadership role, and she proposed something that sounded radical but was altogether doable: ending the shutdown with a general strike. "What is the labor movement waiting for?" she asked. An overwhelming majority of Americans sided with the furloughed workers, so the strike would have had popular support. "It would have been relatively cheap to do and it would have reestablished the labor movement as an important popular social force in millions of Americans' lives," said the economist Richard Wolff. The unions ignored Nelson's proposal. Less than a week later, limited air traffic control workers caused widespread flight delays and airport shutdowns, forcing Republicans to the table. But "it was her call for a general strike that was widely credited for jump-starting the endgame of President Donald Trump's brutal five-week shutdown," wrote Kim

Kelly in *The New Republic*. A much greater disruption to the airline business would happen a little over a year later when the coronavirus sharply reduced air travel, drained billions from company coffers and caused widespread layoffs, forcing the industry to reevaluate its future.

The threat of mass worker resistance, while not acted upon in January 2019, signaled the potential to escalate tactics in a new era of labor militancy, and it was followed up later that year by a dramatic, nearly six-week-long strike by forty-nine thousand autoworkers at General Motors. Organized by United Auto Workers, the carmaker employees ended up winning substantial pay raises, bonuses and a path for temporary workers to gain full-time status, a recognizable victory for the union. The first nationwide strike at GM in over a decade—and the longest automotive walkout in half a century—cost the company around $2 billion and threw a wrench into the economy, causing layoffs across the Midwest just months before the coronavirus pandemic seismically altered the American workforce.

By the sixth week of the nation's pandemic lockdown, in late April 2020, more than twenty-four million people, or one in seven workers, had lost their jobs and applied for unemployment insurance, five times as many people as had filed for unemployment during the worst five-week stretch of the Great Recession. Ultimately some forty million Americans would lose their jobs that spring as a result of the pandemic, plunging livelihoods and the economy into turmoil. But for many employees who didn't get let go and continued showing up to work despite the harrowing health risks, the virus prompted an upsurge of labor demands.

Workers at Whole Foods, for example, decided to ask more of their Amazon-owned employer, so they joined a new, un-unionized organization called Whole Worker to perform a one-day sick-out on March 31. Their demands included hazard pay at double the base hourly rate, guaranteed sick leave for people who self-quarantined, automatic closures of any Whole Foods where an employee tested positive for the virus and other worker-safety measures. For weeks, employees and customers had leveled criticism at the high-end supermarket chain for not doing enough to protect its workers; as a result of the walkout, store employees saw their pay temporarily raised by $2 an hour, with two weeks' paid time off for any Whole Foods employees diagnosed with Covid-19.

Most people didn't feel the measures went far enough, but it was a start. Worker actions and wildcat strikes were becoming more widespread, including by some high-risk nurses and healthcare workers who walked off the job due to a lack of adequate protective equipment. Employees at Instacart, the grocery delivery service, called for a strike and refused to fill orders until the company took more actions to keep them safe. Strikes were meanwhile roiling Amazon warehouses across the country, including, most prominently, a fulfillment center on Staten Island in New York City, where a worker organizer named Chris Smalls was fired after pushing for greater health protections and paid sick leave. By October 2020, Amazon would see more than twenty thousand of its employees test positive for Covid-19.

At Bath Iron Works, a navy shipyard in Maine and the state's fourth largest employer, half the workers stayed home to pressure owners to clean up the shipyard after some employees tested positive for the coronavirus in March. The walkout led that summer to a monthslong strike by the corporation's four thousand three hundred workers, represented by the International Association of Machinists and Aerospace Workers, who opposed management efforts to strip their health insurance, lay off employees and hire more low-wage subcontractors. Bus drivers in Alabama went on strike after not receiving any form of protection against the virus, and workers from General Electric to Barnes and Noble withheld labor to push for safer conditions.

But perhaps the sector that received the most attention during the coronavirus strikes was the fast-food industry, as workers agitating for a more sanitary workplace picked up where the Fight for $15 had left off. According to an SEIU survey of eight hundred McDonald's workers, nearly a quarter reported that they had worked while feeling sick during the pandemic—and half said they had been discouraged or banned from wearing face masks or gloves on the job. As fast-food worker strikes escalated in 2020, "the actions, some of which are spontaneous and all of which have been planned quickly, are beginning to look more and more like a general strike," reported Lauren Kaori Gurley in *Vice*.

Multiple factors have hurt the labor market in recent decades: lower wages, fewer worker protections, weakened union power, more outsourcing, increased automation, skewed tax policies favoring the rich. But the degree to which the middle class collapsed and working Americans lost their financial footing only came into sharp relief following the 2008 financial crash. The pandemic in 2020 exposed those economic fault lines further. The oft-touted American job growth in the decade between the Great Recession and the coronavirus shutdown amounted to a boom in service industry work that paid poverty wages. While two-thirds of the jobs lost in last decade's recession earned a middle-class income, nearly three in five jobs gained back were low-wage positions that brought in less than $14 an hour.

For working people, the numbers just weren't adding up. According to the Economic Policy Institute, employees were illegally shorted about $50 billion in annual wages by their employers through underpayment or unpaid work. Had income stayed on pace with inflation and economic growth over the last forty years, the lowest 90 percent of earners would be receiving an average of around $12,000 more each year. As *The New York Times* editorial board put it: "In effect, every American worker in the bottom 90 percent of the income distribution is sending an annual check for $12,000 to a richer person in the top 10 percent."

The problem of the widening wealth and income gap won't solve itself: it's going to take significant tax reform and systemic changes in the way corporations compensate employees for their labor. In a pre-pandemic report published by the Brookings Institution, entitled "Meet the Low-Wage Workforce," authors Martha Ross and Nicole Bateman revealed that around one in six Americans—about fifty-three million people, or 44 percent of all workers between the ages of eighteen and sixty-four—were low-wage workers getting by on a median wage of $10.22, or annual earnings of less than $18,000. The vocal movement to boost the minimum wage succeeded in raising awareness and, in lots of cases, drove policy changes at the state level that impacted millions of people's lives.

But for many economists, the intense focus on lifting the minimum wage didn't address a core problem. Higher wages were needed for workers across the board, not just those struggling at the bottom. "A minimum wage is a very positive thing, but it doesn't deal with the vast majority of the working class—it doesn't affect the median worker," said Lawrence Mishel. For this reason, to help restrengthen the country's middle class, the scope of the fight for higher wages needs to expand. He went on to say, "I think there's agreement about the rigged economy, but instead of focusing on wages, some on the left are always focusing on the *minimum* wage," which may actually be hurting rather than helping the cause for workers.

In the decade since Occupy Wall Street provided its seminal wake-up call to America's workers, notable changes have occurred. The once-beleaguered labor movement has reemerged in force. Public sentiment has shifted away from the failures of neoliberal, trickle-down economic thinking toward a more populist and progressive approach that favors workers. And the political and financial establishment has also, to a large degree, heard the call. In 2019, the Business Roundtable, which includes chief executives from some of the largest corporations in the country, concluded for the first time that advancing shareholders' interests should not be the single and sole priority of a company; that employers must also invest in their employees and the environment that sustains them. The admission, as laughably obvious though it may seem to many, marked a fundamental revision to the premise that for so many decades steered Wall Street, summed up in Milton Friedman's famous declaration that "the social responsibility of business is to increase its profits," or more succinctly still in the iconic words of Gordon Gekko, from the film *Wall Street*: "Greed is good."

Reinforcing these institutional changes, a new, loud, robust American labor movement has been reenergized in its fight for the 99 percent and is scoring real wins as it helps rebalance the scales of economic power. One of the provisions in the 2010 Dodd-Frank reform bill that Republicans found especially onerous—and Democrats had to fight hard to keep—was a measure that forced companies to annually disclose the pay ratio between CEO and median worker salary. In the wake of Occupy, the AFL-CIO stood unbending as it defended the measure against GOP attacks. "The difference between labor's nonchalance about cutting taxes on the rich in 1963, and the AFL-CIO's leadership in demanding this pay ratio disclosure provision, is very, very striking," said the journalist Pizzigati. "The AFL-CIO led the opposition to that campaign, and I think it's symbolic of the shift in the narrative that Occupy did so much to bring about."

But beyond labor halls and legislative chambers and even classrooms, the narrative shift performed by Occupy Wall Street would leave perhaps its clearest and most lasting impacts on the generation of social justice activists who came out of the movement, and who continue to shape its legacy: the people who were inspired by the global rebellion for equality emanating from Zuccotti Park, and who, as both the creators and inheritors of Generation Occupy, would transform what activism meant and what it could accomplish in America.

NEW YORK IS OAKLAND, OAKLAND IS NEW YORK

OCTOBER 26, 2011

THE NIGHT AFTER POLICE IN OAKLAND, CALIFORNIA, SHOT THE Iraq War veteran and Occupy Oakland protester Scott Olsen, hospitalizing him with a fractured skull from the lead-filled beanbag fired at his head, activists three thousand miles away on Wall Street broke through their own barrier of fear in the face of mounting suppression.

What had happened in Oakland—where police in the pre-dawn hours tore down Occupy's encampment at Oscar Grant Plaza and the next evening launched a violent assault, injuring scores and turning the East Bay Area city into an overnight war zone—marked perhaps the most egregious display of state repression against the overwhelmingly peaceful movement. A decade before the George Floyd protests, we weren't used to seeing police firing rubber bullets, flash-bang grenades and tear gas at nonviolent American protesters. But the incident was by no means isolated. Later, in November, eighteen big-city mayors working closely with the FBI and Department of Homeland Security staged a coordinated crackdown, employing heavy force to clear Occupy camps nationwide. Police continued to unconstitutionally and in many cases brutally suppress Americans' right to protest. Before it was over, by spring of 2012, some seven thousand people would be arrested as lawsuits filed across the country charged police with unlawful conduct and violating civil liberties.

Yet the October night after Olsen was shot, protesters at Zuccotti Park responded in the only way that might have then seemed imaginable: they turned outrage into courage and took over New York City's streets. Faced with a moment that demanded solidarity, Occupy Wall Street reconstituted itself as a revolt that reverberated from coast to coast, finding liberation in the new chant: *"New York is Oakland, Oakland is New York!"* The breakthrough happened shortly after nine when a large crowd of protesters who were being corralled on sidewalks by police escorts made a circle around city hall and, in a decisive instant, lost their fear. First several, then dozens of people burst through police lines, and within moments a mass of hundreds overflowed Broadway, unimpeded by the law. The New York artery belonged to them now, and the call *"Whose streets? Our streets!"* rang out as cheers and chants and the staccato cadence of drums echoed through lower Manhattan. Traffic stalled, taxis sat bumper to bumper as the throng swept up the avenue and protesters weaved and dodged through lanes of immobilized vehicles. Drivers looked out in silence from behind their windshields, some with their windows rolled down in the autumn heat, letting in the smells and sounds of rebellion.

For hours that night we felt we owned the city streets, overrunning police lines that hurriedly assembled to block our path, and making off with their orange kettle nets as souvenirs. Some people were beaten and arrested in the process, but we marched with a sense of triumph. The violent assault on protesters in Oakland had aroused masses of supporters, undaunted by threats, refortified in their defiance. Occupy had issued a direct challenge to the state and now the blue and white lights of helicopters were flashing across the sky, following our dark swarming mass that moved like a wave, loosening and tightening as it streamed through the West Village. Diners and drinkers at outdoor bistros along Bleecker Street stared, some smiling, watching in amazement. As the jubilant parade turned north onto Avenue of the Americas, our power grew. Occupy Wall Street was reinventing what it meant to participate in a democracy.

Two and a half years later, in March 2014, the City of Oakland agreed in a federal lawsuit settlement to pay the military veteran Scott Olsen, nearly killed by police during their attack on city protesters, $4.5 million. Olsen, who was twenty-four years old at the time he was shot, sustained permanent brain damage, which ended his plans to become a computer network and systems administrator, a job he had held at a San Francisco company during the fateful autumn when he chose to stand with Occupy Oakland. On the day the settlement was reached, his attorney, Rachel Lederman, said, "After serving two tours of duty as a United States Marine in Iraq, Scott Olsen could never have imagined that he would be shot in the head by an Oakland police officer while he was peacefully exercising his First Amendment rights in support of the budding Occupy economic justice movement." In the age of Obama, it was a painful lesson that democracy was still coming to the U.S.A.

6

OCCUPY ACTIVISM

A NEW CULTURE OF PROTEST

WATERSHED MOMENT: BROOKE LEHMAN

BROOKE LEHMAN HAS BEEN CALLED A LOT OF THINGS. ANARCHIST Marxist. Communitarian totalitarian. UN operative. Terrorist. In fact, as her name suggests, Lehman is a sixth-generation descendant of the nineteenth-century German Jewish immigrant family that brought us Lehman Brothers—the investment bank whose meltdown on September 15, 2008, triggered the global financial crisis.

But she wasn't exactly one of them, either. Part of the generation that came of age in the first Iraq War and the anti-globalization movement, Lehman had committed herself long ago to a life engaged around social justice activism. In the late nineties, she helped found the Direct Action Network and marched in the Battle of Seattle. She later deepened her skills as an organizer mobilizing protests against the second Iraq War, and by the time Occupy Wall Street came around, Lehman was a seasoned veteran, albeit one with a family history that screamed 1 percent. She was teaching at the Institute for Social Ecology in

Plainfield, Vermont, and when she showed up to get involved at Zuccotti Park, she let discretion be her guide: the goal was to do more listening than talking. "I was trying to not be out front," she told me. "I felt like I was older than most people, and I had the distinct privilege of being an organizer at Occupy Wall Street with the last name Lehman." She had seen the show before and didn't want to fall into a trap. "I think anti-Semitism is pretty real in right-wing media. Everyone wants to characterize the left as being a bunch of spoiled-brat rich Jews, [but] it's not true."

Despite attempts to remain out of the spotlight, Lehman quickly established herself as a mature organizer able to help guide the facilitation working group, coordinate the daily general assembly and participate in delicate, behind-the-scenes discussions that contributed to the movement's rise. Lehman said she recognized early on, sooner than others perhaps, how Occupy Wall Street's more aggressive approach to activism—emphasis on *action*—could reshape the culture of protest in America. "In the generation before Occupy, even during the global justice movement [of the nineties], only a small handful of us regarded direct action as a reasonable response to injustice, and I think post-Occupy it became part of the general vernacular to 'take the streets' in response to all different forms of injustice—whether they be police shootings, school shootings, sexual harassment. All of these moments," she said, referring to successor movements like Black Lives Matter, March for Our Lives and #MeToo, "have led people out of their buildings, out of their private lives and corporate lives and into the public, and I just can't imagine that being the case without Occupy. Now we're in a period where if there is injustice, many people just look on social media to see where to show up. A whole generation is growing up with that muscle in their bones to step out, to do sit-ins, to march and take direct action in response to issues that affect their lives."

Occupy didn't emerge from a vacuum, she added. Rather, it built on the work of decades of social movements that came before it: global justice in the nineties, anti-nuclear in the eighties, anti–Vietnam War in the seventies, and the mother of all social justice struggles, the Civil Rights Movement of the sixties. "They all stand on each other's shoulders," Lehman said, "but I do think Occupy can be seen as the predecessor, or instigator, of this generation of direct action."

À LA CARTE ACTIVISM

LEHMAN HAD ALREADY BEEN WORKING FOR SOME TIME TRYING TO seed the next generation of movement leaders. Four years before Occupy, in 2007, she helped launch a non-profit called The Watershed Center, which hosted social justice organizer retreats and nonviolence training workshops in upstate New York. After Occupy Wall Street's energy began to fade in the winter of 2012, Watershed became an incubator for a new wave of groups, like Occupy Manifest, a project that sought to create focused paths forward for the movement and its organizers. Another initiative sprang from there, called the Wildfire Project, which was started by a talented Occupy Wall Street organizer named Yotam Marom to train grassroots groups building organizational power. Lehman envisioned Watershed as becoming "a feeding ground for the movements," where activists could emphasize tangible goals, clear road maps and long-term strategic planning—precisely the things Occupy had been missing. As an anarchist- and utopian-inspired movement, Occupy was great at defining the present and envisioning the future, "but we were terrible at the transition, [because] there was no strategy to fill in that space: there was no way we were going to go from occupying Zuccotti Park to tearing down the capitalist state," she said. "Occupy was very good at living in the middle zone, where we weren't grounded in best results."

Thus, in a backlash to the Occupy Wall Street experiment, early groups and training organizations emerged from the movement swinging in the other direction. Organizers like Marom adopted some of the lessons and built on the organizing and technology tactics developed at Occupy, but they also established a fundamentally different brand of activism. "Wildfire is distinctly not-anarchistic," said the journalist J. A. Myerson. "They're allergic to leaderlessness. They want to develop leaders and work with organizations." Lehman and the other movement organizers who joined her at Watershed in the aftermath of Occupy had a clear-minded goal: to help launch the next generation of activists. In the process they became mentors advancing a new era of radicalized social justice movements.

The organization that had perhaps the earliest and most visible impact was one that Lehman helped start, in 2013, with another crack organizer from Zuccotti Park named Max Berger, called Momentum. The same group that would become the mobilizing force for Evan Weber and his climate cohort creating the Sunrise Movement, Momentum and its activists arrived at a unique analysis by studying the structures and strategies used in past protest movements: from Gandhian tactics of civil disobedience employed in the Civil Rights struggle to the mass uprisings that fueled the Color Revolutions, and from the anti-globalization and anti–Iraq War protests to the Arab Spring and Black Lives Matter. Rather than fixing on any single strategy—and especially conscious of some of the flaws inherent in the consensus-based, direct-democratic style of protesting at Occupy—Momentum organizers chose from an à la carte menu of options and adopted a range of tactics aimed at creating sustainable movements to drive long-term change. As a result, the structural and organizational failures of Occupy became essential learning tools as young activists discovered more effective ways to lead, incorporating tactical elements from Zuccotti Park while grappling with basic questions such as how hierarchical versus horizontal a structure to create, how centralized versus decentralized a movement to organize, and how much leadership versus how much autonomy activists needed in order to succeed.

REVOLUTIONARY PRAGMATISM

LEHMAN TOLD ME THAT THE SOCIAL MOVEMENTS NURTURED AT Watershed developed a kind of discipline more akin to labor organizing, "versus Occupy, where whoever happens to show up participates." In the wake of Zuccotti Park, activists had learned the importance of creating boundaries and issuing concrete demands. As Nicole Carty, the Occupy Wall Street organizer who joined Momentum, said, "So many people saw the potential of being leaders in their movement or organization in ways you couldn't be a leader at Occupy. In its successes and failures—both what the movement did and what it didn't do—Occupy opened a space for groups to reimagine participation." Very quickly, she told me, the training efforts started to bear fruit. "These movements are pretty powerful, and they have a level of strategy and understanding about how to make change that a lot of current professional organizations and non-profits don't have. Occupy didn't have strategy. The Movement for Black Lives doesn't have strategy. They have policies they care about—but not strategy," whereas the younger movements "have thought about it, they're nimble enough and they have the ability to adapt because they have clear structure for strategic movement building." Occupy's huge intervention was the way it harnessed the internet, "and that's only gotten sharper and better over time," through Gen Z movements like March for Our Lives and the Global Climate Strikes, added Carty. "Social media–native kids who grew up with the internet know how to organize."

By 2019, the most successful example of hybrid organizing tactics developed by Momentum—which combined best practices in grassroots resistance with effective forms of institutional pressure—was the Sunrise Movement. At the same time that it mobilized direct action protests in response to the climate crisis, Sunrise worked with new congressional leaders like Alexandria Ocasio-Cortez to help birth the Green New Deal, demonstrating what Lehman called "maximum vision and maximum program: presenting a long-term vision of what a post-revolutionary society may look like, with the here and now vision" to score tangible wins in the political framework. To have a better shot at achieving their goals, young movements like Sunrise also sought to construct a different language of protest. They recognized the limits of Occupy-style confrontation using revolutionary rhetoric—anti-capitalist, anti-police, anti-system, anti-state—which had ultimately alienated many middle-of-the-roaders and likely helped reduce, rather than expand, participation in the movement by people who gravitated to the message of the 99 percent, but who were turned off by the messenger. The post-Occupy generation of activists had no less a revolutionary critique of the system: they simply learned not to broadcast their position using the same polarizing tone. For Gen X–era activists like Lehman, the more pragmatic style of organizing was something new to wrap their heads around.

"I think it's confusing to people from the global justice movement who are like, 'Wait a second, this is a strategic choice. It's not that they're hiding their revolutionary vision—they're making a conscious choice not to use one in their organizing rhetoric, because they're not the direct descendants of Occupy,'" she said. In contrast to the raw outrage of Occupy, movements that arose in its wake settled on a more tactical approach. "I think the openness of Occupy—and the chaos of Occupy—created the need and the space for these better organized and more effective movements to take shape with strategies toward escalating and winning. It's a different strategy, a different project with a different vision for how to measure success," Lehman added. Ultimately, "Occupy as a movement had an almost impossible vision of success—tearing down the state and capitalism—but we were able to shift the culture in the direction of more anti-capitalist rhetoric, a friendlier atmosphere toward socialism, and bolder action like stopping the Keystone XL pipeline. We didn't achieve what we were trying to achieve, whereas some of these newer movements have instead put forward a vision around shifting immigration policy, around the impeachment of Trump, around the Green New Deal—and they're able to galvanize much clearer movements around tangible policy wins."

Another key contribution that subsequent movements took from Occupy was its novel principle of decentralized organizing. Traditional activist groups, including unions and large, well-organized non-profits, generally follow a centralized model of decision making: directors design an action campaign at the executive or national level, then the group's regional and local affiliates (often in partnership with other ally organizations) work to carry out the plan. The anti–Iraq War movement was a case in point: protests in the winter of 2003 mostly took the form of big marches led by a coalition of organizations with clear executive authority, hierarchies, guidelines and structure-based organizing. Occupy Wall Street, as the first internet-driven global social movement, did just the opposite, creating a decentralized model that enabled every city's Occupy affiliate to act with autonomy: no central authority existed, no one requested approval from the top, there was only a consensus-based general assembly making decisions (or in many cases failing to make decisions) for each Occupy group. As a result, goals articulated at Occupy Santa Fe would differ from concerns voiced at Occupy Boise, protest tactics employed at Occupy New Orleans, strategies agreed upon at Occupy Minneapolis, and so on.

Unleashing the power of social media in movement organizing, Occupy showed what was possible when hundreds of city groups acted creatively, spontaneously, in coordination with, yet fully independent from one another, and marked a clear break from the street politics of the past. But for the generation of younger activists at Watershed, it was evident that the fully decentralized approach contributed both to the movement's rise and to its downfall. Again, they tried to thread the needle with a more balanced strategy. "The boldest movements today are wildly decentralized and youth-based, but are focusing on policy reforms," concluded Lehman. Neither mass, leaderless actions based on horizontal decision making, nor centralized, overly structured organizations like labor unions or non-profits, the nascent groups emerging with Momentum understand the value of coupling militant direct action—strikes, sit-ins, walkouts, occupations—with clear and focused demands for legislative change. Shaped by the experience of Occupy, today's activists represent "something new," she said. "They have a radical analysis of the world, yet are also putting forth what Occupy would have called 'reformist demands,' and

I think these demands are incredibly necessary and part of a revolutionary strategy."

EVOLUTION OF MOVEMENTS: J. A. MYERSON

FOR JOURNALIST AND ORGANIZER J. A. MYERSON, THE DECADE PRE-ceding Occupy was a glum one: not only was there little in the way of protests in the early years of the millennium, but there weren't even venues for young people to engage in activism if they'd wanted to. The Iraq War had had a de-moralizing effect on the public, quieting the anti-globalization movement and numbing Americans to the point where they didn't feel their voice was being listened to, so they stopped trying to be heard. As Myerson put it, "What was somebody to do before Occupy?" The year before protesters descended on Zuc-cotti Park, nationwide opposition had started to build against the Keystone XL pipeline, laying the foundation for the modern climate movement. But apart from that, "if you weren't in a fighting union or a reform caucus, you could be in some marginal socialist party with several hundred members" and that was about it. Responding to the Tea Party's right-wing brand of populism, Occupy came on the scene at what Myerson described as "a low point of the American left." For a generation that hadn't experienced what social and political partic-ipation felt like, the movement presented an irresistible opportunity. "There's a sense in which I was always waiting for Occupy, hungry for Occupy, without knowing it," he said.

Born in 1986 in the Washington Heights neighborhood of Manhattan, Myerson grew up with left-leaning parents from the sixties. His mother was a public school teacher, his father did communications work for labor unions, and both were active in the peace and freedom movements pushing for social justice in Latin America, Africa and Southeast Asia. As a teen, Myerson pro-tested against the Iraq War, and in his senior year of high school he became "a young Deaniac," seizing on the populist message of Democratic Vermont governor and 2004 presidential candidate Howard Dean. In 2008, a few months after Myerson graduated from Bard College, Lehman Brothers collapsed. Less than two months after that Obama got elected, "so that was the world I was spat out into—this new recession and this new political hope." But Myerson's hope quickly eroded. He was appalled at how quickly Obama caved on his signature healthcare reform: "From the very beginning, single-payer was off the table. It wasn't even something used as a bargaining chip, it was excluded at the start of negotiations!" Yet what disturbed him even more was the way Obama failed to rescue millions of homeowners even as he gave a free pass to the Wall Street CEOs whose criminal mortgage-lending practices had wrecked the economy.

In late 2010, Myerson found his way into US Uncut, a group of guerrilla activists who would dress up as bankers and perform skits about tax avoidance, connecting corporate greed to the defunding of libraries, hospitals, and other public institutions. It was through this group that Myerson met people in the summer of 2011 who were engaged in the early planning meetings of Occupy Wall Street. He didn't expect much from it at first. "I was so dispirited then. I was like, okay, another thing, hippies on Wall Street." What he soon discovered was a movement that not only changed him but reshaped the way young people saw themselves as agents of political change.

Myerson, like myself and so many other participants, thrilled in Occupy Wall Street's meteoric rise only to feel walloped a few months later by the movement's swift and premature downfall. The roller coaster trajectory left a lot of people feeling depressed, grasping and at a loss for what should, or could, come next. Myerson cited a graph, developed later by the organization Movement Netlab, which labeled the different phases people experience in popular social movements, starting with largely unobserved actions, then moving through a tension-building stage until, finally, an incident occurs provoking a popular upswell of compassion and outrage, known as the heroic phase. In the case of Occupy, the heroic phase happened after the first week when a New York City police officer pepper sprayed four unarmed white women in the face, igniting the movement. That phase, Myerson explained, is usually followed by "a painful contraction and loss of energy that can be very disillusioning and disorienting and haunting to the people who've just come off the heroic phase." In other words, the Buddhist warning: elation begets despair.

Yet in the decade since Occupy, Myerson has come to interpret the movement and its effects through a different, almost geographic lens, likening the country's growing activism to a series of elevating valleys, as each successive movement builds on the one that came before it. "The idea, the hope, is that from valley to valley there is an increase," he told me. "Before Occupy, let's say we're starting at zero, then with Occupy we land at five, so we have new, higher ground to start from: new publications, new public spaces, new vehicles for coordinating between groups, new infrastructure. After that you have Black Lives Matter, which can attain a higher peak than Occupy had. So through this successive cascade of movement moments we grow our capacity, and over time the ground we're on is much higher than where we started." Occupy, he acknowledged, didn't arise from nowhere. "It was mimicking what was going on in Europe and the Middle East before that," yet "Occupy popularized movements" in a way no activist undertaking had done before, and created new conditions for resistance. "A lot of leaders are doing amazing things in the world right now who cut their teeth at Occupy."

MAKE PROTESTING COOL AGAIN: DANA BALICKI

IN THE DECADES AFTER THE ANTI-WAR AND CIVIL RIGHTS PROtests of the sixties, political activism remained associated with the baby boomer generation. Carrying signs and marching in the streets, rabble-rousing for a cause, became increasingly passé—with notable exceptions. Global anti-nuclear protests in the early eighties brought millions into the streets. The powerful grassroots movement CISPES—Committee in Solidarity with the People of El Salvador—was instrumental in countering Washington's multi-billion-dollar support of a right-wing, oligarchic regime dependent on massacres and death squads to suppress the impoverished people of that country. And with the AIDS epidemic of the eighties, gay activism in the face of the Reagan administration's callous indifference to the suffering and death of thousands of gay men led to the emergence of the LGBTQ community. On October 11, 1987, more than half a million people gathered on the National Mall to view the AIDS Memorial Quilt. The following year, fifteen hundred members of ACT UP shut down the Federal Drug Administration for a day, waving banners that read "Federal Death Administration" and hanging Reagan in effigy.

These and other movements, including the anti-globalization protests of the nineties, were effective and not to be discounted. Nonetheless, to be young and an activist, especially a passionate one, was to locate oneself outside the mainstream, to be out of sync with the zeitgeist. Occupy Wall Street organizer Dana Balicki recalled the anti-activist mood prior to the movement. "In the eighties and nineties, it wasn't cool. It was considered a weird thing, and it was much more homogenous: activists were either old people or they were the folks around the WTO protests," she told me. "In the anti–Iraq War days, I'd say, 'I'm a political activist,' and people would say, 'What?' Men would turn around from me at the bar and say goodbye." But those attitudes seemed to change with Occupy, a movement that, among many contributions, made protesting cool again. "Young people now say, 'Do your thing, it's so much cooler to be a weirdo,' and I think we contributed to that shift." Balicki added, "There are a lot of different ways young people try on and wear the cloak of activism now. For example, it feels very regular to see someone identify as an activist on Instagram, when that wasn't a thing before. Occupy helped pave the way for a whole different normalcy, and it really heartens me that a lot of younger people are now activists."

Born in 1980 in California's San Fernando Valley, Balicki attended Sonoma State University, where she majored in environmental studies and politics. She credited one of her professors there in particular, Peter Phillips—the former director of the non-profit media watchdog Project Censored and author of *Giants: The Global Power Elite*—for radicalizing her politics. Balicki later did communications work for the anti-war group Code Pink and the National Domestic Workers Alliance, and she got involved working with the public relations team at Occupy Wall Street just days before activists were evicted from Zuccotti Park. The movement changed American protest culture, she said, not because it gave the media or public the answers it wanted; on the contrary, it rejected the traditional story line and re-scripted the act of resistance altogether. "People wanted a different story from us: they wanted demands, the stories that they knew about activism and making change. In a lot of ways we refused to give them that, and I think that changed something," she said, echoing the writer Susan Griffin. "The world needs storytellers, and we changed the way people tell stories."

Invoking an original comparison, Balicki likened Occupy's impact on activism to Beyoncé's impact on the music world through her defining album, *Lemonade*. "Not only did she make this incredible work about Blackness, being a woman, love, racism, everything—but she changed the way people listen to and participate in and consume music. She pushed the envelope forward for a lot of artists to address really complex issues in different ways." Occupy Wall Street, said Balicki, "sort of did that, too. We changed the way that people hear and see and understand and process a narrative of resistance. We weren't just an organization with demands and matching T-shirts and banners—we forced people to really *listen* to each other and *see* each other. And we forced people to listen to us, to consume us, in a different way." Occupy's visible, direct influences on American culture and social movements aren't obvious or easy to chart, she added. But ten years removed from Zuccotti, today's activist generation continues to build on that story.

"It's like trying to map the finest spiderweb, or ripples in a pond from years ago. People who say that Occupy didn't accomplish anything are caught in a paradigm of shortsightedness, of moving too fast. It's the easy, results-driven answer: it's the Zuckerberg syndrome," she said, in reference to Facebook founder Mark Zuckerberg's famous, now famously derided, motto: "Move fast and break things." Occupy, for all its faults, put activism in America on a new course. "We were teachers even when we didn't know it. We didn't have a centralizing body, we weren't disciplined, but I think we set a stage and it's great that we made some mistakes because others learned from them and did better," Balicki said. "Occupy was like a lightning bolt striking Earth: we were what we were, and we couldn't have done anything differently. Other movements like March for Our Lives and Alexandria Ocasio-Cortez and Bernie Sanders are a consequence of our actions. People live the impacts from Occupy every day whether they acknowledge it or not."

ACTIVISM ENTERS THE MAINSTREAM: ADAM CHADWICK

TO SAY THAT OCCUPY MADE PROTESTING COOL AGAIN IS, PERHAPS, another way of saying it drove activism into the mainstream. Since the 2011 explosion of marches and occupations brought hundreds of thousands of people into America's streets, protests have become a more habitual form of expression. Motivated initially by a message of economic justice—and later by many other, more specific grievances—people who had never before joined a march, nor even remotely thought of themselves as activists, were suddenly inspired to put down what they were doing and express their dissent. "Looking back on Occupy and where we're at now with the #MeToo movement and Bernie Sanders running [twice] for president and everything that's happened since, it's a real sense that activism has become part of the mainstream," Denver-born filmmaker and Occupy Wall Street activist Adam Chadwick told me. "Whatever topic you're discussing, Black Lives Matter, #MeToo, they're the children of what Occupy started."

Chadwick pointed to his own sister-in-law as an example of the way Occupy helped transform a generation of armchair liberals into protesters. One of the many suburban mothers who joined millions of women and men protesting the inauguration of Donald Trump in January 2017, "she was very pro-

Obama, pro-Hillary, but when Trump was elected she had never participated in any march or anything," Chadwick said, yet "she took my young niece to the Women's March, and she felt like Occupy kind of opened that door." Even before the Trump era, radicalized activism—the thousands who protested fracking wells, tar sands pipelines, oil trains and coal export terminals, not to mention the half million who flooded New York for the People's Climate March—began to look normal. By the time the "alternative facts" presidency had taken root, people marching for science, for an end to gun violence, for higher teacher pay and for racial justice reached into the tens of millions. It's almost easy to forget amid the regularity of demonstrations in the past decade that prior to Occupy Wall Street, masses of ordinary working- and middle-class people simply didn't come out to voice collective anger. The outrage let loose at Zuccotti Park gave people permission to take to the streets, and in a sense they've never gone home.

"Occupy essentially started a conversation. Nobody had answers to anything, but we had questions, and through those questions we opened up a dialogue about what we want from our political leaders, from financial organizations, from corporations who claim to be people. We were having a dialogue about campaign finance reform and breaking up the banks and it spread, just as it was supposed to spread, to topics like for-profit prisons, women's rights, you name it," Chadwick said. "Now protest is in the air and you can participate even if you were a person who didn't before have an open mind to that." Movements like Black Lives Matter and #MeToo would have emerged on their own eventually, he said, "but their structure, their organization, the way those movements have been shaped and conducted and disseminated across social media, with very effective online campaigns and hashtags that are able to go viral—I think they really took their cue from Occupy, and they also learned some lessons from it. The haters like to say it was just a bunch of people in tents who had no demands and failed in their mission. But Occupy had a lasting impact: it got people talking, it spread the conversation, and the conversation is still happening."

REVOLUTIONARY IN EXILE: RODRIGO DORFMAN

FOR LIBERALS AND ACTIVISTS, AND EVEN MORE SO FOR LIFELONG revolutionaries like Rodrigo Dorfman, the reawakening of American protest culture was an overdue, almost redemptive moment. It was also, crucially, an opportunity for people in this country to connect their lately realized experience of injustice with the corruption, oppression and resistance that many other cultures have known for generations. "What happens when you wake up in the morning and you think this is your country, and it's not, and suddenly you realize you are a colony?" asked Dorfman. "Occupy was the day a lot of people realized they lived in a third world country and it was the day they thought, 'I'm willing to put my skin on the line because I feel this matters to me: this country has been taken away and I've known this all along, but now I care because I'm seeing myself reflected in so many people, in everyone else who realizes they're living in exile in a country that has been taken over by multinational corporations.' You're suddenly in exile inside your own country and you're feeling like Black folks have been feeling forever."

Dorfman, who is also a filmmaker, knows something about exile just as he knows what it means to put skin on the line. Born in 1967 in Chile, he came from a family of radicals. His great-grandmother, born in Odessa and educated in Vienna, was Leon Trotsky's secretary at the 1918 peace conference that birthed the Treaty of Brest-Litovsk, ending Russia's participation in World War I. His grandfather, an industrial engineer, helped launch the post–WWII framework that would become the United Nations, and was later accused by Joseph McCarthy of having Communist sympathies, which caused him to immigrate to Chile. Dorfman's father, the renowned author Ariel Dorfman, escaped the Pinochet dictatorship, lived in exile in Amsterdam, then moved the family to the United States, where they settled in North Carolina. The Dorfman legacy was defined by being on the run. "Everyone at some point in their life fled," he told me. "Nobody reached the age of seven in the place where we were born." As for his political convictions, he joked that they were decided long before his birth. "With all of us there's the process of being born into revolutionary consciousness, genetically, celebrated as the fourth or fifth generation of atheist Marxists," a condition that presented its own set of challenges, Dorfman said. "You're born into consciousness and then you have to sustain it, and question it, and deal with that baggage, as opposed to those who come into consciousness [later]."

After attending high school in the States, Dorfman returned to Chile where he worked as a sound person for a guerrilla video collective producing documentaries about real life under Pinochet—not the government-censored version of events. "We would go to shanty towns and churches and hold illegal screenings so people could see what they could not see on TV—it was dangerous, it was illegal, with assemblies of one hundred or more watching films about stories of resistance against the dictatorship, which gave people a reality full of hope and pain so they could see themselves and feel heard and empowered and dignified." When Dorfman returned to the United States as a student attending UC Berkeley in the eighties, he occupied school halls and grounds as part of the anti-apartheid protests that spurred boycotts and divestment from South Africa. "I was fearless because I'd been running from bullets and riot police and military [in Chile]," where one of his friends was doused with gasoline and burned alive, he said. "That's what would have happened to me. I've been careful not to be self-destructive in my search for activism. Somebody could say that sounds very bourgeois, and yeah, if that's what it means, okay. I'm not going to be careless."

When the protests kicked off at Zuccotti Park, Dorfman hoped it would spark a wave—possibly even an era—of resistance across the Americas, North and South. What fascinated him most about Occupy was its sheer amount of "cultural production," as he called it, which spoke to the new language of economic justice. After the movement declined in the winter of 2012, it was natural to see people return to their communities to organize, Dorfman said, because "that was also the understanding: Occupy was a training ground, the way you go train for guerrilla action, feel it, discuss it, then go back to your community and do something." His 2013 documentary, *Occupy the Imagination: Tales of Seduction and Resistance,* examined the movement through the historical lens of the Chilean Revolution, linking Dorfman's personal and political past with the spirit of rebellion on Wall Street. Occupy represented the "reengagement with an ideal I had in my head of the sixties and seventies," he said, and "a reconnection to a feeling of anger, of loss, and an emotion that propels me forward as an immigrant having a stake in the future of this country. It was the first time that I shouted in the streets in a long time—that I really cared enough to actually go beyond my comfort and my distance and my alienation." For him, like for so many others, "Occupy was the creation of an experience in the streets, together, living and protesting in solidarity, that we would take with us into the future."

THE PROTEST ANIMAL: MARTIN KIRK

IN FORGING THAT NEW SENSE OF SOLIDARITY, THE OCCUPY MOVE-ment birthed something perhaps still more elemental in modern American society, arguably even on a biological level, said Martin Kirk, co-founder of the activist organization The Rules. In his words, the generation of activists who chose to wage their future against the unjust prescriptions of the past introduced "the first mutation of a new form of animal: a protest animal." Identifying Occupy at the forefront of a decade of youth-driven social movements, he said, "it was the first of the new breed."

Like Balicki and others, Kirk understood the movement's greatest achievement was its ability to tell the ancient story of inequality in a way that it had never been told, vocalizing a new culture of protest that others would articulate in manifold ways. "Occupy was an early version of the sort of change in narrative and cultural expression that we now have a language around; Black Lives Matter, #MeToo and these other swarming movements picked up the mantle from Occupy," he told me. "They were a consciousness shift, because with Occupy the critique was 'There are no demands.' It was like a shot of adrenaline that recharged the global political consciousness and gave deep, mythical battles fresh relevance. Occupy's absolute power was its narrative power, not its policy power, and what we couldn't read then, we can read now."

Born in 1972 to British parents in Nairobi, Kenya, Kirk grew up mostly in Kuwait where his father worked as an engineer. After earning a degree in modern history, he worked in international development with organizations like Save the Children and Oxfam, but became "profoundly disillusioned" with the non-profit development model, and specifically what he called its "charity logic." "The whole paradigm is wrong," said Kirk, echoing the thesis of Anand Giridharadas's 2018 bestseller, *Winners Take All: The Elite Charade of Changing the World*. "It rests on one faulty assumption: that rich people are morally superior to poor people, and if the rich just give a little bit of their money to the poor, we'll all be fine." Kirk veered into more experimental efforts to address global poverty, working alongside grassroots organizer Alnoor Ladha to co-found The Rules, a group whose smart, viral video campaigns educated millions of viewers about the root causes of poverty and inequality. In the aftermath of Occupy and the decade of social movements it helped spur, Kirk said the continuing rebellion for economic justice and equality won't take the form of a giant "movement of movements," as some have preferred to call it.

Rather, like the decentralized age in which we are now living, he envisioned the next chapter of protest emerging in the 2020s powered by an overwhelming force of collective movements working together. "I think it's already here actually, re-scripting the whole economic logic," he said. "I think there's an enormous movement happening in an almost unseen way in the mainstream media, held together by values and radical principles of environmental sustainability and justice, and when the shit hits the fan in a massive way with the climate, they'll say, 'People have been building a community for twenty years, and here it is.' Occupy set the scene and prepared minds for Black Lives Matter, #MeToo and global movements like #YoSoy132 in Mexico, where you can see their whole approach to change born from what was happening in Occupy. You have to break through barriers and that's what Occupy did: it broke through a consciousness barrier, it showed a different way of doing things, and it showed the systemic struggle that we all face."

OCCUPY PHILANTHROPY: LEAH HUNT-HENDRIX

IN THE SPRING OF 2012, AS OCCUPY WALL STREET WAS UNRAVEL-ing, Leah Hunt-Hendrix joined several hundred movement activists attending the Occupy Manifest retreat at The Watershed Center in upstate New York. Like many Zuccotti Park organizers, Hunt-Hendrix was a college-educated millennial, already at work on her PhD in Religion, Ethics and Politics at Princeton University. And like Brooke Lehman, she came from a family associated with extreme wealth: Hunt-Hendrix's grandfather was the Texas oil tycoon H. L. Hunt, whose company and fortune the family still manages. The goal at the Manifest retreat was to begin building enduring organizations that activists could carry back to their communities, and Hunt-Hendrix recalled getting an important piece of advice from her friend Max Berger, who would soon found Momentum. "He was like, 'You should organize your community: you should go organize rich people. Fundraising sucks but we need money, and those are your people—you know them.' I was like, 'Yeah, I can do that.'"

So Hunt-Hendrix got to work contacting some of the wealthy, left-leaning people she knew and talked up the idea of a donor network to help fund activism. She reached out to individuals "who got the importance of social movements, and even have an anti-capitalist lens—because a lot of them didn't make their money, they inherited it, and they see how it's destructive in their lives and in their families, and they want a different world," she said. "I knew two people, and they knew one person, and it just grew, literally, one by one." In 2013, Hunt-Hendrix launched Solidaire, a radical funders organization that over the next seven years helped several hundred wealthy donors give away $40 million to grassroots movements fighting for economic and racial justice. Solidaire saw its role as supporting projects that mainstream funders deemed "too radical, too urgent, too risky." The groups that received money and resources included the Movement for Black Lives, Standing Rock, OUR Walmart and Momentum, among others. Since activists couldn't be out protesting year-round, she said, Solidaire aimed to be a "connective tissue that holds people together between all the movement moments," helping organizers build power to deliver more lasting results.

In the decade since Occupy, Hunt-Hendrix spotted a clear continuity between the movement and more recent strains of activism it helped spawn—from #MeToo and the March for Our Lives to the progressive reorganization of the Democratic Party. "I see a direct through line from Occupy to the Movement for Black Lives to Standing Rock to Bernie Sanders to Justice Democrats and AOC," she said. In many cases, those movements incorporated the same individuals who learned and improved their organizing skills at Zuccotti Park and then continued working together to drive the next phase of protest activism. "There are hundreds of people from Occupy who have kept working and have led to so many of the big moments we've seen in the past years. Occupy developed a new generation of activists and helped them develop their understanding of power in social movements—but also corporate power and who we're up against," Hunt-Hendrix told me. Indeed, Occupy's economic critique and its organizing model shaped a generation, as did its example of being "more confrontational, and putting the wrench in the gears." But it took an evolution of movements, each building on the ones that came before it, to realize notable success a decade on. "Occupy didn't know what to do about leadership and what kind of positive, constructive demands to have, and now we're getting around to recognizing that it is really helpful to identity leaders because you can hold them accountable. The movements are getting better."

It has long been a right-wing trope to call liberals hypocrites when, through activism or philanthropy, they denounce the affluence and privilege from which they sprang. But for Hunt-Hendrix, using her position of influence to steer wealth away from the 1 percent toward organizations calling for institutional racial and economic and environmental change made sense. "I think it's so much more fulfilling to be on the right side of history, and to be in communities that are based on real common struggle and shared mission, rather than just hanging out on a yacht by yourself. The benefits of coming from a family with a lot of wealth don't outweigh the costs on the rest of society," she said. In 2017, in response to the election of Donald Trump, Hunt-Hendrix founded the donor network Way To Win, which fundraised for grassroots electoral organizations to support hundreds of progressive candidates on the city, state and national levels. By 2020, the group had raised more than $100 million helping influence elections across ten battleground states. "People have different roles to play," she added, "and there's no way I can justify extreme wealth, so it seemed obvious and important to get involved addressing economic inequality—because the 1 percent have the most responsibility in trying to change that."

THE EIGHT STAGES OF PROTEST: KEVIN ZEESE AND MARGARET FLOWERS

SOCIAL MOVEMENTS ARE COMPLEX CREATURES THAT CANNOT ALways be understood over a trajectory of a few months or even years. And when they're as novel and illuminating and powerful as Occupy Wall Street, sometimes decades must pass before the results truly reveal themselves. "Movements take a long time to unfold, a generation or more, and I think the Occupy impact is still unfolding—it can take twenty to thirty years," the late lawyer, peace activist and organizer Kevin Zeese told me when we spoke in 2019, the year before he died of a heart attack at sixty-four. "It's not like you do an encampment for a month and suddenly everything changes. The 2020s are going to be when you really see it, because this movement is reaching a level of maturity and breadth, and the various issues we're dealing with are reaching crisis level proportion where they can't be ignored any longer."

Zeese and his partner, Margaret Flowers, a pediatrician and longtime advocate for single-payer healthcare, had been fixtures in the American activist community for decades, so they knew what patience looked like. The pair frequently mobilized on the front lines of political issues that weren't even considered issues until they helped bring them to light. On September 17, 2011, as several thousand activists marched through lower Manhattan and established the first night of camp at Zuccotti Park, Zeese and Flowers were already weeks into the planning stages for a separate, independent occupation of Freedom Plaza in Washington, D.C., located steps away from the White House. Their hope was to ignite a nationwide rebellion, modeled after that spring's uprisings in Spain, Greece and across the Arab world. As it turned out, Occupy Wall Street beat them to the punch by about a week. "When we were organizing Occupy in D.C., we were talking to all these groups and everyone was thinking the same thing, it was in the air almost: everyone was feeling that they had been using all the traditional tools of advocacy and it wasn't working, things weren't changing. We had to do something different, and Occupy was a manifestation of that," Flowers told me.

For months, the pair's leadership helped anchor one of the two Occupy encampments in the capital (the other one, populated by a rowdier, more anarchist-aligned crew, sat a few blocks to the northwest at McPherson Square). After Occupy, the couple and their grassroots organization, Popular Resistance, led the first direct action protests against the Trans-Pacific Partnership, drawing attention to the "NAFTA on steroids" trade deal years before Bernie Sanders and Donald Trump would both make it their punching bag in the 2016 presidential primaries. The couple later galvanized one of the earliest and loudest public campaigns to preserve net neutrality, which, for a time at least, succeeded in stopping the Federal Communications Commission's further deregulation of big telecom corporations. During the Trump years, Zeese and Flowers carved out a special niche, in some ways parallel to the work being done at Momentum, by running an activist training school where they emphasized the long-haul nature of strategic movement building, and popularized a theory known as the Eight Stages of Social Movements.

First floated by the activist icon Bill Moyer in the 1980s, his "movement action plan" described the eight stages of a successful social movement's evolution. During the first three stages, Zeese explained to me, protesters are helping build the popular recognition that a social problem exists. Small groups become gradually larger numbers of people documenting and publicizing the impacts of the institutional failures they're addressing. As public anger mounts and conditions ripen for revolt, events come to a head in the fourth stage, known as the takeoff—what we remember J. A. Myerson referred to as the "heroic phase." Occupy Wall Street represented a classic example of the takeoff, as people in hundreds of cities across America and the planet erupted in outrage over economic inequality and corporate corruption of the political system. Critically important in this stage, Zeese said, is the fact that "people see they're not alone, that others are willing to stand up, and that is what's most contagious."

What follows is the fifth stage, known as the landing, or the perception of failure, in which mainstream culture interprets and describes the movement as a defeat because it failed to achieve its stated goals. It isn't a defeat at all. At this point, "the politicians say you lost and did nothing," Zeese said, but in reality, "we're just getting started. Movements evolve. We put issues on the agenda and got majority support for them. We also let each other know we exist, and that we're willing to stand up and fight." The sixth and longest stage—and arguably the one we're still in today, a decade after Occupy—is called "majority times." This is when the movement achieves majority support on the issues and builds toward a national consensus. Take any cause that progressives deem important, said Zeese—Medicare for All, Green New Deal, debt-free college, $15 minimum wage, tighter gun laws, criminal justice reform—and what you see, over and over, are polls showing an overwhelming majority of Americans, between 60 and 80 percent, supporting measures that ten years ago were way off the mainstream radar.

"On issue after issue that came up during Occupy, we're reaching majority times and moving toward national consensus," he told me. Once public opinion firmly picks a side, it sets the stage for transformational change. And what follows is the seventh stage, known as winning consensus, at which point the movement approaches success. "The takeoff crystalized trends that had been building. Now the public agrees with us, and the election of AOC and the Sanders campaign reflect the movement achieving majority times and consensus." In the eighth stage, the movement consolidates its success and politically implements the changes it sought to bring about.

MOVEMENTS TAKE ALL KINDS OF FORMS, AND FOR ZEESE, OCCUPY Wall Street followed in the courageous tradition of the lunch counter sit-ins and the Montgomery bus boycott that fueled the Civil Rights Movement. He also considered it a natural successor to the Poor People's Campaign led by Martin Luther King Jr. But the historical event that Occupy most clearly evoked, said Zeese, was a resistance movement that many Americans may not be familiar with, known as the Bonus March, which he called "the most successful occupation in history." The Bonus March was initiated by World War I veterans who, in the summer of 1932 amid a heated presidential race between Herbert Hoover and Franklin Delano Roosevelt, arrived by the tens of thousands in Washington, D.C., to demand the postwar "bonus" payments they had been promised. The veterans were scheduled to receive their bonus in the 1940s, but the terrible hardship of the Great Depression forced their decision to wait no more, so they came with their families from every corner of the country. Some drove in from Oregon, others walked in from Pennsylvania, with the single purpose of occupying the capital until they received their pay. The House of Representatives gave in to their demands and approved the early payments, but the Senate rejected the measure. When Congress announced it was leaving for summer recess, the Bonus marchers stayed put.

In Zeese's words, "They built ramshackle encampments out of cardboard boxes and pieces of wood. Some lived out of their cars, others put up tents, and all were committed to the occupation." The nation's highest decorated marine,

Smedley Butler, called the Bonus protesters the most patriotic people in the country and encouraged them to stand strong. Finally, the pressure was too much for Hoover, who tasked generals MacArthur, Eisenhower and Patton with removing the marchers. In a scene of barbarism—now strangely reminiscent, in symbolic terms, of Donald Trump's decision on June 1, 2020, to order the military to tear gas and violently remove peaceful protesters from Lafayette Square to make way for his Bible photo op—the generals "assembled military troops with bayonets, tear gas and horses, and they attacked the World War I vets in the middle of an election year. A baby was bayoneted, people were killed, the Bonus marchers were forced out of D.C.," said Zeese. FDR told his advisers, "We've just won the election," and a few months later he triumphed in a landslide. But the Bonus marchers "didn't win just from doing that protest," Zeese added. "They started a movement," one that presaged the sweeping changes of the Roosevelt era.

What happened at Occupy Wall Street should similarly not be seen as a one-off event, but more as the marker of a new era of protest in which popular demands will, over time, transition into long-awaited policy reforms. "We've seen in the last decade a growing culture of resistance," said Flowers. "It was kind of bare before Occupy, with small protests happening around the country. Then Occupy was this huge, visible revolt and since then we've seen a real maturing of movements in the U.S. People are now thinking very strategically, with so many groups organizing and sharing the tools and analyses they've developed." With multiple crises—economic, racial, environmental—reaching a tipping point, and now perhaps pushed over the edge by the health and financial catastrophe unleashed by the coronavirus, the 2020s pose a "tremendous opportunity" for systemic change, she said. "The climate crisis makes it clear the clock is ticking very quickly. The economic insecurity and wealth divide just keeps growing. If we have a vision and are prepared for what we want to accomplish, this could be a very transformative decade."

Zeese agreed that the growing numbers of people who are now entering and participating in activist politics signal that the Occupy movement may be reaching its later stages of evolution. "We're getting majorities and supermajorities of support on all fronts and the movement is getting more and more precise about what the demands are, getting deeper into issues like healthcare, wage increase, climate remedies," he said. Timing also plays a critical role. "While the roots of Occupy came before Obama, the Occupy 'takeoff' moment happened under Obama because he raised expectations, he said 'hope,' he said 'change,' then he didn't deliver and people revolted." Under Trump, those pressures built further. "A lot of people voted for Trump who are economically struggling, who believed he would raise their lives up, and he actually did the opposite," which is why it is only a matter of time before the movement's next, more powerful stage arrives, said Zeese, perhaps in the form of a climate change rebellion or a sustained, working-class-led revolt like the Yellow Vests in France. For the Democratic Party, simply winning in 2020 won't be enough. "The movement will grow even more because people's expectations are high" under a Joe Biden presidency—much higher, in fact, than when Obama entered office.

The gaping inequalities that were exposed and the societal rupture caused by Covid-19, together with demands for a systemic overhaul of policies to ensure racial justice, could begin to force the large-scale transformation that Occupy Wall Street envisioned. "You're starting to see the impact of Occupy on electoral politics, economic policy, climate policy—but the most important impacts of Occupy are still ahead," said Zeese, a one-time U.S. Senate candidate who, as a lawyer in the eighties, was a leading advocate of medical marijuana and decriminalizing drugs. In terms of sheer numbers, Occupy wasn't a game-changer, he told me. It inspired an estimated three hundred thousand supporters nationwide to become active with the movement. Even so, "we only had one-tenth of one percent of the public participating, and look at the impact it had." According to Zeese and Flowers, the magic number is 3.5 percent: when that portion of the population engages in active resistance and civil disobedience, through strikes, boycotts, blockades and the rest, no modern regime on Earth has been able to hold on to power. The tens of millions of protesters, from all ages and backgrounds, who took the streets in the summer of 2020 to declare Black Lives Matter indicate that those numbers are already there. The bigger question, it seems, is what will emerge on the other side of the protests. "We have to keep educating, organizing and mobilizing people," Zeese said. "The 2020s have incredible potential to realize what Occupy put on the agenda and to achieve its goals, because the percent [of activists] is growing, we have national consensus growing, we have crises that can't be ignored—and people are expecting results now."

MOVEMENT TIMES

OCCUPY WALL STREET RANG THE BELL, AND THE SOUND OF ITS echo reverberated through the decade, growing louder and more distinct with each passing year. Occupy, it has been widely acknowledged, had plenty of flaws. At its core it was a movement constrained by its own contradictions: filled with leaders who declared themselves leaderless, governed by a consensus-based structure that failed to reach consensus, seeking to transform politics while refusing to become political. Yet for everything that Occupy got wrong, the movement radicalized a generation of activists who forced social, economic, racial and climate justice to the center of the conversation, inaugurating a new era of protest. The Fight for $15 demanded a higher minimum wage; Black Lives Matter demanded that police stop killing unarmed Black people; the People's Climate March demanded that we save our planet; the Standing Rock water protectors demanded the closure of a pipeline; the Dreamers demanded citizenship; the March for Our Lives demanded an end to gun violence; the #MeToo movement demanded an end to gender abuse and discrimination; the Women's March demanded resistance to the Donald Trump presidency; the Sunrise Movement demanded a Green New Deal. As the Occupy veteran and Momentum organizer Nicole Carty told me, "These are different times we're in now: these are movement times."

Whereas Carty's millennial generation—not to mention the Gen X crowd before them—had to invent the mood of modern protest, "now what you have is a whole generation that is growing up in movement times, which explains all the escalation you're seeing and the work that's happening among very young people who were still kids during Occupy," she said. "I didn't grow up with that. I remember people protesting the Iraq War, but the early 2000s were a period of closed civic space," and what Occupy represented was "a public reemergence of movements as vehicles for political change for my generation." In the Blue Wave of 2018, the anti-Trump movement broadly known as The Resistance capitalized on a decentralized approach to activism pioneered at Occupy and reflected a culmination of the protest energy that originated at Zuccotti Park. According to Carty, organizers with Indivisible—the grassroots movement that led the charge to save the Affordable Care Act after the 2016 election—reached out to Momentum to discuss structuring strategies, "because we were familiar with those structures more than the traditional non-profit left. Between Occupy, the Movement for Black Lives and The Resistance, there's a clear line—The Resistance represents a mainstreamification" of those movements, she added. "Yes, it's electoral, and yes, it's political, [because] they're trying to use popular escalation as a means of creating political power."

The legacy of Occupy has cropped up in some other unexpected ways that indicate the seismic impact it had on the way Americans see resistance as a political tactic. "It's a mistake to think of Occupy as just a point in time," said Vlad Teichberg, who launched the Global Revolution TV livestream that became a central platform fueling the movement's rise. "It's not like we invented the fight against inequality, but what was different was tactical: we were going to do a protest that doesn't end. It's one thing when you show up and wave flags for a day," he told me, but "it's a whole different story when you're there forever in front of the gates: when you occupy. Look what happened in the summer of 2019 when Immigration and Customs Enforcement started separating children: the ICE centers around the country got occupied, people sat in front of those places getting information out and trying to stop the injustice against our immigrant neighbors. Occupy is a verb, an idea of how to do things—and it needs to come back."

The Zuccotti Park organizer Tamara Shapiro agreed that Occupy's impacts continue to shape the landscape of activism and politics. "A new generation grew up under Occupy. It was a petri dish where all of these experiments were starting," she said. The movement, like a storm surge, became "a wave that was moving, and that wave kept going. Occupy was an incredibly important, lasting power because of what came after. It's not just Occupy, it's the whole generation that it kicked off." Echoing Zeese's long view of history, the radio host Egberto Willies said he believed it's still too soon to accurately assess the impacts of the movement—particularly when it comes to the climate crisis. "The Occupy legacy continues because we're still building on that legacy. All of the activism that you're seeing out here now, those tentacles are right there in Occupy," Willies told me. "Occupy gave permission, it gave a spine, to a lot of other movements to exist. We forgot about civil disobedience but we see that it's now back in vogue, [because] Occupy reminded us that it's okay to have civil disobedience—and now it's actually existential because of climate change. We're talking about our existence: it's reached the point where our corporations are killing us, and we're now going to fight. Occupy said, 'We can do something about it.'"

The feelings of injustice and inequality that are politically motivating people to protest today are the same ones that got them out into the streets a decade ago. Except now, said Carty, the stakes are that much higher. "People don't have faith in our government, they feel the establishment is corrupt," she said. The youth movements that are emerging provide an antidote to those feelings, because they "are built around moral truths, expressing the unfairness, and playing on the Occupy language of the ruling class. We can't unlearn the 99 percent. We can't unlearn some things we've learned in the past couple of years about systemic racism. There's no going back, really."

OCCUPY'S RACIAL JUSTICE PROBLEM

NICOLE CARTY'S EXPERIENCE OF OCCUPY, HOWEVER, ALSO TELLS A different, important story about the movement and its legacy. In the summer of 2011, as America was stumbling through the Great Recession, Carty received her bachelor's degree from Brown University and, like most college grads at the time, had little luck finding work. She had moved to New York and was living with a friend in Williamsburg when Occupy Wall Street erupted that September, and she quickly joined the movement. "We graduated into the worst economy in a generation, so not only did Occupy speak to us, but it was relevant to see young people talking about income inequality," she said. Born in 1988 in Atlanta to a mother from the Caribbean and an African American father who had grown up in the South under Jim Crow, Carty shared the age, but not the skin color, of most of the protesters showing up at Zuccotti Park. She got involved with the facilitation team, helping train people to steer the movement's consensus-based decision-making process, and she also joined the People of Color caucus. But Carty quickly discovered there wasn't a whole lot of room at Occupy Wall Street for voices like hers. "Occupy was very ambitious and had a lot of beautiful things about it, but it suffered from a tyranny of structurelessness," she said. "White men made a lot of decisions. People talked over women and didn't listen to them. I wasn't really listened to."

That Occupy had a problem earning African American support was clear. With its anarchist ethos and its reputation as a movement fomented by college-educated white kids, the scene at Zuccotti didn't speak to most people of color, nor did it try. According to the journalist Nathan Schneider, author of *Thank You, Anarchy: Notes from the Occupy Apocalypse,* Occupy Wall Street resisted efforts to incorporate racial questions into its economic critique from the outset. "There were crucial ways that its blindness as a movement were outgrowths of the whiteness of the participation—a kind of ideology and set of habits and implicit practice," Schneider told me. One event stood out for him in particular. On the second Saturday of the movement, when a number of activists had assembled in Union Square to voice outrage over Georgia's execution of a Black man named Troy Davis, many Occupy participants failed to support the march and stand with the Black protesters. "People were like, 'What? We're here to protest banks,' and that to me was a critical moment of conflict," recalled Schneider, because "it made bare how white the composition of the Occupy movement was. It was evident very early on that this group wasn't inclined in many cases to see economic justice with a racial analysis."

For Egberto Willies, the lack of diversity at Occupy presented a problem because it contradicted the movement's core premise that it genuinely represented the 99 percent. As he put it, "I was a Black guy in Occupy, which was mostly white people." Willies was born in Panama and earned his mechanical engineering degree from the University of Texas at Austin, before starting his own software company. In 2008, inspired by Barack Obama's presidential campaign, he began writing political blogs that pushed him deeper into activism, and in 2010 he co-founded the Coffee Party—an ironic, progressive response to the Tea Party whose goal, he said, was to "create an environment where people could have civil discussion, Republican, Democrat or otherwise, and sit down for coffee together to discuss real politics without all the animosity." When the Occupy movement came his way, Willies jumped in, leading marches at Occupy Houston and helping establish Occupy Kingwood in a conservative Houston suburb. But from the start, the movement's race problem bothered him. "The country is fortysomething percent non-white, so the way you galvanize the entire country is you center your movement in such a manner that Black folk, Latinos, Asians, all these people actually feel like they're part of it—and not just there because we want to show we have Black or Latino faces," he said. "If an Occupy is going to be successful in the future, it needs to have everybody in the movement."

A month into Occupy Wall Street, as police abuse mounted in New York City and across the nation with beatings, arrests, surveillance and other efforts by law enforcement to suppress the movement, protesters found themselves focusing less attention on the banks and more attention on evading and responding to police aggression. And as the movement racked up thousands of jail sentences and on-camera incidents of pepper sprayings and other violence, the country got exposed to a new level of police brutality and heavy-handed law enforcement rarely glimpsed in modern America by the white population. It was nothing, of course, compared to the violent experience Black people had been enduring for decades and centuries, a reality that was put starkly before the nation, in the summer of 2014, when a white police officer shot and killed an unarmed Black teenager named Michael Brown in Ferguson, Missouri, launching the Black Lives Matter movement.

The uprising over racial injustice, which would evolve into the largest protest movement in American history, shared a number of things in common with Occupy. Yet "Black Lives Matter was free from the 2011 story—free from the idea that you would just occupy a space and then you'd win," said Schneider. "There were similarities between the movements, but there was a different logic and it became a kind of cleansing moment, where people who had been involved in Occupy and [seen] its racial blinders were able to get involved in Black Lives Matter and take on the part that had been missing so directly. I remember seeing Occupy people in Black Lives Matter and feeling that this was a correction for them."

As different as the movements were in demographics, messaging, tactics and other ways, Occupy Wall Street and Black Lives Matter drew some fundamental connections. "I think in many ways Occupy and the Movement for Black Lives have a piece of what the other one is missing," said Carty. "Occupy didn't have any racial analysis: it was missing racial economics and exploitation. Then you look at the Movement for Black Lives, which at the very beginning was just a conversation about police and murder. It was very visible and understandable and an entry point for the discussion, but it didn't speak to the root of the problem—that deeply ingrained racist inequality exists in our country today because our economic system perpetuates and legitimizes that racism. It took a long time before the Movement for Black Lives moved to a place that was deeper: from police versus Black people to 'The police are the way the state enforces the racist hierarchy, and police are the symptom, not the cause.' Occupy pointed the finger at the police, but the Movement for Black Lives deepened the story."

THE MOVEMENT IN FERGUSON

IN AUGUST 2014, A FEW DAYS AFTER MICHAEL BROWN'S KILLING, then program director of the Working Families Party, Maurice Mitchell, traveled to Ferguson to help protesters organizing what became Black Lives Matter. Three weeks earlier, New York City cops on Staten Island had stopped Eric Garner, a forty-four-year-old Black man selling cigarettes without a tax label, and put him in a choke hold during which he gasped eleven times, "I can't breathe," before suffocating to death. Caught on film, Garner's murder ignited outrage and protests, and after the eighteen-year-old Brown was shot in Missouri on August 9, and his body left lying for four hours on the hot asphalt, Black people in his city had seen enough. Americans were suddenly back out in the streets by the thousands to demand an end to police killings of young unarmed Black men. Mitchell saw natural parallels between Occupy and what he called the "organic Black rebellion" taking shape in Ferguson. But from the start, he said, the movement's protesters were acutely aware that they needed to correct some of the basic mistakes made by Occupy and chart a different path: moving away from a structureless, leaderless, consensus-based form of activism toward clear demands with a unified message to force changes in law enforcement. "I think a clarity came out of seeing what happened at Occupy," Mitchell said.

"Leadership matters and Occupy had no leaders. It was like, 'Why can't we just be honest that there *are* leaders?' So we wanted to make an intervention around that: to create a leaderful movement that focused on the leadership of working-class young Black people," Mitchell told me. "We were open to different models of decision making, and we agreed with Occupy's assessment that hierarchical, top-down structures limit creativity and can replicate the oppression that we're trying to challenge. But we decided we're not going to do that: we're going to be much more flexible and nimble. Building power for everyday Black people—that is our goal—so we're not going to focus on form or structure, we're going to focus on function and outcome. The clarity that we need demands was definitely born out of witnessing a social movement *without* demands, so seeing how Occupy went down was helpful in orienting us where we wanted to go."

The strategy was a smart one, and it delivered results. As Black Lives Matter exploded overnight into a nationwide movement, one whose focus would later broaden into the Movement for Black Lives, it coalesced around a series of spokespeople who articulated core demands to address racial injustice and police violence in Black communities. Among their central goals: defund city police budgets, invest more money in poor Black neighborhoods, establish greater community control over police departments, and deliver justice for the individuals wrongfully killed by law enforcement. A large share of the U.S. public embraced the movement and its call for racial justice, echoing the early mainstream success of Occupy Wall Street in reshaping the national conversation around inequality. And part of the reason Black Lives Matter was able to spread its message so quickly and powerfully was because it built on the groundwork established at Zuccotti Park.

For one, Black Lives Matter immediately adopted the decentralized organizing model pioneered by Occupy Wall Street. This meant that despite elements of movement leadership developing among the activists in Ferguson, every city chapter, from Los Angeles to Baltimore, had autonomy to choose whatever strategy and style and timing of protests were deemed effective. The freedom enabled community organizers and activist coalitions to clarify their demands and engage both in the streets and in policy circles on a local level. At the same time, Black Lives Matter benefitted from the livestream, social media organizing and other technology tools developed at Occupy.

"Black Lives Matter mobilized the resources that had been left behind by

Occupy," J. A. Myerson said, and then built on them through a more disciplined organizing structure. "As a tactical model of ways to resist, I think Occupy was influential, but Black Lives Matter ascended to heights Occupy never achieved. Occupy created all of these tools and networks and pieces of infrastructure that were useful—for example, backend communication strategies like Maestro conference calling. But I think Black Lives Matter did a better job of forming organizations for collective action, rather than rudderless autonomous gatherings." As Nicole Carty put it: "Occupy is the first social movement in the U.S. that really used the internet to spread its message, from Twitter to livestreams—and the model it created, replicating chapters all over and showing what it looks like to have a decentralized movement, made Black Lives Matter more possible. Whether people want to say it influenced the movement or not, Black Lives Matter improved upon that model."

Using digital and social media networks to masterful effect, Black Lives Matter activists shared cell phone–recorded footage of police brutality and peaceful protests to create a succession of viral moments that fueled public outrage and enlarged the movement. Charlotte Alter, author of *The Ones We've Been Waiting For*, wrote, "As the videos and photos of racist police violence spread across the internet, a massive and nimble new racial justice movement grew around them that could rapidly respond to new incidents as they arose. And, just as Occupy did with income inequality, Black Lives Matter gave a new and compelling framework to describe the systemic racism that had persisted for half a century after the civil rights movement." The way both movements turned impassioned slogans into viral memes was notable—*We are the 99 percent* for Occupy; *I can't breathe* and *Hands up, don't shoot* for Black Lives Matter—further signaling the generational connection they shared. "Both Occupy and Black Lives Matter were about problems that disproportionately affected young people—it was young people whose financial futures were decimated by the financial crisis, and it was young Black people who were most likely to experience police violence."

But it wasn't only Occupy-pioneered technology and messaging tactics that helped grow Black Lives Matter. Occupy individuals also stepped in to play an important role, lending visibility and exposure to the Ferguson movement as it expanded in its early days. One of those people was Vlad Teichberg, the founder of Global Revolution TV, who told me that "when Michael Brown got killed, I went to [our] three-hundred-person media group and said, 'We have to amplify this,' so we started tweeting to Ferguson, doing the first livestreams through our centralized media collective, and it got a huge push from us that reached around thirty-five million people." It was one of Zuccotti Park's most able and charismatic organizers, Nelini Stamp, who, after the 2012 killing of the unarmed teenager Trayvon Martin in Sanford, Florida, helped form the Black youth-led group Dream Defenders, an organization that would become one of the pillars of the Movement for Black Lives. An Ohio student association that helped birth Occupy Columbus later transformed into a racial justice protest in response to the November 2014 killing of Tamir Rice, a twelve-year-old boy shot by police on a Cleveland playground while holding a toy gun. The next month, after a Staten Island grand jury failed to indict the officer who killed Eric Garner, Occupy Wall Street organizers helped stage a twenty-five-thousand-person protest march for Black Lives Matter in New York. "When it came to putting together a march in two weeks' time, a lot of Occupy people and infrastructure ended up getting pulled in: our arts network, banner makers, direct action, march logistics. The tactic was built in large part on Occupy," said Carty.

Unlike Occupy, which failed as a movement to produce visible policy wins, Black Lives Matter succeeded early in moving the needle: it spurred a wave of decriminalization laws, greater enforcement of police accountability, near-ubiquitous use of body cameras, and an increase in jail sentences for cops found guilty of killing unarmed Black men. "For the first time in my lifetime you're seeing prosecutions and convictions of police who were involved in racist killings or racial abuse. It's not the full solution, but it's a step toward that," said Kevin Zeese. The Black Lives Matter protests that continued six years later, with the national outpouring of unity and calls for racial justice after the May 2020 killing of George Floyd in Minneapolis, further impacted the political landscape—for starters, by helping to secure Kamala Harris as the first African American woman to serve as vice president of the United States. For Martin Kirk, the noisy, disruptive activism of Occupy had created a new frame of reference that made the events in Ferguson, and what followed them, much more possible. "Occupy changed the environment and it radicalized the environment, and that helped pave the ground for Black Lives Matter," he said. "Black people have been standing up forever," but even "the Civil Rights Movement didn't go global," he told me. By contrast, "Occupy went global, which hadn't been done before," and in its wake, "Black Lives Matter has gone global. It saw how Occupy worked, and it was focused, with leaders, with a centralized message and a coherence throughout the process."

Maurice Mitchell, who would later become national director of the Working Families Party, agreed that Occupy Wall Street played an essential role helping reorient the country to see powerful social movements as the key ingredient driving change. "If you look at the Movement for Black Lives, the immigrant rights movement and The Resistance following the 2016 election, Occupy is part of this continuum that has shifted our political culture in the U.S., and has created a different readiness of everyday working people to engage directly with democracy through the tactics of protest, direct action and mobilization. That, to me, is a lasting contribution," he said. Perhaps most important, Occupy showed Black Lives Matter, and movements that came after, the value of uniting in the street with collective demands—transforming the cynicism that maintains status quo politics into an urgent call for systemic reform. The lesson the movement imparted was clear, he added: "Either I can engage in intellectual debates, in all kinds of conversations, in political education—or the other thing is that I can just *do* my politics through intense public actions, and through actions that show my politics, I give other people permission to take similar actions. Through participation in social movements, individuals collectively end up doing amazing things that they otherwise never thought would have been possible: they become politicized at a social scale in the thousands and millions, occupying spaces all over the county and all over the world in acts of mass rebellion."

FROM THE WOMEN'S MARCH TO #METOO

WHEN MORE THAN FOUR MILLION PEOPLE TOOK TO THE STREETS for the Women's March on January 21, 2017, it looked as though the new face of American protest had arrived, and it even had a name: The Resistance. On the day after Donald Trump's ominous inauguration speech about "American carnage," a spectacle of pink, homespun pussy hats bobbing in our nation's towns and cities seemed to shake the country from its post-electoral malaise, and girded people for the four-year battle ahead. In some ways it evoked Occupy—a raw, universal sense of outrage channeling a joyous, collective energy—except much bigger. The Women's March also featured some of the organizing hallmarks of Occupy: grassroots organizing had happened online, mostly through social media, with protests taking on a decentralized, city-by-city character. Months after the Women's March, in spring and summer, Indivisible's highly organized, highly decentralized movement of coast-to-coast congressional protests helped torpedo Republicans' efforts to abolish and replace Obamacare. But it wasn't until that fall, in October 2017, when the #MeToo movement erupted and took on a new target, which by now people felt more familiar in denouncing: sleazy, abusive males of the 1 percent.

Once dozens of women came forward to accuse the Hollywood film producer Harvey Weinstein of predatory sexual behavior including assault and rape, the floodgates opened and they haven't closed. From the Fox News media mogul and conservative icon Roger Ailes to news hosts like Bill O'Reilly and Matt Lauer, the actor Bill Cosby, the Alabama senate candidate Roy Moore, the comedian Louis C.K. and dozens of others, famous, rich, powerful men were suddenly toppled from their pedestals as women exposed decades-held secrets: stories of sexual harassment, abuse and misconduct. Like #OccupyWall-

Street, #MeToo started as a hashtag and quickly became a global phenomenon as issues like gender equality, workplace fairness and women's pay took on new relevance. On a more profound level, observers drew connections between the movements because of the inequality narrative they shared. For the feminist author Susan Griffin, Occupy helped lay the foundation for #MeToo, since it "so dramatized financial inequality" that by the time celebrity feminists came along to talk about equal pay and conditions for women, people were prepared with an economic and class critique to hear their message.

"Occupy raised class consciousness" in a way that put gender justice in the broader context of the 99 percent, Griffin told me. "When #MeToo gained notice and leaders like Jane Fonda and Gloria Steinem were interviewed, they were very careful to say, 'We're privileged, and this is happening to women who are waitresses and secretaries and behind the counter at McDonald's, and lots of working-class women who have less protection than we do.' It brought awareness to the issue that men feel entitled to have unequal pay scales in every profession," she said. "Fonda and Steinem both had class consciousness before #MeToo, but it became a national issue and they were speaking to an audience that had already thought about class and inequity because Occupy brought it forward. Occupy was empowering implicitly to every movement, not just to itself."

Mirroring the unfair economic experience that people shared at Occupy Wall Street, #MeToo gave women a chance to finally say out loud what others have known all along, starting a cascade effect. "I think what happens with these movements is not so much that an idea has been put into people's heads, but that they feel permission to speak about it because others are feeling the same thing. It's not that women began to notice or began to feel these things: it's that we began to talk to each other, to tell each other our stories, and we began to feel a legitimacy, a possibility of social change," Griffin added. Building upon the plant-based metaphor used by others, she agreed that Occupy's larger transformative impacts, while already visible in some ways, haven't yet necessarily been felt. "Occupy planted seeds all over the place, and some of them maybe haven't even germinated yet, but they're there in the ground, working their way. Movements don't grow incrementally in a measured [sense]: they grow and grow, and then suddenly grow exponentially, and people make the mistake thinking that they came from nowhere. Consciousness is not predictable by questions and answers, or data collection. There's no way to count somebody who saw something about Occupy on the news or walked past it, and then five years later runs for office or writes a book or starts an organization."

The labor journalist and editor of Inequality.org, Sam Pizzigati, acknowledged that it may not be possible to draw a straight line from Occupy to successor movements like #MeToo, given their essential differences in style and substance. But he agreed that without Occupy, which crystallized the economic argument against the 1 percent, #MeToo could not have taken root as suddenly and virally as it did. "It's hard to point to a direct cause and effect from one movement to another, but what Occupy did, by changing the ideological climate, was to create an environment where all sorts of movements could grow," he said. "It was exciting, it created a new sense of empowerment among people, and you can't overestimate the importance of that. When you think about #MeToo, would we have been able to succeed in knocking off Harvey Weinstein and these moguls if the Occupy movement hadn't first delegitimized the 1 percent in the public mind? You can't say Occupy created that success, but I think Occupy prepared the ground for that sort of success."

WE'RE IN THE MARCH FOR OUR LIVES

IN DECEMBER 2012, A YEAR AFTER OCCUPY WALL STREET, THE MAS-sacre at Sandy Hook Elementary School in Newtown, Connecticut, claimed the lives of twenty children and six staff members, an unspeakable tragedy that nonetheless failed to stir Senate Republicans, and even many Democrats, to pass legislation addressing gun violence. It was par for the course in Washington, where generations of lawmakers funded by and fearful of the National Rifle Association and its army of gun lobbyists on Capitol Hill weren't about to act on sensible arms control measures—background checks, a ban on assault weapons and high-capacity magazines—even if it killed them. The epidemic of mass shootings in recent decades has left a tapestry of tombstones blanketing the nation: Columbine, Virginia Tech, Orlando, Las Vegas, Dayton, El Paso, Charleston, the list goes on. After each incident, state and federal GOP legislators offered their "thoughts and prayers" to victims' families and stated they were "grieving" with communities torn apart by violent mass shootings. But despite polls showing that 80 percent of Americans demanded changes in the nation's gun laws, nothing, it seemed, could make elected officials act.

Then, in February 2018, after a teenage gunman wielding an AR-15 semi-automatic rifle killed fourteen students and three staff at Marjory Stoneman Douglas High School, in Parkland, Florida, the equation changed. Young people had had enough and they took action. They walked out of school. They confronted their state legislators and city governments and the gun lobby directly. They demanded that the country see them—see the destruction to their lives abetted by irresponsible and cowardly congresspeople who were unwilling to stand up to the gun industry and protect citizens by passing even basic legislation banning military-caliber weaponry from America's streets. The following month, Florida governor Rick Scott managed to sign a bill that lifted the age for purchasing a rifle in Florida from eighteen to twenty-one, instituted background checks and waiting periods for gun buyers, banned bump stocks, and made it harder for mentally unstable people to obtain guns. But the measures were too little, too late, and overnight, fueled by hashtags like #NeverAgain and #EnoughIsEnough, a group of teenage students from Parkland ignited the March for Our Lives—a distributed, social media–fueled movement that brought half a million protesters to Washington as millions more marched nationwide and globally on March 24, 2018, signaling the beginning of the end of NRA-dominated politics in America.

Spurred by tragedy and outrage, America's youngest generation—as yet undefined except to be called Generation Z—had arrived at its inflection point. To become an activist at sixteen, at twelve, at seven, became a sensible, meaningful identity, one that more and more adolescents would embrace. Their numbers scaled dramatically the following year when millions of high school students left class and led the planet in a week of Global Climate Strikes. With their lives and the habitable future of the Earth on the line, no response except protest any longer seemed to make sense. Rebellion was now in the bloodstream of America as Gen Z organized for the common goal of survival. And so a generation that is perhaps already best defined by its closeness with technology and its mortal fear for the future turned with a greater urgency to the culture of resistance: through our screens, on our streets, in our lives. In the metaphor of social movements as a sequence of elevating valleys that build on one another's height, the new generation was starting from a place of mastery over its digital organizing environment—a sphere that Occupy Wall Street, one decade before, was on the cusp of discovering.

SHUTTING DOWN THE PORTS

DECEMBER 12, 2011

SEVERAL HOURS BEFORE DAWN, I HOPPED A RIDE WITH TWO GUYS from Occupy Santa Rosa and we drove south to Oakland. The rain had stopped, it was still dark out, approaching five thirty, when we reached the city BART station and joined a thousand people already assembled there, bundled in coats and scarves, holding banners, picket signs, megaphones, musical instruments. By six we were marching west on Seventh Street toward the Port of Oakland. Scores of protesters rode along on bicycles and activists from Food Not Bombs distributed scalding cups of coffee that we sipped while we walked. The streets smelled warm, fresh, as steam rose off the ground and the cadence of our footsteps punctured the early morning silence. But as we passed immense cargo lots filled with shipping containers stacked five and six stories high, the movement's plan to close the port, it seemed to me, was not all that well conceived. The majority of workers with the International Longshore and Warehouse Union—the very men on whose behalf Occupy had mobilized that day, from Seattle to San Diego, to shut down the West Coast shipping industry—did not support the strike. Occupy Oakland organizers claimed they had tried to meet with union bosses to win support and were either rebuffed or ignored, so they went ahead and planned the action anyway. There was a provision in the ILWU contract that allowed workers to strike if they felt their safety was at risk, so a cadre of the union's most militant longshoremen stepped in to assist. Heading toward winter, in the aftermath of nationwide park evictions that had noticeably quieted the movement, activists billed the ports shutdown as the moment "Occupy Strikes Back." Something big needed to happen, a resurgence of some kind. No one was ready to admit, nor was it in any way yet clear, that Occupy might be over.

After police officers had violently cleared Zuccotti Park in the middle of the night on November 15, and following our publication of the climactic fifth issue of *The Occupied Wall Street Journal*, I had flown back to California in an attempt to gain some perspective. I immersed myself in the redwoods, taking twilight walks along the Russian River as I sought to understand what had happened to the country, and to me, over the past ten weeks. One afternoon I went out to visit my Buddhist friend, Gabe, who lived in a secluded studio on his mother's property, surrounded by apple orchards outside the town of Sebastopol. Like a lot of people then, Gabe wanted to know what was next for Occupy. I couldn't tell him, and sensing my agitation as we drank tea in his garden, he offered advice: "Maintain sovereignty over your mind," he told me. "Do not surrender your peace." I wanted to tell Gabe it was too late for all that, my peace was shattered, my mind was upended, but I understood what he was after: sovereignty is the inverse of chaos. Gabe led me later through an oak forest that his family had owned for generations, and as we climbed through the brambles he was mostly silent. At the crest of a hill he finally spoke and his meaning was clear. Occupy had achieved something important by "raising consciousness," he said, but it needed to amount to more than protest. Stating the obvious, in a calmly removed tone that contrasted with my troubled one, Gabe reminded me of a spirit of balance I sensed I had lost long ago, if I had ever possessed it at all.

Because of course, he was right. Occupy had opened a door, which we were all now looking through, asking what stood on the other side. We had changed the conversation and transformed the language itself. We had invited people to think and act differently about what it meant to participate in democracy. But now the public was hungry for a plan. People wanted concrete proposals, realistic solutions; they wanted to engage and they were prepared to act if Occupy would direct them toward some useful, constructive end that did not involve marching in streets and sleeping in parks. We needed to grow beyond ourselves if we hoped to challenge the institutions that had been dictating our lives, for so long, with little disturbance.

That December, Occupy organizers on the West Coast thought they had found the answer by taking the fight against Wall Street to the waterfront. Sixty percent of American trade went in and out of the ports located across California, Oregon and Washington. At issue was a labor conflict with Export Grain Terminal, or EGT, a transnational corporation controlled by Goldman Sachs that was in a lockout with longshoremen over wages and conditions at the port of Longview, Washington, located on the Columbia River. Occupy sought to boost the workers' cause and bring attention to the grain profiteering conglomerate. So it coordinated a strike that stretched from Los Angeles through Oakland to Portland, Olympia and Tacoma. A number of longshoremen backed the action, but the majority opposed it because, they argued, it would cost thousands of shipping, trucking and port workers their day's wages while hardly making a dent in Goldman's multi-billion-dollar grain trade. The movement needed to sit down with union leadership and form a deeper alliance with the rank and file. It also needed to communicate to the public why the strike mattered. Occupy did neither.

Peter Olney, who was then the ILWU's organizing director for the West Coast, had spent time at Occupy San Francisco helping rally people against foreclosures in the Bayview district. He'd even convened a discussion with the AFL-CIO and national unions in an attempt to get organized labor to support the movement, with little success. "Occupy provided a spark. It was a cultural political phenomenon. It was cool," Olney later told me. "It laid the basis for other organizing, whether it was the teacher strikes, the Verizon strikes, the GM autoworkers." At its core, the movement had "raised the issues of economic inequality, the 99 versus the 1 percent—it named the enemy, it led to the power of the movement around Bernie Sanders and what he's been able to do." But while "the movement tapped into the energy and frustration, there was no strategic game plan," he said. Heavily burdened by its anarchist rejection of leadership, it had essentially limited its organizing capacity to the amount people could get done while sitting around in a park or public square, Olney added. In the end, "some members of ILWU supported Occupy and the actions of amassing in front of our marine terminals and closing them down," but the strike's success was "based more on the traditions and the history of the ILWU than the support of Occupy: if you put a thousand people in front of a marine terminal, it's going to shut down."

AFTER WALKING FOR FORTY-FIVE MINUTES, STILL IN THE PRE-dawn dark, we reached the port and split into four groups, each with many hundreds who dispersed and formed picket circles at four berths across the port. By seven in the morning, trucks were stalled, unable to enter the docks as people continued to show up and our numbers grew. The pickets moved in slow circles; some people played instruments or banged out rhythms on bucket drums while the chant rang out, "*Whose port? Our port!*" and riot police stood by, motionless, hands on their belts, awaiting orders for what to do next. Minutes stretched into hours under the gray morning light until finally, sometime after ten, cheers erupted when Boots Riley, the famous singer of The Coup and a commanding figure at Occupy Oakland, received a text from Local 21 leadership announcing the Longview port in Washington had closed. Soon, the call came in that ILWU in Oakland had called off work and gone home, and Portland quickly followed. A Black longshoreman standing in the crowd beamed. "I'm in support of the protest. I'm part of the 99 percent," he told me. "I didn't cross the picket lines and I'm totally grateful for what you guys did."

But as I moved away from the protest toward the long line of cargo vehicles stalled outside the dock, I heard a different opinion. A forty-five-year-old truck driver named Rich, from Modesto in the Central Valley, was sitting in his cab with a sour look on his face. Heavy-set, with a rust-colored goatee, he told me he was pulling a fifty-thousand-pound container filled with dog food bound for Malaysia. Truckers like him, not corporate giants like Goldman Sachs and the Export Grain Terminal, were the real victims of the shutdown, he said. "They cost me four hundred dollars today. I bring two loads in here daily and pocket two hundred after fuel. I'm not rich by any means, I make fifty-two thousand a year working fifteen- and sixteen-hour days. I make enough to support my family." Nodding at the young Occupy protesters who were marching in their picket, Rich added, "I don't think they're doing any good. They say they're helping us, but I don't see how if they're costing us our wages. They're hurting truckers and local businesses. They should be electing different people into office, not blocking trucks from going into ports." Then he looked at me hard and told me the real problem was illegal immigrants taking away American jobs. "We're the little guys, they're picking on the little guys. They should be getting the big guys. It hurts my kids at Christmastime. Explain it to a six-year-old why Dad didn't get a check this week. I live check to check, I'm not a 1 percenter who can afford to lose a day's wage. I don't even have a bank account I'm so broke. Taking a day's wage from me is a big, big deal."

The shutdown of the ports drew nationwide attention, sending a powerful message three weeks before the New Year that Occupy, though expelled from the parks, wasn't gone by a long shot. Nobody yet knew at that point what the movement was or wasn't capable of; we still hadn't come to the staggering conclusion that our consensus-based disunity and lack of leadership would get us nowhere toward charting a structurally coherent future. Solidarity port actions that day ricocheted from Anchorage to Hawaii and as far away as Japan, where rank-and-file longshoremen turned out. The strike also, more importantly, brought EGT to the negotiating table to finally resolve its contract with the union. It seemed as though the tide might be turning. Occupy was finding its feet, preparing to enter into the second round against Wall Street and the corporate class. But like a boxer without a coach, the flailing that ensued showed why discipline, planning and strategy—particularly when faced with the immense power of the 1 percent—was key to winning the fight.

7

OCCUPY TECHNOLOGY

THE WHOLE WORLD IS WATCHING

DIGITAL ACTIVISTS CONVERGE

IT WAS SOMETIME DURING THE SECOND IRAQ WAR, WHILE HE WAS studying for his communication arts degree at the University of Wisconsin, Madison, that Harry Waisbren realized he could use the internet as a political tool for change. Born in 1985 and raised in Milwaukee, Waisbren was a freshman when the war broke out in 2003. Facebook and Twitter didn't exist yet; progressive blogs and web-based organizing were just coming into vogue. That fall, activists with the organization MoveOn revolutionized online politics, mobilizing an army of grassroots volunteers to propel the firebrand governor of Vermont, Howard Dean, into the top tier of the Democratic presidential primaries. Dean's digitally enhanced campaign shattered party fundraising totals, hauling in a then-record $14.8 million in the third quarter of 2003 and demonstrating, for the first time, how online small-dollar donations could reshape elections.

Waisbren became a budding journalist and activist who co-hosted a Madison radio show, worked at a community access TV station and helped coordinate a conference for Iraq Veterans Against the War. As he organized, he saw the potential of applying a "media-first approach" to politics. "Massive rallies weren't covered much, and that's when I got into digital activism, using social media as a counterweight to the traditional media propaganda that was stifling and silencing what would have otherwise been fervent anti-war activism," he told me. Waisbren understood, perhaps earlier than most people, that as online tools began to make everyday people's voices louder, it became "just as important to spread and amplify great activism, as it was to organize itself."

By the time Waisbren graduated, America was knee-deep in the financial crisis. He spent a year "trying desperately to find meaningful work" before moving back in with his parents. Then, in the fall of 2010, he landed an online organizing fellowship with Greenpeace that brought him to New York City. He tuned in that winter to the Arab Spring, but he was more riveted to—and personally invested in—the pro-union uprising that had transformed his old town Madison into a giant populist encampment. "I wasn't able to go back in person, but I spent an enormous amount of time following the livestreams and news, and that's when I first started learning about occupation as a tactic," Waisbren said. "When you say 'occupation' you think of a sit-down strike. But the big difference I saw was that by using internet and social media, we were able to spread the word in a way that was revolutionary: it was a buildup that got bigger and bigger, as more people shared it online and then they went to check out the hundreds of thousands of people at these rallies. It was proof of concept for me: it was the testing ground."

Just a year younger than Waisbren, Justin Wedes was another tech-savvy, Midwestern millennial living in New York City as the 2011 protests hit high gear. A Detroit native, Wedes had studied physics and linguistics at the University of Michigan before moving to Brooklyn just prior to the 2008 crash to pursue a high school science teaching fellowship. Living in comfortable Park Slope, he would commute to a poor part of Red Hook where he worked with immigrant youth, dropouts and the so-called hard to teach kids in the projects.

The inequality he experienced "was really my personal, political awakening," and Wedes soon got involved with the United Federation of Teachers fighting against city budget cuts and overcrowded classrooms. In the summer of 2011, he joined the national organizing team of US Uncut—the same rowdy, theatrical group of activists that J. A. Myerson had become a part of—which sought to rouse a left-wing response to the Tea Party by opposing austerity policies, corporate bailouts, foreclosure evictions and tax cuts for the rich. Wedes honed his online activist skills and connected with others who were busy organizing the September park takeover that would become Occupy Wall Street. Meanwhile, Waisbren that summer joined the cadre of protesters from New Yorkers Against Budget Cuts who launched Bloombergville, the encampment forerunner to Zuccotti Park.

A third techtivist who was primed for the eruption of Occupy—more experienced, more prone to taking risk, and perhaps the most digitally brilliant figure of the movement—was Vlad Teichberg. Born in Moscow in 1971, Teichberg came to the United States when he was ten and grew up in Rego Park, Queens. As a mathematics major studying at Princeton during the first Iraq War, he founded the free campus newspaper *Information Gulf,* which documented American pro-war propaganda in the media. After college, Teichberg went to work on Wall Street, where he became an expert in exotic derivatives, probability and market models. While creating complex products for Bankers Trust, Deutsche Bank, HSBC and others throughout the nineties, he saw up close the way "globalization was being sold to us, not as the oppressive thing that it has become, [but one] that would eradicate inequality." Finally, feeling disenchanted with the status quo, Teichberg decided that "we need to change the system from the inside," so he stealthily went about trying to do it.

Following the September 11 attacks, concerned with what he saw as the country's "sharp turn to fascism" under George W. Bush, Teichberg and several dozen others formed an underground New York media network called the Glass Bead Collective. The group experimented with culture jamming, flash mobs and guerilla media actions—he called it an early "New York version of Pussy Riot"—and also produced a documentary, *Watch This*, about police violence and repression at the 2004 Republican National Convention in Minneapolis. Teichberg continued to work as a big money guy by day and a subversive "citizen media expert" by night, doing sophisticated graphic editing work using viral online footage—skills that would pave the way for the digital breakout achieved at Occupy Wall Street.

In May 2011, when the Indignados flooded the streets and squares of Spain, Teichberg was in Madrid to launch Spanish Revolution TV, a livestream channel that contributed to the movement's exploding popularity. "Spanish media started labeling all the protests, saying, 'It's just about a bunch of homeless people in the squares,' so we started broadcasting from the square and that went viral—it counteracted the narrative—and people started taking squares all over the country," he said. Teichberg seized on an important lesson: "If they go in and they lie about you, and pretend you don't exist, they have a problem, actually, because if they make a mistake defining you, you can define yourself."

THIS REVOLUTION IS BEING TELEVISED

THE SPANISH EXPERIENCE PUT TEICHBERG IN THE DIGITAL VAN-guard, positioning him to do something similar—except this time, on a bigger scale—when the action broke out four months later at Zuccotti Park. Straight off, he and his online media collective launched Global Revolution TV, a twenty-four-hour livestream channel that broadcast Occupy to the world in real time. "We knew Occupy Wall Street was going to be censored and ignored in the mainstream media, but if we got a signal up, and kept it up, it would create a consistent beacon of reality that would contradict the corporate world," he told me. "And it worked. For one week we were censored, then we broke through the media blockade because of that stupid cop who tear-gassed those girls, and that went viral. The number of people watching us every day grew and grew exponentially, it became a social phenomenon [where] we were averaging twenty to thirty thousand people watching at any given moment." One of those people was Harry Waisbren, who started to follow the movement's dramatic Twitter feeds and livestream being produced in a way he had never seen technology used before. The televised social media was "providing entry points for people," Waisbren said, "especially for people going into something that was high-risk, and the harrowing livestreams at Occupy Wall Street along with the response from NYPD made me realize something big was going on there, and I had to get involved."

Waisbren joined Occupy Wall Street's tech operations working group and became another digital creator of the movement helping manage its public-facing channels, like the Twitter handle @OccupyWallStreetNYC and the website OccupyWallSt.net. He also worked to collate the first giant email list, generated from tens of thousands who visited the park and who would receive the movement's weekly newsletter, *Your Inbox Occupied*. Wedes was also busy using Twitter and Facebook to crowdfund cash and food donations for the protesters—some quality restaurant fare, with particular focus on a "pizza delivery tactic" he had seen work to great effect when he visited the Wisconsin capitol occupation a half year earlier. "If people are going to stay in one place, they gotta eat," Wedes told me, and "coming from my cultural Jewish background, I know that one way to get people to stick around is to feed them, and feed them well." Internet technology anchored the organizing networks at Zuccotti, where activists used Google groups and hangouts for reliable communication and put Google Docs to novel political use, since suddenly, "you could write a manifesto with a thousand people." During the movement's peak days, Wedes played a notable role helping steer what became known as the Tweet boat, a coalition of Twitter users whose continuous, dramatic updates from the streets read like a sports play-by-play on Wall Street, inviting a growing global audience along for the ride.

"The linking of tremendously powerful digital tools and people's inherent desires to organize politically really came to fruition with Occupy. The tools now existed to be able to build this movement together online, and then coalesce in real space and make visible those online networks," Wedes said. "I don't think a movement before Occupy could really claim to have been so thoroughly broadcast in real time, from so many angles and with such a rich, multimedia view from the ground, giving people at home and all over the world a chance to *be there*. It quickly became apparent that for all of the activity that was happening in the streets and in the park, there was even more activity and energy and buzz happening online, and we wanted to find a way to connect all of the people who saw the promise of this movement—to experience and feel the emotions and excitement in an easy, digestible way—and tweets became a really good mechanism."

An even more powerful mechanism, it turned out, was the technology that Teichberg, Waisbren and others were just then developing into a popular vehicle for social and political change: livestream video. Today, activists understand instinctively how to use social media to draw mass viewership to protest movements as they're happening. Take, for example, the eight-minute, forty-six-second video of George Floyd's killing, followed by the superbly documented Black Lives Matter upheaval of 2020; or the millions of viewers who followed the Global Climate Strike walkouts the year prior; or the millions more who tuned in to the March for Our Lives protesting gun violence the year before that.

Live footage captured in the streets is now the way many people routinely process and connect to social movements. But a decade ago, the activists at Occupy Wall Street were inventing that digital playbook from scratch. Admittedly, the production wasn't always tip-top. A lot of factors went into producing a good livestream at Occupy, Waisbren told me, from having the right cell phone camera and video equipment to maintaining a good enough internet connection. When a hundred—or a thousand—cell phones were suddenly in use at the same time at the same place, straining the ability of wireless networks to handle the data clog, Waisbren and others worked diligently to sustain the feed for long enough, and at a high enough quality, that the stream didn't constantly cut in and out. The whole idea was to keep people tuned in, using video "as compelling as possible, to build up thousands of viewers," and it wasn't enough just to show the feed. Occupy also relied on legions of people tweeting it out, sharing it on Facebook and driving traffic to generate an organic, viral following. "It's one thing to have a great livestream," he said, "but if nobody's watching it, how much impact did it really have?"

The media makers at Zuccotti Park were testing a novel concept: whether, by holding and building an audience in real time online, they could inspire greater numbers of people to move offline and join the movement in the streets, creating a self-reinforcing protest loop. A model example was the filmmaker Abraham Heisler, who felt drawn to Occupy Wall Street after he watched a video clip on YouTube the first week. "You had people documenting in real time what was going on—people protesting the rampant greed on Wall Street, the fact that nobody was held accountable for all the shit that went on in 2008—and I was inspired," he told me, "so I started making videos, and that brought more people." Early on, Heisler saw hundreds of activists running around with cameras, shooting footage independently with no centralized structure. So he helped launch a collective, Occupy TVNY, whose clean, professionally shot and edited videos powerfully conveyed the movement, distilling its message in the call for economic justice. After Occupy TVNY's first news clip topped one hundred thousand views in the first twenty-four hours, its YouTube channel took off. Following the October 1 mass arrests on the Brooklyn Bridge, the actor and activist Mark Ruffalo approached Heisler and asked him for footage to take to Lawrence O'Donnell at MSNBC. "We were respected," Heisler said. The immediacy of the visuals was in many ways at the heart of the movement's appeal. As he put it, "I don't know if Occupy would have been possible without the technology."

The grassroots organizer and founder of The Engage Network, Marianne Manilov, said Occupy's innovative "ground to digital" approach broke with organizing models of the past, inducing more activism through what she called the movement's "field to online to field" tactic of engagement. As opposed to big non-profit organizations, in which "a group of people got in a room, decided what to put out in digital, then put it in the field and people picked it up and it spread," Manilov said, the opposite occurred at Occupy Wall Street. "I was seeing things created that were never created before—the idea that you could do something on the ground, then put it online, and around the world within twenty-four hours people would echo that." Through its creative new genre of protest documentary media, the movement seized control of the narrative, circumventing the news broadcast cycle as livestreams from Occupy reached, according to Teichberg, an estimated audience of three hundred million people over the course of the autumn.

Live feed technology, though still in its infancy at Zuccotti Park, was nonetheless already popular and sophisticated enough to help the movement in several tactical ways: not only showing Occupy to viewers who would become radicalized participants, but, at the same time, assisting protesters who were out marching and doing direct actions against the banks. "The idea that you could have a camera, a smartphone, and people linked up to hotspots and TriCasters for mobile live broadcasts—and that those people marching in the streets could carry thousands of people with them online in a real live broadcast—this all gave people who were home an opportunity to be part of the protest: to be the eyes and ears of the movement, watching and tuning in and engaging and showing their support," Wedes said. "Then, if a livestreamer was in a march and people elsewhere had knowledge of the location of the police, or if a group of protesters had been separated from the main group, livestreamers could communicate in their comments, on their feeds, to others on the ground in a sort of real-life video game." During months of tense showdowns between Occupy activists and police, the technology made real one of the movement's marquee slogans: *The whole world is watching.* For the first time in human history, it actually was.

That fact, perhaps more than any other, made Occupy Wall Street an original movement among movements. Protesters were no longer protesting alone: they were bringing Americans and everyone else with them on the journey, absorbing millions of viewers in their challenge to take on the 1 percent. A few livestreamers, like the in-action camera personality Tim Pool, became small celebrities, bringing global visibility to the movement at the same time that they brought it to themselves. Yet Occupy's vigorous use of technology also provoked what Waisbren considered a breakthrough in consciousness, catapulting people "past the psychological barrier, [by] taking an otherwise passive supporter who might share something on their Facebook profile, and getting them to come out into the streets," he said. "Livestreaming and social media is a big part of helping people break through the learned helplessness that otherwise keeps them on their couch feeling there's nothing that they can do to make this a better world."

REVERSE SURVEILLANCE

THE LIBERATION OF SOCIAL MEDIA TECHNOLOGY AT OCCUPY COULD also be seen as a response to people's growing unease over encroaching police and government surveillance in the new century. A decade earlier, following the September 11 attacks, the American security state under George W. Bush vastly enlarged its scope. The creation of a militarized Department of Homeland Security, and the routine federal tracking of citizens' cell phone and online communications—a practice that was long suspected, and which the National Security Agency whistleblower Edward Snowden later revealed with startling depth and clarity—impacted the way activists felt freely able to organize and mobilize public dissent. But with the eruption of Occupy, surveillance technology was suddenly turned on its head: instead of being passive objects of government monitoring, the movement taught citizens how to use that same technology to safeguard themselves. "There was a lot of concern at Occupy about surveillance, cameras on streets, undercover surveillance within the movement," Wedes told me, but at the same time, "there was a genuine feeling that these tools could also be turned against the state—that activists could use cameras to film police brutality, so the same tools that were being used to intimidate and coerce certain behaviors from citizens could also be used by citizens" to counter government repression.

Again, it was a matter of millennials realizing their ability to harness the skills and power of their generation, through the superior use of technology, to disrupt and ultimately change the policing status quo. "My parents' generation, many of whom fought against wiretapping and all the intrusions of the surveillance state, harbored a real fear and apprehension about surveillance, whereas my generation grew up knowing nothing different: it was normalized," Wedes said. By the time of Occupy Wall Street, "people understood, 'okay, everyone's being surveilled—let's surveil back!' That was one of the driving motives of Occupy: we can't turn off the cameras, we can't stop the infiltration and the undercovers, but we can use these tools to both promote the cause and, on a physical level, to protect each other and ourselves."

The online organizing entity that received perhaps the most government scrutiny during Occupy Wall Street was the artful, leaderless hacker collective Anonymous. Three months preceding the occupation of Zuccotti Park, the group—which many would later associate with the Guy Fawkes masks popularized at Occupy—called for a similar-style swarm and takeover of public space across U.S. cities. Then, after the Canadian magazine *Adbusters* issued its call on July 13, 2011, for a peaceful demonstration to #OccupyWallStreet, Anonymous dialed up the heat; hacktivists quickly spread the information across Twitter, blogs, a discussion forum known as Internet Relay Chat, and, most visibly, through video clips posted to YouTube. The group's most explicit announcement, which not only caught the attention of activists worldwide but also set off alarm bells at the Department of Homeland Security, came in the form of a one-minute video, uploaded on August 23, entitled "Hello Wall Street." The video declared: "On September 17, Anonymous will flood into lower Manhattan, set up tents, kitchens, peaceful barricades and occupy Wall Street for a few months. Once there, we shall incessantly repeat one simple demand in a plurality of voices: We want freedom. This is a nonviolent protest. We do not encourage violence in any way. The abuse and corruption of corporations, banks and governments ends here. Join us. We are Anonymous. We are legion. We do not forgive. We do not forget. Wall Street, expect us."

The temptations, and the benefits, of deploying media technology to challenge governments and corporations were obvious, but so were the risks. A little over half a year later, an arrested hacker turned FBI informant named Hector Monsegur, facing 124 years in prison, helped U.S. authorities arrest several dozen cyber activists across Europe and South America, dealing a blow to the movement. Although he operated in a different, more openly political sphere of activism, Vlad Teichberg might have suffered a similar fate as a leading technologist at Occupy Wall Street, and in the global resistance that began with the Arab Spring and the 15-M movement in Spain. After Occupy ended, Teichberg moved to Madrid, had a child, and focused his attention on helping expose European governments' harsh treatment of migrants arriving from the Middle East. He worked with the group Hack Borders, in some instances helping smuggle cameras into refugee camps, and made "a lot of enemies," he said. In particular, "the Russians hated us." Teichberg understood that his movements were being tracked and his activities monitored. For years, he and his girlfriend endured lengthy interrogations each time they re-entered the United States. After the 2016 election he tried to organize a project called TrumpLeaks.org. Before it got off the ground, some fellow activists in Italy, who were trying to set up a secure drop box to solicit anonymous information about Trump, were visited by the FBI.

"I think what we do means something to the state," he told me, speaking of Global Revolution TV's digital muckraking success. "We were independent media that couldn't be controlled: we identified voices in the street, people directly in these uprisings, and we curated to amplify these voices to a huge audience, speaking to the world and bypassing the mainstream media." Police repression swept the movement off the streets. But the basic principles that spurred Occupy, he added, have not only endured but strengthened with time. "Occupy is about ideas of equality, that we're all equal, and it's a desire for a fairer world. It's about radical humanism. So much violence was used to suppress Occupy, and the movement wasn't prepared for that violence. [But] we need Occupy to exist, because we need an alternative. There is a vision of America being presented to the population right now that revolves around us respecting each other rather than hating each other. I think we're already winning," he said, in 2019, looking ahead to the post-Trump era. "We can be great by treating people great."

THE TECHNOLOGY LEGACY

THE DIGITAL STRATEGIES DEVELOPED BY TEICHBERG, WAISBREN, Wedes and many others helped shape a decade of social movement organizing in America. Tech-fueled protests had already taken root prior to Occupy Wall Street, noted Waisbren. "It started with the Arab Spring, using Facebook, Twitter and YouTube to spread the word about mass protests. It came through the Wisconsin occupation," he said, but "then it took off with Occupy, and it continues through the progressive-led movements." The most powerful example of viral livestream coverage occurred three years later, at Black Lives Matter, as young people of color elevated video sharing to the next level. They filmed police officers to hold them accountable for acts of brutality and murder, and filmed their own peaceful, nationwide protests in response. "The process of having an inspirational action, where you have camera people and dedicated individuals document with video and photos and distribute strategically through social media—that process is something that Black Lives Matter did masterfully," Waisbren said. Through use of livestream in Ferguson and other cities, Wedes agreed, activists were "really challenging the behavior of police in communities of color, because all of a sudden people could see the way police were responding violently to protesters, and it wasn't pretty."

By the time the Standing Rock movement got underway, in 2016, young people understood how to use technology at their fingertips to help transform even an isolated protest—in this case, a remote encampment led by Native

Americans on the plains of North Dakota—into a sustained, national story. At that point, said Waisbren, "activists across the gamut recognized that they don't need to ask permission, and that with just a small group of dedicated individuals using social media, they can make their cause spread virally." Indeed, protesters' growing command of social media for live movement coverage would become the hallmark of a generation, from #YoSoy132 in Mexico to the #MeToo movement, the March for Our Lives and the Global Climate Strikes. "Occupy was a watershed moment—a political coming of age for millennials," Wedes told me. "My generation, the so-called digital natives, brought to the fight all of these tools that we grew up embracing, and I think there was just an organic digital layer to everything. All these emerging, networked social movements evolved hyper-rapidly by watching each other and duplicating some of the best practices in terms of technology, collaborative tools, and mimicking the street tactics of livestreaming. Occupy was like a sandbox for testing this activist tool kit."

For the millennial author Charlotte Alter, the movement's digital contributions reshaped the way today's generation approaches political organizing, and redefined what activism looks like. "Aside from laying the foundations for a revival of American progressivism, Occupy also demonstrated how the internet—and the sense of radical democratization that went with it—would transform protest movements in the early twenty-first century," she wrote in *The Ones We've Been Waiting For*. In the post-Zuccotti era, "social media would become an entirely new arena for mass protest, a digital version of the streets, where activists could organize themselves and their ideas with many leaders and few rules."

The activist Martin Kirk interpreted the digital impacts of Occupy on an even deeper psychological level, crediting the movement with a fundamental shift in the way political ideas are spread, solutions are considered, and change is produced. "Occupy was the first expression of this new modern, memetic social media warfare," he said, generating a kind of "hive mind" behavior in our culture whereby "ideas are being passed from one brain to another in real time, and that [becomes] the ground from which policy naturally grows. Inevitably hashtags and memes would have happened, because that's the medium we're now in, but you can say Occupy taught us about how these things worked, and showed us the first taste of the future." Using the abundance and rapid evolution of digital tools deployed to protests, the Occupy generation effectively sped up, and forced, a new media and policy discussion. "With the rise of social media in particular, what we're seeing is the conversation space that used to happen at a certain scale is happening at a much larger scale, and it's driving the news agenda. The boundary between Twitter and conventional media has been leveled, [but] if you think back to 2011, it was all still very new."

And the evolution keeps happening. In the decade since Harry Waisbren helped pioneer the use of livestream during protests at Zuccotti Park, video's political value has advanced to the point that activists can now produce "social media's version of cable news, where we have multiple camera feeds and can mix back and forth, we put chyrons on the screen like you're watching CNN, and make a good enough user experience that audiences tune in for long periods of time to these compelling and inspirational actions and speeches and rallies," he said. During Bernie Sanders's 2019 run for the Democratic nomination, Waisbren helped organize the live feed at a series of town halls featuring Michael Moore, Van Jones, Elizabeth Warren and Alexandria Ocasio-Cortez—events that further fueled Sanders's viral online campaign. "We'd put on a compelling show, then distribute it through our different networks and pick up viewership that would beat cable news, with millions of total viewers."

Many of the ground-to-digital organizers who helped make Occupy a worldwide movement didn't end their efforts that autumn in Manhattan. On the contrary, Occupy became "an umbrella brand where all sorts of movement efforts could grow and turn into their own offshoots. The individuals and the networks would go on and start new projects, and you'd keep seeing them over and over at the cutting edge: the same people who were in Occupy Wall Street were in Black Lives Matter, the People's Climate March, the Sunrise Movement. Some of the top activists of this generation got their start at Occupy Wall Street," Waisbren said, "and the network they developed with the people they met continues to this day. There are activists and dedicated citizens that believe a better world is possible, but we need a better media to make it happen."

THE 1 PERCENT ARE GETTING ARRESTED

MARCH 24, 2012

THE SKY WAS GRAY, ALMOST DRIZZLING, ON THE SPRING MORNING when I showed up at my friend's Crown Heights apartment and greeted the others who were waiting. I wore a dark suit, a starched white shirt and a striped maroon tie. My hair was cut short and my face shaved clean in the hope that I could pass for a guy making six figures. When you're going to get arrested in front of TV cameras on the lawn of the United Nations, you want to do it right. Never underestimate the power of a good suit.

My four accomplices—two men, two women—were likewise dressed as bankers. Logistics prepared, props ready, now all we had to do was play our part: executives in the 1 percent. Our Occupy working group's campaign, Disrupt Dirty Power, sought to connect the dots from Wall Street banks to the fossil fuel companies they bankrolled, revealing the links between big finance and the corporations driving climate change. We had assembled half a dozen small white tents in the apartment's backyard, each painted with a bright corporate logo: Koch Industries, ExxonMobil, BP, Citibank, Bank of America, JPMorgan Chase. Two other guys went to pick up a van while the five of us sat around the kitchen looking tense. I filled a glass of water from the sink and drank it down, then drank another. One woman, Lil, small and composed, fiddled with readjustments to her suit. Around ten o'clock our friends returned with the van, loaded in the tents and set off for Manhattan as the five of us walked out and caught the 4 train to Grand Central.

We were early so we stopped at an Irish pub around East Forty-Fourth Street and Third Avenue, where some of us ordered soup and all of us had whiskey to fortify our spirits. A big march scheduled for that afternoon at Union Square, part of the Million Hoodie movement to protest the killing of the unarmed teenager Trayvon Martin in Florida, had shifted the NYPD focus downtown. Meanwhile, about a hundred Occupy protesters were gathered at Dag Hammarskjöld Plaza on Forty-Seventh Street, across from United Nations headquarters, to demand stronger government action fighting climate change.

We sat at the pub for a long time waiting for a phone call from the drivers. When it came, we walked quickly north to Forty-Sixth Street and met the van that had just pulled up. From there, everything happened fast. We unloaded the tents, carrying them awkwardly on our shoulders as we made our way toward the UN. We hustled down Second Avenue past a barber shop, a deli, a shoe repair, a pet store. Our lead organizer, Toby, kept his eyes on the clock and slowed us down to prevent us from arriving too soon. We walked with raucous laughter now, a band of guerrillas in corporate suits comically juggling the tents in our arms like giant beach balls. After turning east on Forty-Fourth Street we began the final descent, past the UNICEF courtyard, past Cushman & Wakefield Management and, finally, past the UN Plaza Tower where the flags came into view and one could see the tall white wall in front of the towering, aqua-green facade that housed the thousand windowed cubicles of the United Nations.

The last hundred yards felt like a sprint. Pumped with adrenaline, we beat the crossing light and dashed across First Avenue, leaped over the short hedge wall and entered the narrow green strip of lawn that was our destination. At that moment, the crowd of protesters who had gathered for the rally at Dag Hammarskjöld Plaza turned onto First Avenue and came marching in our direction, drums beating, chants echoing. A dozen cops kept pace with them and didn't at first notice as we positioned the tents on the lawn and took our places beside them. Police finally realized what was happening, left the protesters and ran toward us, but by then it was too late. We had arranged the tent logos of the banks and oil companies to face the street, with the looming structure of the United Nations building behind them. Television cameras rolled and cheers rose up from the crowd as the cops closed in. They surrounded us on the lawn and told us to leave, warning that we would be arrested. We didn't budge but stood beside our tents: stone-faced executives occupying the grounds of the United Nations. Bankers occupying the climate emergency. The cuffs came out and police pushed us toward the center of the lawn as shouts erupted from the protesters: "*The 1 percent are getting arrested! Arrest the 1 percent!*" Then a white police van rolled up. We were loaded in and driven to the Seventeenth Precinct, between Lexington and Third Avenue, where we were booked and held in jail through nightfall.

8

OCCUPY WORLD

A GLOBAL WAVE BEGINS

ROOTS OF INTERNATIONAL UNREST: SARA BURKE

IN THE SUMMER OF 2008, A MONTH BEFORE THE COLLAPSE OF LEH-man Brothers set off the global financial crisis, Sara Burke took a job as a policy analyst researching international equity issues with the Friedrich-Ebert-Stiftung, a publicly funded German think tank in New York. A self-described "renegade economics journalist" covering the intersection between finance and social justice, Burke could see the writing on the wall. "I was already reading upsetting things about the housing market, runs on banks in the U.K., weird swap lines between central banks," she said. One of her first tasks at FES was to help organize a conference on financial regulation, which quickly morphed into a discussion about the economic meltdown. In Burke's retelling, the 2011 global unrest that produced Occupy had its origins in the bureaucratic missteps and institutional shortsightedness she observed up close following the 2008 financial crash, when governments and giant lending bodies like the International Monetary Fund and World Bank dealt with the crisis by essentially *not* dealing with it. When the G20 nations assembled in dramatic fashion that fall to "save the global economy," they agreed to a series of quick-fix stimulus policies to inject money into their economies and prop up the teetering pillars of the financial system. For two years, stimulus spending was the closest thing to stability the world's richest countries could provide. But then something happened, said Burke, which changed the playing field.

In the fall of 2010, at the G20 summit in Toronto, the global financial stimulus agreement collapsed over European fears that the PIIGS nations—Portugal, Italy, Ireland, Greece and Spain—were taking on unmanageable levels of debt. Suddenly, Germany and the so-called Troika, composed of the IMF, European Commission and European Central Bank, turned the tables on the poorer EU member states and reversed course on spending. Shifting abruptly to austerity, bankers and the political institutions in Brussels blamed Mediterranean countries' skyrocketing debt on their own people's irresponsible behavior rather than on the socialized bailout of the banks two years prior. The message, said Burke, was clear: poor people were to pay the price for an economic crash caused by the 1 percent.

In contrast to Europe, America and the BRICS nations—Brazil, Russia, India, China and South Africa—continued using stimulus to bolster their economies. The Obama administration, in fact, kept injecting money into the financial system long after many experts thought that he would, through the ongoing Troubled Asset Relief Program and even more so through the Federal Reserve's quantitative easing program, which pumped four and a half trillion dollars into the U.S. economy. Europe during that time did just the opposite: instead of adding new money to the system, it took money out in the name of belt-tightening, a "pro-cyclical policy that just increased the problem of lower growth and rising debt," said Burke. As a wave of deeply unpopular austerity measures swept across southern Europe and fanned outward through Africa and Latin America, shrunken budgets contracted further, the recession worsened, youth unemployment grew and people's suffering increased.

Prior to those dangerous austerity cuts, protests had already begun to destabilize different parts of the planet in 2006 and 2007, when a spike in the global commodities market—caused by droughts and other disruptive climate events, and compounded by financial speculation at Goldman Sachs and elsewhere—sent food and energy prices soaring. From Mexico to India, from Kenya to Morocco and Senegal, people on the brink of starvation rebelled because they could no longer afford to eat. Across the Global South in the lead-up to the crash, a heightened sense of desperation caused by tightening markets provoked "a kind of ritualized struggle between populations and governments," Burke said, "where there's a subsistence level of human need and a tacit agreement that [leaders] will not let people fall below this floor."

The social contract in the age of globalization was fraying, Burke told me. "People completely lost trust in the authorities. Populations had bought into the idea that if you work hard and are upright, you're going to be able to develop and flourish. It's the idea of social mobility—the hope that your children will be able to have a better life than you had—and I think this is what's been shattered and stomped on again and again since the 2008 crisis, because it was never resolved properly, in a socially just way, in any country." The popular anger that exploded in 2011—starting with the Arab Spring, and followed by uprisings in Spain and Greece, then later Israel and Chile—reflected the growing consensus that regimes were no longer functional because they had failed to provide adequate opportunities for work and survival, and ensure a basic level of dignity for their populations. People en masse gave up on "technocrats or politicians of any kind anymore to represent them." Through with listening to the men in dark suits, the public demanded a reset—a rebalancing of the scales of economic justice.

And in the worldwide rebellions that year, Burke said, "Occupy was the fulcrum. They spoke truth to power in a way that refused to allow the message about inequality to be co-opted or spun. The whole idea that they wouldn't reduce it to just a list of demands or a political platform was powerful—it made experts stop and scratch their heads and say, 'We don't understand, what's going on? Why won't you just tell us what you want? What do you mean you don't want the world to be unequal?' And it brought the usual algorithm to a complete standstill."

BORN IN 1963 IN LUBBOCK, TEXAS, BURKE BOUNCED AROUND THE West with her family—Oklahoma City, Wichita, Houston, Denver—before she dropped out her junior year of high school and ran away to Santa Fe. She later earned a BA from Reed College in Oregon and worked as an artist in the 1980s, then enrolled in graduate school at Stanford to study documentary filmmaking. Drawn to explore themes of wealth inequality, Burke accompanied a classmate to the Philippines to work as her cinematographer on a film about Imelda Marcos—the outlandishly rich wife of the country's deposed president—and the role of women transforming politics. She felt riveted, if confounded, in her encounters with the former first lady. "I was fascinated that someone could talk as though they had the right to shape things and make decisions that would change millions of people's lives, that would impact people on a mass scale, and who thought about people as putty," she told me. Seeing Smokey Mountain, the city of garbage above Manila populated by families scavenging for their survival, awakened a sense of socioeconomic urgency that would guide Burke's future work. "I wanted to understand where real poverty came from, why some people have very little and others have way too much," she said, "and how we got to a place with this kind of inequality."

Burke went on to study economics at The New School in Manhattan, and when the second Iraq War got underway she launched a muckraking news site called Gloves Off, exploring political and economic issues through an activist lens. In 2010, she joined anti-corporate protests organized by people involved with US Uncut, and after the brief Bloombergville encampment in the summer of 2011, Burke offered up her Staten Island home to about twenty activists, who lived on her porch for days. When the Occupy movement happened, it brought fresh focus to Burke's global research on inequality. During several months in the autumn of 2011, Occupy entered and became part of the political culture in hundreds of cities around the world. Across Africa and Asia and Oceania, throughout Latin America and in nations that spanned Europe, the movement's message resonated, reflecting a readiness by the global population—including those living in powerful financial centers like Tokyo, Frankfurt, London and Zurich—to declare solidarity with the 99 percent. A decentralized global economic justice movement unlike any that had come before, Occupy Wall Street embodied the shared suffering and universal anger caused by a financial crash whose corporate culprits were never punished.

In the aftermath of the 2008 crisis, two World Bank researchers, Branko Milanovic and Christoph Lakner, had embarked on a study of the economic winners and losers in the early twenty-first century. Their work resulted in a famous 2013 graph, known as the elephant curve, which charted how different countries, and different classes within those countries, fared in the two decades leading up to the crash. The graph started with the global poor, primarily in Africa and Southeast Asia, who saw their incomes rise only slightly during that period. The poorest nations represent the elephant's tail. Stronger, larger developing countries like India, Indonesia, South Africa and Brazil experienced better growth, reflected in gains made by an expanding middle class; they represent the elephant's rear and back as it ascends in a steady upward trajectory. Then, at the elephant's head, the line plummets sharply downward, representing the falling fortunes of middle- and lower-class people in the developed economies of Europe, the United States and Japan, who saw wage growth stagnate and who felt hardest squeezed by the crisis. But the final, most revealing portion of the graph is the elephant's trunk, which makes a U-shape, shooting straight back up into the air, reflecting the massive growth accrued to the top 1 and top .01 percent.

The elephant curve served as an institutional wake-up call. Where global banks and financial lenders seemed previously oblivious to all the clamor around rising inequality, suddenly many insider economists were forced to admit that, in fact, widening wealth and income disparity was not only a systemic problem, but a worsening crisis. The same year the graph appeared, and two years after the eruption of Occupy Wall Street, Burke and her research team at the Friedrich-Ebert-Stiftung produced a working paper entitled "World Protests: 2006–2013," which analyzed nearly 850 protests occurring across eighty-four countries during the previous eight years. The authors wrote, "There have been periods in history when large numbers of people rebelled demanding change, such as in 1848, 1917 or 1968; today we are experiencing another period of rising outrage and discontent, and some of the largest protests in world history." The study sought to reveal some of the common causes behind so many global uprisings, tying rising economic inequality and specific popular grievances (like falling wages and higher food and housing costs) with government failures to provide an adequate social safety net. Burke's research showed a steady growth in annual protests—from 59 in 2006 to 112 in the first half of 2013, including a sharp increase in 2010 after austerity measures around the world went into effect. It especially reflected rising disillusionment in democracies where people felt their governments had failed to represent their economic needs and interests.

Burke pointed to a classic example in Tunisia, the birthplace of the Arab Spring, "which wasn't a country marked by extreme poverty. It had a very educated youth class who were highly trained and internet savvy, but there was no mobility for them, no jobs, and on top of it, the richest of the rich were flaunting their wealth like nobody's business." Burke explained how extreme anger started to build "between those who weren't the poorest of the poor, but middle-class people who didn't see any possibility for improvement in their lives, or realizing the promise of their education." But "the thing that really struck us was the failure of political representation: we saw more calls for real democracy than any demands of any kind anywhere in the world, and they came from every type of political system—from advanced democracies to authoritarian systems like China—so there was something linking all of that, and this picture begins to explain what sets the stage for the discontent of the Occupy movement."

It was in the winter of 2012, just months after Occupy peaked, when some of the world's biggest financial stakeholders, starting with the Davos crowd, began to reverse course. Long-term adherents to free-market orthodoxy—who viewed inequality not only as necessary, but desirable, because it encouraged wealth-making, which drove innovation—began to agree that an ever-widening wealth gap might not be so good for the global economy after all. In their book *Confronting Inequality: How Societies Can Choose Inclusive Growth*, Jonathan D. Ostry, Prakash Loungani and Andrew Berg, three top economists at the IMF, would later make the convincing argument that government policies, which had contributed over decades to rising inequality, had in fact harmed long-term growth and weakened the economy, not strengthened it.

The economists instead proposed "inclusive growth" models aimed at reducing inequality, which they declared were necessary to effectively save capitalism from itself. Countries were now encouraged to empower themselves through capital control, enacting policies that kept the national wealth from being sucked out by international finance and corporations. Economists urged nations to redistribute wealth through social programs, expand the safety net, invest in education, healthcare, research and infrastructure, and limit executive compensation, among other measures. Only recently, the mere mention of redistribution had invoked comparisons to the *Communist Manifesto*. Countries were now being advised by leading thinkers at the IMF to pursue those redistributive policies.

As more respected economists moved left, a larger shift also occurred in their financial perspective, moving away from a macroeconomic view of markets to more of a focus on the ways economic policies personally affected people, their families and their communities. This signaled a larger transformation taking place within the world's most powerful financial bodies, and "what's really interesting, ten years down the line," said Burke, "is that the mandate of these institutions, including the World Bank and the Organisation for Economic Co-operation and Development, has changed to the degree that they consider their following neoliberal policies all these years to have been wrongheaded." Burke, who worked closely with the IMF, said that to the organization's credit, it actually started to research the economic impacts of inequality in 2009, two years prior to the global protest movements. More recently, she said, those same institutions have moved their focus away from Big Banks toward Big Tech, where trillion-dollar corporations regularly paid zero in taxes, starving countries of vital domestic revenue and further exacerbating inequality. Worried less about Too Big to Fail banks and more about Too Big to Touch corporations, institutional elites were finally "asking questions like, 'Is Google too big?' 'Is Amazon too big? 'Is Alibaba too big?' 'Are these giant monopolies, bigger than we've ever seen, the greatest threats to the health of the system?'"

As if to hammer home the point, a whistleblower concerned about rising inequality in 2016 leaked eleven and a half million documents from the Panamanian law firm Mossack Fonseca, at one time the fourth biggest provider of offshore financial services on Earth. Investigated and published by the International Consortium of Investigative Journalists, the trove known as the Panama Papers exposed for the first time in such detail the existence of hundreds of thousands of tax-sheltered entities and how they operated. The following year, the consortium released a follow-up, the Paradise Papers, which revealed in more specific ways how the global 1 percent—politicians and famous figures among them—worked diligently to hide their excess wealth overseas. The exposures fueled greater outrage and increased scrutiny on tax havens, secret corporate wealth, profit-shifting and illicit financial flows.

Many countries today still don't report their tax data because they're often too poor to collect it. And for the countries that do report, much of the tax information they deliver is inaccurate. Since the United Nations cannot legally compel countries to divulge their financial records, global data on wealth and income inequality remains scattershot. In India, for example, household surveys tabulate how much rice and milk and eggs people consume, "but the rich aren't going to answer the questions about how many homes they own," Burke said. Other countries, like China, may collect the data but aren't necessarily sharing what they've found, so globally, she said, we're left with a leaky system where "you don't capture the status of the poor, because they don't pay, and you don't capture what the rich pay because their money stays hidden. The very, very wealthy cannot be compelled to disclose their wealth, [and] billionaires are not going to tell you about the things that they don't want you to know."

2012: STUDENT REBELLION IN THE AMERICAS

AS OCCUPY WALL STREET RESHAPED THE GLOBAL FINANCIAL DIS-cussion, it also had a widening ripple effect on political and social movements across the planet, starting with the trio of university student upheavals it fueled in the Western hemisphere. In November 2011, while Zuccotti Park was still at its height, tens of thousands of students in Canada were staging an occupation of their own, six hours north of Manhattan in Quebec's largest city, Montreal. The students had rejected a 75 percent tuition fee hike proposed by the Quebec Cabinet and stormed McGill University's administrative building. By December they had assembled a student union coalition, known as CLASSE, which was preparing for a mass student strike. That winter, as Occupy Wall Street faded from view, the movement emerging a few hundred miles to the north seemed to repurpose the spirit of revolt. Protests swept across cities and towns in Canada's second most populous province, where thousands of students wore small red felt or paper squares, the symbol of the protest, on their winter coats. Montreal residents who supported the movement produced nightly *concerts de casseroles*, beating pots and pans from their balconies as the protests escalated through February and March.

The students occupied bridges and targeted powerful economic symbols like the Quebec Liquor Board. Confrontations between students and police escalated into violence, including the use of rubber bullets, tear gas and flash-bang grenades, which hospitalized numerous protesters. By spring, more than three-quarters of the province's college students were on strike over the fee increase, and in May 2012, the movement mobilized mass marches that included labor unions, opposition political parties, teachers, lawyers and a large swath of the Quebecois population. The Maple Spring, as the monthslong protests came to be known, resulted in thousands of arrests and sustained global news coverage. The National Assembly of Quebec tried to curtail the strikes by passing an emergency law to outlaw protests near university grounds, with penalties greater than $100,000 for anyone in violation. But on the hundredth day of the strike, May 22, students flouted the law and nearly half a million protesters filled Montreal's streets in the largest act of civil disobedience in Canadian history. When the nationalist Parti Québécois came to power later that summer, it repealed the emergency anti-protest law and ended the tuition fee hike. The students had achieved their goals. In September 2012, they returned to class.

The Montreal uprising signaled a first protest win in the post-Occupy era, and the impacts reverberated south. In Chile, university students had already staged mass demonstrations in the months leading up to Occupy Wall Street when hundreds of thousands of young people in mid-2011 marched against inequalities in the country's underfunded education system. Long seen as South America's financial success story, Chile had built a robust economy since 1990, when Augusto Pinochet's seventeen-year-long dictatorship came to an end and democracy was restored. But for all its growth, the country had failed to build new publicly funded universities, creating what many considered a form of segregation—"educational apartheid." Increasing numbers of students who couldn't pay faced extreme student debt or were shut out from higher learning altogether while the children of wealthy families enjoyed full access to elite, privately run institutions. In response, Chilean students rebelled, at times violently, sparking street clashes with police as they demanded quality public schooling and an end to the voucher-paid, for-profit universities that comprised half the country's education system.

The protests in the capital, Santiago, reflected young people's anger over growing inequalities and the outsized role of corporations influencing government decisions. Soon, the demonstrations expanded beyond the academic sphere to impact other vital areas of the economy: transport workers demanded better job security; copper miners went on strike for higher wages; environmentalists mobilized to save a pristine Patagonian river from a hydroelectric dam. As José Joaquín Brunner, a former minister in Chile's government, told the BBC at the time: "The unrest goes beyond education, even if education is the reason why it's suddenly burst into the open." Still, it was the student crisis that was front and center, and as in Quebec, Santiago's noisy *cacerolazos*, or saucepan protests, became a popular, powerful way for everyday people to support the movement.

Led by a charismatic twenty-three-year-old named Camila Vallejo—she would later become a Chilean Communist Party fixture and a Chamber of Deputies member representing the Twenty-Sixth District of La Florida, Santiago—the student uprising had issued three core demands: better state funding of education, a fairer admissions process, and free public education. In April 2012, Chile's education minister offered to eliminate private banks from the student loan process and slash interest rates on loans from 6 to 2 percent. But students rejected the plan, refusing to "trade debt for debt," as another student leader and future member of Chile's parliament, Gabriel Boric, put it. In the months that followed, known as the Chilean Winter, hundreds of thousands of students continued to march in Santiago, occupying schools and universities, showing that they were dug in and not going anywhere. Finally, after two years of sustained conflict, Michelle Bachelet of the Socialist Party was re-elected president in 2013 on a promise to establish free and universal access to higher education. By 2016, the country had launched a tuition-free policy, known as *gratuidad,* that allowed a new generation of low- and middle-income students to attend universities and technical training schools, remapping Chile's educational landscape.

The third student uprising, and one that would become most closely associated with Occupy Wall Street, was #YoSoy132, dubbed the Mexican Spring or, by some, the "Mexican Occupy movement." It began simply enough on May 11, 2012, in the capital, Mexico City, where Enrique Peña Nieto, then a candidate for president, visited the prestigious Ibero-American University to talk about his campaign platform. At one point, students asked Peña Nieto to explain the violent police action he had authorized in 2006, as governor of the State of Mexico, when a dispute over the rights of flower vendors at a local marketplace had exploded into protests resulting in beatings, more than two hundred arrests, police sexual assaults against dozens of women, and two deaths. In his reply, Peña Nieto defended and legitimized the police response, eliciting jeers from students in the crowd, some of whom recorded and posted the raucous clip on social media.

After Mexico's major television networks and newspapers reported that the dissenters at Peña Nieto's speech weren't students at all, but political plants and opposition rivals, 131 Ibero-American students organized through Facebook to produce a video showing each person holding up their university identity card, proudly proclaiming their school affiliation. Uploaded to YouTube, the video went viral on Twitter and protests erupted as tens of thousands of young people across Mexico's private and public education systems declared their solidarity, "Yo Soy 132"—I am number 132. "We caught them off balance. The video put a face to the individual protesters," Rodrigo Serrano, one of the organizers, told the *NACLA Report*. Suddenly, "the paradigm shifted from representative democracy to participatory democracy, because [the politicians] don't represent us."

YoSoy132 launched a nationwide movement aimed at democratizing the media and raising voter awareness. Through Occupy-style, decentralized digital organizing over the next two months, students across the capital and in dozens of Mexican cities staged demonstrations, marches and sit-ins to protest Peña Nieto, the ruling Institutional Revolutionary Party (PRI), and a corporate media establishment that backed both. Ten days before the election, YoSoy132 succeeded in pulling off an internet-only broadcast of a presidential debate, proving the movement's skill not only at mobilizing in the streets but at disrupting the media status quo. On July 1, Peña Nieto beat Andrés Manuel López Obrador in an election marred by fraud, vote buying, illegal campaign spending and manipulated election data, all of which favored the PRI candidate.

For weeks, tens of thousands of Mexicans packed the Zócalo in central Mexico City to protest what had all the hallmarks of a second consecutive stolen election (following López Obrador's widely contested loss to Felipe Calderón in 2006). The results stood, but six years later, in 2018, AMLO, as he was called, returned for a third campaign and that time he won, delivering Mexico its first left-populist, anti-establishment presidency in modern memory. In the process, YoSoy132 had awakened the country to a new language and strategy of dissent, challenging the corporate, political and media classes as a new generation demanded to be heard. "The students who developed YoSoy132 were really direct descendants of Occupy," said Burke. They were "middle-class students, they went to a private university, so it's again that story of squeezing out the middle. They said, 'No, we really have something to say. You *have* to listen to us.'"

2013: FROM GEZI TO BRAZIL

THE FOLLOWING YEAR, IN THE SPRING OF 2013, OCCUPY'S INTERnational legacy took on more lasting shape when a new park protest sprang up in a place no one expected: at the crossroads of East and West, on the Bosphorus separating Europe from Asia, in the Turkish metropolis Istanbul. Occupy Gezi ignited one week before *The Guardian* launched its explosive exposé about America's secret mass surveillance programs, based on information provided by the NSA contractor-turned-whistleblower Edward Snowden. The protest didn't garner much Western media attention at first. A few dozen environmentalists had simply showed up on the evening of May 27 and camped out in Gezi Park, part of the city's historic Taksim Square. Their hope was to prevent the bulldozing of six hundred trees that would be sacrificed for a new shopping mall, luxury apartments and a faux-sultanate military barrack. Turkey's prime minister Recep Tayyip Erdoğan had been in power already for a decade, and his Islamist-rooted Justice and Development Party was in the process of curtailing basic secular freedoms starting with a free press and free speech. Erdoğan appealed to his religious base by banning the sale and consumption of alcohol at night, jailing people for blasphemy, imposing harsh restrictions on religious freedom, threatening to make abortions all but impossible to obtain and, perhaps most improbably, attempting to outlaw kissing in public.

Yet even as he sought to tighten his authoritarian grip in 2013, polls showed two-thirds of the country opposed Erdoğan's bid to rewrite the Turkish constitution and give the office of the presidency more sweeping powers. Meanwhile, a growing environmental movement was challenging the ongoing destruction of the Black Sea region where mines, waste dumps, coal plants, hydroelectric dams and other hazardous developments had been built in the name of progress. Growth in Turkey had slowed, unemployment stood high, and the country's expanding involvement in the war in Syria was unpopular. A few days before Gezi, a Turkish hacker group called RedHack released documents showing the government had known about but done nothing to prevent a recent terror attack, in which two car bombs killed fifty-two people in the Turkish town of Reyhanli, near the Syrian border. Frustrations were at a tipping point. Then, all it took was a park.

Like Occupy Wall Street and so many of the social movements we've seen in recent years, it wasn't so much the initial protest as the government's violent overreaction that generated a groundswell of popular support. Occupy Gezi— also called *Gezi Derinisi*, or Gezi Resistance—began that warm May night as a peaceful environmental sit-in, but the next day, when protesters blocking the bulldozers refused to leave, police raided the park using tear gas as they burned people's tents. The scene fueled nationwide outrage, and the photograph of a young woman in a red dress bravely standing her ground as police peppersprayed her in the face captured the world's imagination. The Gezi protesters put out calls for support, to which people responded, showing up en masse for a park occupation that lasted several days until the morning of May 31, when riot police launched a harsher assault. Firing tear gas and water cannons, they arrested dozens and injured more than one hundred, hospitalizing many protesters while erecting barricades around the park to prevent people's re-entry.

The next day, as thousands marched across the Bosphorus Bridge and merged into massive crowds making their way through the city, Erdoğan took a misstep when he approved plans to move a political rally that afternoon to Taksim Square. Once police had vacated Taksim to make way for the rally, thousands of protesters poured back into the park. The whiplash of events was palpable, wrote *The New Yorker*'s Elif Batuman, as "over the course of the week, Occupy Gezi transformed from what felt like a festival, with yoga, barbecues, and concerts, into what feels like a war, with barricades, plastic bullets, and gas attacks." The protesters at Occupy Gezi demanded the preservation of the park, an end to police violence, the right to free assembly, and a halt to the sale of public natural resources. Sensing the situation starting to slip beyond his control, Erdoğan declared on television that what the Turkish people were reading on Twitter were lies, and that the clashes were the result of "a few looters." In response, protesters reappropriated the term *çapulcu*, or looters, which became a widely used moniker on social media adopted by those who sympathized with the Gezi uprising.

Apart from the extreme violence inflicted on Istanbul's protesters, Occupy Gezi had a lot of things in common with Occupy Wall Street. Gezi Park had no leaders and no strategic plan beyond occupation. More than half the protesters were under thirty (at Zuccotti the average age was around twenty-five). Both occupations featured a food center offering donated meals, a medical center, musical concerts and a library (Gezi claimed to hold over five thousand books; on the night Occupy Wall Street was dismantled, police threw away more than fifty-five hundred books from The People's Library.) In Istanbul, as in New York, the protesters came without political affiliations or ties to organizations. In neither place did activists openly support or even identify with a party, but instead represented people across the left-right spectrum. At Occupy Gezi, wrote Victor Kotsev in *The Atlantic*, "all of Turkey was represented: the young and the old, the secular and the religious, the soccer hooligans and the blind, anarchists, communists, nationalists, Kurds, gays, feminists, and students."

But the connections didn't end there. In the first week at Occupy, there had been no news coverage. Likewise, Turkish media ignored the Gezi protests for as long as they could, enabling park activists to tell their own story through the expert use of social media. And also like Occupy, each time the state responded with brutal displays of violence, the protests grew and spread—in Gezi's case, bringing hundreds of thousands of people into Istanbul's streets, and erupting in thousands of strikes and protests nationwide, involving some three and a half million people (more than 4 percent of the Turkish population) in ninety cities across nearly all eighty-one provinces. Widespread concerns about Erdoğan's autocratic rule, the growing Islamist influence in government, and the complicity of Turkish media, had drawn "more than students and intellectuals" to the protests, wrote *Der Spiegel*. "Families with children, women in headscarves, men in suits, hipsters in sneakers, pharmacists, tea-house proprietors—all are taking to the streets to register their displeasure."

Hundreds of cities around the world protested in solidarity with the movement at Gezi Park, which police cleared after about two weeks. In the aftermath, President Abdullah Gül announced the suspension of government plans to demolish and redevelop the park, and an investigation was opened into police brutality, with some officers relieved of duty as a result of their actions during the protests. After more than three thousand arrests, eight thousand injuries and at least twenty-two deaths nationwide, Gezi marked the world's biggest protest event since Occupy. Many saw it as a direct continuation. "Occupy people went over and talked to folks at Occupy Gezi, and people from Gezi came to Occupy," the Momentum trainer Nicole Carty told me, because "Occupy was everywhere." For Sara Burke, the events in Istanbul helped crystallize what activists at Zuccotti had accomplished as movements worldwide began to gain momentum. "Gezi seemed to mark the moment when something changed," she said, when "it was clear that Occupy wasn't just a flash in the pan—that the demand to have people's space was universal."

THE WIDENING SNOWDEN REVELATIONS AND THE UPRISING THAT consumed Turkey were a lot to digest that June, yet the news kept coming. On the other side of the planet, in Brazil, the recently elected mayor of São Paulo, Fernando Haddad, announced a hike in the cost of city transit. It wasn't a huge amount—from 3 reals to 3.20, or about a buck thirty-five—but it led to an explosion of protests known as the Free Fare Movement, which later some referred to as the Brazilian Spring. In the way the Turkish people's rebellion in Gezi Park became the catalyst for much wider expressions of dissent against the Erdoğan regime, Brazil's transit fare protests turned out to be about much more than the price of a city bus ticket: they were, at their core, about inequality.

In 2013, South America's biggest nation was in the throes of planning, and building, to host the world's two largest sporting events back-to-back: the 2014 World Cup and the 2016 Olympics in Rio de Janeiro. It was to be the country's coming out party after a record boom based on soaring Chinese demand for commodities like sugar, soy, beef, iron and oil. Brazil's average annual growth topped 5 percent between 2000 and 2012, putting it temporarily ahead of Britain as the world's sixth largest economy. During his popular eight-year presidency, Workers' Party leader Luiz Inácio Lula da Silva helped lift tens of millions of Brazilians out of poverty. But even as the country glowed with new wealth and aspired to join the elite club of nations, Brazil failed to invest in education, healthcare, infrastructure and other basic social services, exacerbating an already highly unequal class structure. Despite more people entering the middle class, the fault lines on inequality were growing and so were the demands to stop rampant corruption. Then, in 2013, financial scandals and budget overruns exploded into view as the country rushed to construct and renovate twelve football stadiums in time for the World Cup, which carried a shocking price tag of $15 billion. (The final outlay for the Rio Olympics two years later would exceed $13 billion.) The breaking point arrived when the cost of a transportation ticket in São Paulo rose twenty cents.

The first revolt, known as the Bus Rebellion, had happened the previous summer in Natal, in northeastern Brazil, where protesters forced officials to cancel that city's planned rate hikes. In the spring of 2013, the action shifted south to the cities of Porto Alegre and Goiania. There, some protests turned violent but likewise achieved their goals: both local governments backed down, eliminating the new transit costs. It was only on June 6, when the mayor of Latin America's largest city tried to impose the same type of increase, that Brazil's regional urban uprisings coalesced into a national one. In response, massive crowds poured onto Avenida Paulista, kicking off a month of protests that brought an estimated two million Brazilians into the streets across more than one hundred cities—from Florianópolis in the south, to Manaus deep in the Amazon interior, to the many urban centers ringing the northeast, like Belem, Recife and Salvador. Within days of the outbreak, the mayors of São Paulo and Rio de Janeiro rescinded the transit fare hikes, though it did little to quell the discontent that had boiled over into the largest demonstrations the country had seen since the reestablishment of democracy in 1985.

Marches and protests occurred in conjunction with soccer matches, fusing Brazilians' love for their national sport with scorn for their leaders. Again, social media played an instrumental role in helping protesters launch and communicate their actions, but it was in the streets where the movement was made. "Twenty cents was just the start," read signs that were held aloft in São Paulo. As one protester, a twenty-nine-year-old civil servant named Savina Santos, told Reuters: "What am I protesting for? You should ask what I'm not protesting for! We need political reform, tax reform, an end to corruption, better schools, better transportation. We are not in a position to be hosting the World Cup." Though the anti-transit fare protests began peacefully, police overreacted by firing tear gas and rubber bullets, injuring scores and further escalating the violence. At different points, protesters smashed windows, burned cars and took over government buildings in a visible outpouring of rage at an economic and political system that had left them behind.

Observers drew some clear connections between the Brazil protests and Occupy, not least because many of the demonstrators explicitly identified with the movement on Wall Street. Activists in Complexo do Alemão, a favela in Rio de Janeiro known for its high levels of crime and drug trafficking, decried police brutality and called themselves Occupy Alemão. For Sara Burke, the protests reflected the core grievance of inequality articulated several years earlier at Occupy, which was now specific to the Brazilian context "where people are saying, 'I can't afford the transportation, I live in a favela, I have a middle-class job—why don't I deserve to have working sanitation and a decent transit system, where it doesn't take me four hours to commute back and forth every day?'"

Writing in *The New York Times*, Simon Romero and William Neuman reported that Brazil, erupting amid a global wave of protests, found itself suddenly "upended by an amorphous, leaderless popular uprising with one unifying theme: an angry, and sometimes violent, rejection of politics as usual." The identification with worldwide social upheavals was evident, they wrote, as was the government's inability to apply a fix. "Much like the Occupy movement in the United States, the anticorruption protests that shook India in recent years, the demonstrations over living standards in Israel or the fury in European nations like Greece, the demonstrators in Brazil are fed up with traditional political structures, challenging the governing party and the opposition alike. And their demands are so diffuse that they have left Brazil's leaders confounded as to how to satisfy them."

2014: EUROPEAN MOVEMENTS BECOME PARTIES

THE DIVERSE MOVEMENTS THAT AROSE OVER THE PAST DECADE, while in some ways unevenly connected, shared at least one basic feature: they all demanded justice in the form of a more honest political representation. Often, the struggles carried steep human costs. In December 2011, exactly twelve weeks after the first Occupiers had showed up at Zuccotti Park, tens of thousands of Russians poured into the streets of Moscow and cities across the country—the largest protests seen there since the fall of the Soviet Union— to denounce ballot-rigging in that month's parliamentary elections. The For Fair Elections demonstrations, later dubbed the Snow Revolution, continued through the month and led to more than a thousand arrests, posing the loudest democratic challenge to date to then prime minister Vladimir Putin, who had declared his intension to seek a third term as president. During ongoing protests in 2012, hundreds of Russian opposition movement leaders were arrested, including Boris Nemtsov—a prominent physicist, politician, and Kremlin critic, whom hired assassins would shoot dead on a Moscow bridge in 2015—and Alexei Navalny, a charismatic lawyer and anti-corruption activist who would be nearly killed in August 2020 after the Russian Federal Security Service allegedly helped poison him using the advanced nerve agent Novichok.

Following the Gezi and Brazil protests of mid-2013, a more sustained and successful rebellion would occur that fall, some five hundred miles southwest of Moscow, when hundreds of thousands of Ukrainian protesters occupied the Maidan, or Independence Square, in Ukraine's capital, Kyiv. After the government of President Viktor Yanukovych had canceled the signing of an association agreement with the European Union, aligning the country more firmly with Russia, popular grievances exploded targeting Ukraine's corrupt, antidemocratic regime. Protesters mounted barricades, seized control of state buildings, and engaged in violent clashes with police that lasted for months during the bitterly cold winter, resulting in many hundreds of deaths. In February 2014, Yanukovych was ousted and fled the country, the protesters proclaimed victory as parliament called for new elections, and Euromaidan, also known as the Revolution of Dignity, came to symbolize the growing power of people's democratic demands in an era of globalized resistance.

The system at its core was corrupt, declared the new generation of protesters, which is why tweaking this or that law would no longer do. From the perspective of many of the activists at Occupy Wall Street, the protest had seemed to be the point. "Occupy brilliantly articulated a crisis of inequality that was such an urgent threat to not just any particular democracy, but to *Democracy*, that people poured into the street. It said, 'We're not going to solve one particular facet of the dilemma with inequality—where, for instance, if we just solve the foreclosure crisis things will be okay, or if we limit executive compensation pay things will be okay,'" Burke told me. "What Occupy really said was 'We take issue with the whole thing.'" But where the Occupy movement didn't take the next step of founding a party, electing candidates and transforming its protest power into political change, others, mainly in Europe, seized on their moment to do so. "What has developed in various ways since 2011 is that the very inequality Occupy originally identified has become now a much more explicitly political fight, [as] we've seen political movements and parties develop, and move more directly into the political realm."

The earliest example of this occurred in Spain, where in the aftermath of the 15-M movement in spring 2011, activists quickly pivoted from the streets and public squares to Madrid backroom meetings where they redesigned themselves into a political party to win power. Los Indignados had gained a global following when they took over more than fifty plazas around the country, on May 15, a week before local elections, demanding "real democracy now" and an end to government controlled by financial interests. Emerging at a moment when 40 percent of Spain's youth remained unemployed, the movement, which followed only a couple of months after the Arab Spring, presented a new style of direct-democratic decision making. As Diego Beas wrote about 15-M in *The Guardian*, "The movement has studiously avoided engaging with ideological agendas, unions and, most importantly, professional politicians . . . city square by city square, individual meeting by individual meeting, thousands of citizens have come together in a networked approach to politics that is fresh and engaging because it defies, above anything else, the hierarchical approach favored by vested interests." But after police brutally cleared the encampments from the parks that summer, the Spanish public was left wondering—similar to the way Americans would wonder after Occupy—where the protesters and their movement had gone. Soon, they had an answer.

In January 2014, activists led by Pablo Iglesias, a television personality and political science professor from Madrid's Complutense University, launched the Podemos party, whose platform sought to oppose austerity policies, restructure the country's debt, crack down on corruption and improve public education, housing and healthcare. In May 2014, backed by a coalition of intellectuals, unions and political allies on the Spanish left, Podemos—*We Can*—won 8 percent of the national vote as five of its members got elected to the European Parliament.

Podemos representatives' first act was to cut their €8,000 monthly parliamentary salaries to less than €2,000—an amount still three times the minimum wage at that point in Spain. A popular Citizens Assembly invited people nationwide to submit principles they wanted the party to adopt. Membership that year grew to nearly two hundred thousand. The following year, Podemos saw its first big city wins when it helped elect the housing rights activist Ada Colau as mayor of Barcelona, and the progressive judge Manuela Carmena as mayor of Madrid. In December 2015, the party solidified its place at the center of Spanish politics when it captured 21 percent of the national vote in the general election, winning sixty-nine seats to become the third largest party in parliament and the country's most successful third party in the post-Franco era.

Podemos had a bold plan: it sought to raise taxes on corporations and the rich, increase the minimum wage, shrink the workweek to thirty-four hours, cap property rental prices, and force banks to reimburse government for bailout funds they received during the financial crisis and recession. But rather than succeed in passing any landmark legislation, the party instead helped to prevent the formation of a ruling coalition, the absence of which brought Spain's government to a deadlocked standstill. The results weren't what the party's supporters had in mind. After shaking up the status quo, Podemos led the way for an era of political newcomers, from the center-right Ciudadanos to the ultranationalist, anti-immigrant Vox party. A series of missteps and intra-party conflicts further diminished Podemos's glow; by 2019, in the country's fourth election in four years, Podemos had merged, with other leftist groups to form Unidas Podemos, which came in fourth in parliament, winning fewer seats than Vox but enough to form a ruling coalition with the Spanish Socialist Workers' Party.

Even if Podemos in the initial years failed to secure wins that built on protest momentum and its promises from the streets, the party demonstrated something that hadn't been done by a movement within the global Left. As the Occupy London media organizer Ronan McNern said of 15-M's political transformation: "They went into power, and they got power."

WHILE PODEMOS WAS SURGING TO PROMINENCE IN THE MIDDLE OF the last decade, Greek anti-austerity protests fueled the rise of an even more powerful political movement led by the Coalition of the Radical Left, or Syr-iza. Founded in 2004 by an alliance of ecologists, communists, democratic socialists and workers, the Syriza party had consistently garnered around 5 percent support. But by 2010, the Greek economy was in tatters. Mired in debt by hundreds of billions of euros, the country agreed to numerous rounds of austerity imposed by EU creditors, who forced Greece to privatize state assets, "restructure" its healthcare and welfare systems, raise taxes across the board and make deep cuts to social spending. Economic misery grew and strikes became a regular feature of life in Greece, where more than half the popula-tion under thirty remained without work. In 2011, the number of suicides in the country sharply rose, and suddenly, ideas that a few years earlier seemed radical or even unthinkable—for instance, allowing Greece to default on its loans and abandon the EU in the form of a "Grexit"—found growing support.

Seizing the moment, Syriza positioned itself as the party able to offer fresh, populist solutions from the left, and in 2012 it won 16 percent of the vote to become the second largest force in Greek parliament. Following several more economically disastrous years for the country, in January 2015, Syriza took 36 percent of the vote to win majority control of parliament on a promise to abolish the EU austerity contract, raise taxes on Greece's oligarchs, and lead the nation out of the debt crisis. The question loomed whether Greece, the birthplace of Western democracy, would step forward and succeed in rewriting the rules. Alexis Tsipras, the party's leader, took over as prime minister and appointed a new generation of reformers who set out to rebuild the Greek state.

The most visible among them was his choice for finance minister, Yanis Varoufakis, a dashing Marxist economist who had taught at the University of Texas at Austin, and earned instant celebrity status when he took on the EU financial chiefs. Rejecting the austerity terms of agreement, Varoufakis likened the Troika's treatment of Greece to "a fiscal waterboarding," and compared the country's bailout conditions to a modern Versailles Treaty—one where Germany, this time, was making others pay. According to *The New Yorker*'s Ian Parker, during a meeting at the White House, President Obama told Varoufakis he didn't envy him the task of trying to dig Greece out of its deepening hole of debt, to which Varoufakis responded: "You inherited a mess when you came to office, but at least you have your central bank behind you. We inherited a mess and we have a [European Central Bank] trying to choke us." Obama reportedly admitted to Varoufakis that Washington's agreement to bail out Wall Street was like taking "political poison," and advised the Greek finance minister to "swallow bitter stuff" in the interests of the nation.

In June 2015, Tsipras called a referendum to let the Greek people decide whether to accept more austerity concessions in exchange for billions in further loans. The people issued an overwhelming "No": 61 percent voted against versus 39 percent in favor, more than a three-fifths majority. Yet Tsipras, the former anti-austerity crusader, ignored public will and settled on another three-year bailout agreement—including even more onerous austerity measures than the version Greek voters had rejected. Varoufakis, who left government, dubbed the agreement "Greece's Terms of Surrender" and later transitioned the rebellion against Europe's financial and political elite into a new phase with the launch of an organization called the Democracy in Europe Movement 2025, or DiEM25. Led by progressives committed to saving the EU by, among other things, instituting a Green New Deal for Europe, DiEM25 in some ways resembled the "political revolution" that Bernie Sanders introduced to the United States in 2016. The two movements fused with the creation of a new alliance in 2019 called the Progressive International.

For Sara Burke, the trend was striking. "We've seen Bernie and Varoufakis launch a new international movement, and the question is: Can these social movements put pressure on the political class at an international level, too?" she said. Greece had failed in its effort to stand up to the European financial powers. But "we need the development of international political movements to go beyond the limitations of national governance, and the Progressive International is a recognition that we have to have an international political movement, not just a social movement. Don't underestimate the progressive fuel to reform institutions."

EUROPE'S THIRD AND PERHAPS MOST QUIXOTIC POPULIST POLITI-cal movement to emerge from the 2011 protest era was the Five Star Movement of Italy, which rose in 2013 to challenge and fundamentally reshape the Italian political establishment. Five Star had begun in Milan in 2009 out of the office of an internet consulting firm called Casaleggio Associati, run by the web strategist Gianroberto Casaleggio. Some years earlier, in 2005, the comedian and blogger Beppe Grillo had effectively launched the movement when he railed against the corruption of Italy's parliament and called for a new era of social networking to transform politics. From those grassroots, internet-based origins (the "Friends of Beppe Grillo" held numerous national meetings), the movement built a committed following around ecological, de-growth, anti-establishment, anti-corruption and anti-globalist principles. The group ran candidates in local and regional elections for several years, winning only small percentages of the vote each time. But in the aftermath of the 2011 European and Occupy uprisings, its ideas came into vogue.

Part protest movement and part politics, Five Star's genius, according to the former *Adbusters* editor Micah White, was its skill "blending horizontalism with verticalism: a hybridization of populist direct democracy with closed membership." The stars in the name represented the five core demands in the movement platform: sustainable transportation, sustainable development, a free and open internet, publicly owned water and, in the most general sense, environmentalism. The Five Star Movement never fit neatly into either the left or the right; it later earned a major following for its Euroskeptic and anti-immigrant views. But perhaps most significantly, it spoke to the populist anger that was brewing in Italy where, like its Mediterranean neighbors, people were drowning in unemployment and felt they were paying an unfair price for the Euro debt crisis. In 2013, four years after its formal founding, the movement exploded on the scene, shocking pollsters as it won over eight and a half million votes—more than a quarter of the total—to become Italy's second biggest party.

Five Star went on to receive 21 percent of the vote in the 2014 European parliamentary elections, but its views were seen as too risky to allow for alliances with parties on either the left or the right. Like Podemos in Spain, it refused to join a national coalition, and also suffered from persistent infighting and dissension within the organization, contributing to the further logjam in Italian politics. Two of its members, Virginia Raggi and Chiara Appendino, went on in 2016 to become the mayors of Rome and Turin, respectively, and the Five Star Movement won nearly 38 percent of the vote to become the largest individual party in parliament in 2018. Efforts at coalition building failed with the center-left Democratic Party led by Matteo Renzi. Finally, to the chagrin of many former supporters, Five Star found a home with the anti-immigrant Northern League party, whose so-called government of change ruled in coalition for about a year.

In looking at the emergence of Podemos, Syriza and the Five Star Movement, a pattern seems to emerge—as it does throughout history—in which young radical voices calling for a shakeup of the status quo ultimately find their way into office and then, to greater or lesser degrees, fail to deliver on the transformational change they promised. Nonetheless, the remarkably fast rise of all three parties, the way they used their decentralized activist networks to fuel their growing popularity, and the fact that many of their once-radical ideas have become accepted as mainstream, reflect some of the systemic changes that the movements helped bring about.

Occupy, as Micah White put it in *The End of Protest,* "was a wake-up call to break the script of contemporary protest and rethink the principles of achieving social change through collective action." In response to that global social moment, he wrote, "the rise of Syriza in Greece, the Five Star Movement in Italy and Podemos in Spain reveals a trend toward internet-enabled people's parties that ascend at dazzling speed." Indeed, it was perhaps the sheer novelty and momentum of these parties, rather than their deft management of the political halls of power, that so far has made the most lasting impact. As Burke said, "Hopefully we'll see an emerging dynamic where progressive social movements can hold progressive political parties to account, and where the parties can actually be legitimate enough to say they represent the movements." Occupy teetered "right on the edge" of politics without actually entering it, she added. "It was all-embracing, a new revelation—it wasn't something that people were comfortable confining to the typical political debate. Now we have political parties that have been directly influenced by Occupy—like Podemos, maybe Syriza, maybe Five Star—while others have veered off into right-wing populism."

2015: GLOBAL GRIEVANCES TURN TO THE RIGHT

AS BURKE AND HER RESEARCH TEAM AT THE FRIEDRICH-EBERT-Stiftung continued to study the rise of global protests and their causes, they ran into another, more uncomfortable discovery. Whether in reaction to the left-wing populism birthed in 2011, or as a different response to some of the same grievances raised in those protests, a global right-wing insurgency was likewise emerging—and not only competing for attention but, in many instances, organizing politically with greater speed and effectiveness than its left-wing counterpart. Tapping into a mood of nationalism and xenophobia that was growing across Europe, Latin America and the United States, reactionary populist movements rose to prominence over the last decade by flipping the protest playbook on its head. As Burke recalled, it was around 2013 when she and her colleagues spotted a trend of right-wing protests gathering momentum worldwide. "We started noticing something we called 'denial of rights,' where in addition to all of these positive protests [supporting] what we think of as rights, we were also seeing protests that were about suppressing the rights of other people," from immigrants to leftists to LGBTQ people, she said. The pendulum was swinging backward, this time echoing global grievances of the far right.

The left-populist protests of 2011, like 15-M and Occupy, may not have been the direct cause of an emergent right wing, Burke told me. But the movements "unleashed" a darker side of the public's frustrations with the status quo, in most cases reflecting white populations' fears that they were being swallowed up by immigrants and multiculturalism and left behind by the global economy. The new right-wing movements were only partly distinguishable by the variety of labels they adopted, or which others gave to them: nationalist, ultranationalist, ethnonationalist, neofascist, right-wing populist, identitarian, anti-Islam, anti-immigrant. But what they all shared was an underlying rage, because deeper beneath, "maybe it was simply part of a larger discontent about inequality and the uneven shifting of wealth into the hands of the rich," said Burke, yet finally, "what they see is dark people getting more, and themselves getting less, and they're so easily manipulated to believe that."

Following the debt crisis and the global recession, simmering right-wing populism in Europe found its moment with the migrant crisis of 2015. After more than one million refugees entered the continent, fleeing from war and instability in Afghanistan, Syria, Iraq and elsewhere, the anti-immigrant backlash was swift—and had direct, visible impacts on Europe's policies and culture. In Britain, the nationalist U.K. Independence Party was instrumental in pushing the 2016 vote for Brexit past the finish line. In Germany, massive demonstrations by Patriotic Europeans Against the Islamization of the Occident, or Pegida, lent street muscle to the new far-right Alternative for Germany, which by 2017 became the third-most-represented party in the Bundestag. In the Mediterranean countries, powerful ultra-right or openly fascist parties seemed to emerge in tandem with those on the left: the Golden Dawn in Greece, the Vox party in Spain, the Northern League in Italy. Across the rest of Europe, right-wing extremism had equally found its place at the ballot box—from Poland's Law and Justice party and France's National Front, to the Party for Freedom in Holland, the Finns Party in Finland, and the Fidesz and Jobbik ultra-right parties in Hungary. Within a few years of Occupy, rather than countries moving farther to the left, a nationalist, xenophobic populism had redefined Europe's political landscape.

A similar pattern emerged in the United States, where resentment and fear of immigrants coupled with growing economic frustrations among white, working-class voters delivered Donald Trump a nationalist, "America First" victory in 2016. But for Burke, a more illustrative example of the global right-wing backlash occurred in Brazil. After the transit fare protests shook the nation in 2013, people talked about wealth redistribution and greater economic inclusion; yet simultaneously, a nationalist movement based on exclusion gathered force. In 2014, right-wing populists aligned with the Free Brazil Movement began to dominate the streets, holding widely attended protests that reshaped the national discussion. Fueled by a reactionary middle-class base whose libertarian principles correlated with the Tea Party in the United States, the movement whipped up public anger over corruption charges. It called for the destruction of the Workers' Party, specifically the takedown of its leader, President Dilma Rousseff, a goal it ultimately achieved en route to electing an ultra-right former army captain, Jair Bolsonaro, to the presidency in 2018. "Part of the fight to bring down inequality involves choices and trade-offs," Burke said, "and so far those trade-offs have not required the super wealthy and corporations to pay their share." In Brazil, as a result, "we're seeing the middle class get squeezed and that's fueling populist movements, which have also been taken advantage of by nimble, right-wing populist parties with smart social media capacities."

In a more complex crossover between left- and right-wing populism, the Yellow Vest movement appeared on the streets of France in the fall of 2018. Spurred by rising fuel costs and government tax reforms, which people said fell too heavily on the shoulders of workers and the middle class, the movement staged mass marches and nationwide road blockades that caused repeated shutdowns of Paris as protesters clashed with police. Calling for economic justice, higher taxes on the rich, a raise of the minimum wage, greater government accountability and an end to austerity measures, the Yellow Vests, like Occupy before them, represented voices across the political spectrum and employed many of the same decentralized protesting tactics. As Burke put it, the movement's "politics are up for grabs, because it is where the right and the left sort of meet. The collapse of upward mobility and middle-class aspirations—the collapse of the social contract—leaves people vulnerable to organizations both right and left, and I think the grievances of the Yellow Vests are something that we have to listen to." White discontent may have also played a role in the movement, but what really motivated people was "an uncompromised rage at the unfair and broken status quo. The protests have tried to stay somewhat distant from parties or leaders per se, because the point is to pressure them, not to become them. One of the reasons these movements have grown, from Occupy to the Yellow Vests, is a mistrust of experts, of technocrats."

The Yellow Vests raged in France throughout 2019, and in March 2020 they made headlines by defying stay-at-home measures on the eve of local elections amid the coronavirus pandemic. The late organizer Kevin Zeese said he saw powerful parallels between Occupy and the Yellow Vests, which emerged as a genuinely working-class movement opposing privatization, globalization and neoliberal policies that have driven ever more wealth toward the 1 percent. "They want better wages and an end to homelessness. The Yellow Vests are an aggressive, anti-neoliberal movement that stands for dealing with climate change, economic insecurity, better healthcare," Zeese told me. "They were angry about [French president Emmanuel] Macron giving massive tax breaks to the wealthiest in France and then increasing taxes on people who drive to work. They said, 'Don't put climate change on our backs, put it on the backs of those who've made money.' It was a working-class revolt against burdening the working class when they should have been burdening those who made money off the status quo."

2019: REVOLUTION IN HONG KONG

PERHAPS THE MOST ENDURING GLOBAL LEGACY OF OCCUPY, THE pro-democracy uprising known as Occupy Central with Love and Peace, began in September 2014 in Hong Kong. After the Chinese Communist Party in Beijing attempted to change Hong Kong's electoral laws, stripping the special administrative region's citizens of the right to elect their own chief executive and legislative council, young people flooded the streets and took over the city's financial district. Led by the Hong Kong Federation of Students and the vanguard group Scholarism, tens of thousands of mostly young protesters occupied major roadways, bringing business, schools and much of Hong Kong daily life to a standstill. Young organizers like Joshua Wong emerged as courageous spokespeople as the call for democratic rights in Hong Kong reverberated globally. For three months, the movement sustained a successful civil disobedience campaign that became known as the Umbrella Movement because of the way protesters used umbrellas as shields to defend themselves en masse against water cannons fired by police. The activists were met with harsh repression; scenes of tear gas, beatings and other forms of police brutality were transmitted around the world in real time using similar livestream and social media tactics as those developed by Occupy. People saw Hong Kong in many ways as Occupy's natural successor.

"Occupy most certainly helped spur the Occupy Central movement in Hong Kong," said Nicole Carty, who was invited to the city in 2013, one year prior to the movement, to train student leaders and other activists in strategies of direct-democratic organizing. "Hong Kongers were taking a lot of lessons from Occupy in planning this massive escalation to push for democratic rights," she told me. The protesters planned the movement "to trigger this occupation." Commenting in 2015 on the global impacts of Occupy, Ross Perlin wrote in *Dissent* magazine, "Tiny Zuccotti inspired a global archipelago of Occupy offshoots, but Turkey's Occupy Gezi and Hong Kong's more recent Occupy movement mark an inflection point. Sustained, fiercely local mass movements are tapping into and extending a new global language of protest." According to Perlin, the Occupy movement had devised what resembled a one-size-fits-all formula for social movement activism. "Occupy is serving as an open-source template for dissent, a transparent and adaptable playbook for organizing global movements with diverse aims and values," he wrote. "By turns autonomous and hyperconnected, the template is an uncanny fit for our precarious, plugged-in life."

After enduring harsh repression from the state in the fall of 2014, the rebellion in Hong Kong subsided in 2015. There were periodic outbursts of protester activity over the next few years. Then, in March 2019, the pro-democracy movement sprang back to life in response to the Hong Kong government's introduction of a bill allowing extraditions to mainland China. People surged into the streets as fresh demonstrations roiled the country. The protests drew hundreds of thousands that summer, posing a direct challenge to the Beijing-appointed regime. In October, the government instituted an anti-mask law as part of a broader crackdown, arresting many prominent activists and lawmakers. Protests continued, the extradition bill was withdrawn, and Hong Kongers appeared to be gaining momentum. But in the summer of 2020, as the world dealt with the coronavirus pandemic, China's Communist Party passed restrictive legislation outlawing any public forms of dissent, including protesting, holding signs or chanting anti-China slogans. The repression from Beijing was a bitter pill to swallow for the generational pro-democracy movement that had laid it all on the line.

Occupy Central and the Hong Kong rebellion revealed Occupy's expansion into a global hybrid movement that condemned the excesses of either the capitalist or communist systems when they trampled on people's essential rights. "Hong Kong was inspired by Occupy," said Burke, and "we see what's at stake for them in the transformation from an open society to the kind of totalitarian regulation and observation that they get under the Chinese government." In the case of Hong Kong, people were fighting for something different from Occupy Wall Street. "It wasn't about inequality of an economic nature," Burke told me. "It boiled down to freedom and real democracy."

The dramatic action in Hong Kong was just one of many mass mobilizations organized by protesters globally in 2019, which became known as the year of the protest. From the youth-led Global Climate Strikes to "Arab Spring 2.0" protests that rocked the Arab world from Algeria to Lebanon, social movements were in ascent. "The impression from the mainstream [media] is that everything died down, and now it's risen up again," Burke added. Protests today may be different in some ways from the kind that spread across the planet a decade ago. Specifically, she said, "the kinds of protest that we're seeing now aren't necessarily grounded in a transformational vision of greater equality for everyone, [but] are asserting rights that have been denied to different groups." Nonetheless, "there are a lot of linkages and direct contacts between what was going on in the Occupy era and what might be going on right now."

2020: THE YEAR EVERYTHING CHANGED

IN LATE JUNE 2020, FOLLOWING A MONTH OF NATIONWIDE PRO-tests against systemic racism and police violence over the killing of George

Floyd by Minneapolis police, thousands of Black Lives Matter activists camped out in New York City as part of a campaign they called Occupy City Hall. The effort to push New York lawmakers to cut $1 billion from the city police department failed, but the message their protest sent was clear: the biggest social justice movements of their generation were, in some elemental sense, now a part of one another. For Burke, seeing the heavy participation of white people in the Black Lives Matter movement indicated the growing power of its message. The movement had also spread internationally: racist policing was no longer just America's problem, it was the world's. "The concern about Black lives wasn't limited to the U.S. It was taken up in other countries like Germany, Holland, the U.K. and France, [showing] the lack of support that people of color feel from police everywhere," she told me. "Putting white bodies in between the police and Black bodies" reflected a new level of solidarity that "would not even have been imaginable this time last year. We seem to be in a time where the unimaginable can suddenly become imaginable."

Like the racial justice protests, the coronavirus pandemic exposed deep fissures of inequality in America, especially the economic disparity when it came to healthcare. Looking back on the first two decades of the millennium, Burke identified three major crisis points—the first two of which had provoked different forms of restructuring. In 2001, following the attacks of 9/11, came legal restructuring with the Patriot Act and the buildup of the surveillance state. The crash in 2008 produced financial restructuring with Dodd-Frank and tighter international lending laws. Following 2020, Burke said, the restructuring would happen on a much broader scale, due to the "socio-ecological economic transformation" that more and more people were demanding.

"I think we don't have any idea yet how deep the economic crisis we're on the cusp of really is, and the depth of the restructuring that could follow," she said. "This crisis may be forcing us to reexamine the institutions, because if they can't deliver, and we have democracies that don't seem real, people are going to be very angry in a way that may not be as creative an anger as Occupy was—it might be messier anger, like 'How much more of this shit are you going to make us take?'" The 2008 financial crash and its fallout helped crystallize for people the ways that the political and economic systems are not working for them, providing them a clear rationale to demand change. "There will be simmering anger from the Occupy generation, which has already been hard hit by these global crises as they're trying to get their lives off the ground," Burke concluded. "What a lot of the ongoing protest movements since Occupy have in common is this sense of betrayal by the elites. It's causing a lot of anger. Today's generation doesn't want safety: they want justice. I think we're going to see an era where we're forced to focus on why people are upset, and the failure, again and again, to come up with a just economic system."

THE OCCUPY CARAVAN

JULY 4, 2012

DURING THE WINTER OF 2012, THE NUMBER OF OCCUPY ACTIVISTS dwindled as plans for a movement comeback faltered. The autumn closure of the encampments had presented organizers with an opportunity to retreat indoors and advance from their initial goal of "liberating space" to a more realistic vision offering social and economic solutions. Many held out the hope that Occupy Wall Street would revive and recreate itself to launch a second act. But the evolution never occurred because the activists from Zuccotti Park had no blueprint for moving forward, and could not agree on the need or the strategy to create one. Leaderless, structureless, directionless, Occupy came apart over the course of several seasons, although it took some people, myself included, longer to reckon with the results. I wasn't ready to leave the movement. In April 2012, I joined a dozen activists to launch Occupy.com, a news site fusing protest coverage and political analysis to deepen the discussion around economic and social justice. On May Day, Occupy Wall Street's last big march drew thirty thousand people into the streets of Manhattan in what felt like the unofficial send-off for a movement that had lost its focus and organizing power.

After the march, some of us who didn't know what we'd be doing or where we'd be going next, hit the road. In early June 2012, I returned to California to help lead a mad three-week, twenty-city journey across America called the Occupy Caravan. Assisted by a $10,000 donation from Ben Cohen of Ben & Jerry's, the caravan set off from two cities, Oakland and Los Angeles, en route to the Occupy National Gathering happening in Philadelphia in the lead-up to the Fourth of July. From the mountains to the plains, our motley crew of several dozen activists sought to reawaken the movement across the heartland. The slogan of the trip, "This Land Is Our Land," honored the one-hundred-year anniversary of the birth of legendary folk music and social justice icon Woody Guthrie. In a tribute to Guthrie, we designed the itinerary so that the two flanks of the caravan converged halfway across the country in Okemah, Oklahoma, the singer's hometown.

In each city that our troupe landed—Reno, Salt Lake, Denver through the country's middle; Las Vegas, Albuquerque, Amarillo across the south—Occupy groups provided a rowdy, food-filled welcome with coordinated and newsworthy protests. Camping in forests and cities, crashing on couches as we traversed the continent, we marched on Koch Industries headquarters in Wichita; disrupted an oil conference in New Orleans; and protested against home foreclosures at PNC Bank in Atlanta, Bank of America headquarters in Charlotte, and the governor's residence in Raleigh. We even demonstrated in the sweltering late June heat of Washington, D.C., where we swarmed the United States Postal Service headquarters to demand that Congress fund rather than privatize the nation's centuries-old mail service.

Our journey was a lot like Occupy: colorful and chaotic, inspiring and self-defeating. As a driver and organizer, I felt bound in my leadership role to enforce some rules of the road, but my attempts to maintain order were met by disruptive and at times violent challenges from anarchists who inflicted a

unique brand of mayhem on our road trip. In one incident that occurred outside a warehouse where we were sleeping in Little Rock, Arkansas, my refusal
to hand over the vehicle keys to a defiant twenty-year-old activist ended with
his kicking a dent into our Toyota rental van as people rushed in to stop our
fight. (The traveler, who called me "authoritarian" and "a fascist," was eventually ejected from the trip by consensus and deposited at a Greyhound station
in Atlanta). Later, in Asheville, North Carolina, an Occupier with bipolar disorder threw a violent late-night tantrum in the basement of our elderly host
couple's home after I asked him to turn down his music.

What I had experienced in New York was reinforced on the caravan: the
sense of frustration and difficulty working with anarchists to build an effective social movement. According to Peter Gelderloos, author of *The Failure
of Nonviolence: From the Arab Spring to Occupy*, "Anarchists generally believe
in a social revolution, which means the destruction of the existing political
structure and all coercive hierarchies, without the imposition of a new political
structure, therefore allowing everyone to organize themselves freely." Organizing themselves "freely" meant that the anarchist elements at Occupy took
guidance and direction from no one; at the same time, by rejecting any form
of leadership, they obstructed and impeded others' efforts to craft a coherent road map for the movement. Fears—both paranoid and legitimate—that
forces within the Democratic establishment and progressive institutions were
seeking to co-opt Occupy further served to hamper the movement's growth.

As a result, during the winter and spring months of 2012, Occupy Wall
Street became a painful exercise in process over progress, as strategic planning
increasingly took a back seat to discussions about protocol and consensus-
based decision making. Long before our caravan undertaking, anarchist con-
tingents had forced movement organizers into a monthslong debate around
so-called diversity of tactics in response to police violence. In February, after
Occupy members had engaged in televised property destruction in Oakland,
the journalist Chris Hedges published a controversial article in *Truthdig* calling black bloc anarchists "the cancer of Occupy." Most people in the move-

ment agreed that a minority's willingness to commit violence was hurting the cause of economic justice. But without any hierarchy, structure or organization to enforce rules of behavior, Occupy organizers had no method to prevent or punish those forms of "direct action" that disrupted, rather than enhanced, their message.

During the Occupy National Gathering that took place that summer around Washington Square and Independence Mall in downtown Philadelphia, hundreds of activists participated in five days of marches, trainings, assemblies and performances, which culminated in a night of tumult on July Fourth. As thousands of revelers converged on Benjamin Franklin Parkway to watch the fireworks, Occupy protesters faced off with baton-and-shield-wielding police, engaging in an hours-long game of cat and mouse in the crowded streets where activists had hoped to spark a citywide protest. Suddenly, in the distance, shots rang out. People started running as excitement became replaced by fear. We later learned that two people, unrelated to Occupy, had been shot that night. The experience in Philadelphia felt like a premonition, a warning of greater volatility ahead.

Exhausted by the growing sense of disorder and discord, I withdrew from the movement. I retreated that summer to my father's house on the Saranac River in upstate New York, trying to figure out next steps. I spent time walking in the Adirondack foothills, grateful for the opportunity to lose myself in nature. I attempted to write, but the experience was too close and too fresh to see clearly. My recovery from Occupy took time. It wasn't easy abandoning the hopes that I, like many others, had invested in the movement. I also wasn't ready to give up. The resistance had begun; now it was time to bring solutions into being. I continued working as the editor of Occupy.com, managing a team of national and global correspondents reporting through a lens of the 99 percent. These writers and activists narrated the growing number of stories about popular resistance and reforms gathering strength across America and around the world. People eventually started picking up the threads, as Occupy evolved into many other movements.

In the fall of 2012, a year behind schedule, I returned to Europe to take care of my divorce. I then moved back to California and got on with my life. I started a family, published a novel and began teaching journalism at a local community college. All that time, as a participant in the movement's evolution, I never took my eyes off the stage that Occupy had set for a decade of sweeping political and social change. The Occupy movement had ended, yet the ideas, projects and networks that people developed at Zuccotti Park were only getting started. Seeds had been planted. Now many of them were beginning to flourish with remarkable results, a divergent blossoming that continues to grow.

9

OCCUPY FUTURE

THE SOLUTIONARIES

STUDENT DEBT RESISTANCE: THOMAS GOKEY

THOMAS GOKEY GRADUATED WITH A MASTER'S DEGREE FROM THE Art Institute of Chicago saddled with $70,000 in student debt. As an adjunct professor teaching studio art at Syracuse University, Gokey spent a lot of time thinking about the economic hole he was in. He even began an independent research project, hoping to "figure out some creative solution" that would make the problem go away. Beyond his own financial concerns, Gokey said, "I saw how much debt my students were going into, and I saw how much I was getting paid—roughly minimum wage—and it didn't make sense." Millennials graduated owing nearly four times as much debt as students from Generation X, and Gokey wanted to know: "Why do my students need to take on $60,000 of debt for a degree?"

In the fall of 2011, he had taken a leave of absence to focus on an art project, and was in the middle of reading David Graeber's seminal book, *Debt: The First 5,000 Years*, when Occupy hit the headlines. Gokey didn't hesitate.

He hopped a Greyhound bus to New York City, where he knew no one, "and went down to Zuccotti with a backpack and a sleeping bag. I showed up after the sun had set," he recalled, "it was raining at the time and they weren't allowing tents, so I just slept in the rain that night, and kept doing that because it just kept raining." Over the next few days, he had countless conversations in the park, each of which seemed to return to the basic question of "Where exactly do we have power and leverage over Wall Street?" Gokey realized, "every month when we pay our debts, that's how we cooperate" with the big banks, and at one point, a "big switch flipped in my head." The way he had been thinking about student debt was wrong, because it was no longer a personal problem requiring a personal solution. Rather, "within forty-eight hours of being in Zuccotti, it was 'We need a mass debt strike.' Instead of figuring out a clever way to pay it off," Gokey concluded, "we need to all refuse to pay it."

On November 17, 2011, two days after Occupy protesters were evicted from Zuccotti Park, Gokey got arrested in a large civil disobedience action on Wall Street. He and his comrades spent a couple days in jail plotting the next steps of a movement that no longer had a home. To exercise real power over the banks, Gokey believed, people needed to put the Gandhian model of nonviolent resistance to the test by organizing mass non-cooperation with the system. Though most American consumers didn't realize it, the debt that consumed them was also a form of leverage that they could use against the banks. If thousands—and ultimately millions—withheld payments on medical bills, credit cards and student debt, it would "cut off the flow of money and power," and "liberate all of that wealth to do other things." Gokey wasn't alone in his thinking. "One of the things that Occupy did was have all of these really creative, brilliant, dedicated people come out of the woodwork and find each other," he said. With the encampment cleared, Gokey and other organizers agreed: it was time to act on student debt.

A short time later, the Occupy Student Debt working group declared an ambitious target: to get one million people to stop paying their student debt. In the spring of 2012, after the May Day march, movement activists created a new organization called Strike Debt explicitly committed to debt resistance. As student debt in the United States surpassed $1 trillion, the group did something original: it invited young people to publicly share their stories and personal shame around debt, enabling a generation to open up about the stigma for the first time. "They had never talked about it before and now they were talking about this thing that was controlling their lives," said Gokey.

David Graeber, one of the architects of the phrase *We are the 99 percent* and a towering mind in the global left community of political economics, died suddenly of necrotizing pancreatitis in September 2020 at the age of fifty-nine. It was Graeber who had sent Gokey an email explaining the basic idea of how debt abolishment worked. "At first I read and didn't understand the email," Gokey told me, "then a couple of weeks later I went back to it and I was scratching my head, it seemed too good to be true, so I asked [Graeber] some follow-up questions. Then I just went down the rabbit hole." Gokey spent the summer studying and learning how to buy debt on the secondary market. He would cold-call debt buyers and conduct informal interviews asking them about how they did their jobs. Most of them got impatient and hung up. The work tended to attract a personality type, people "looking for quick money all of the time," he told me. "Nobody gets into the debt buying business because they're a good guy."

In September 2012, Strike Debt published one of the Occupy movement's defining documents: a 122-page book called *The Debt Resistors' Operations Manual*, which declared its aim "to provide specific tactics for understanding and fighting against the debt system so that we can all reclaim our lives and our communities." The book explained how all of the major forms of debt worked—from credit scores and credit cards to medical, student, housing and municipal debt—and laid out in detail how the debt collection business operated. The manual shared resources and tips about ways that people could individually fight back against paying debts and collectively resist making those payments as a society.

That fall, Strike Debt launched the Rolling Jubilee, a fundraising project to purchase and abolish a portion of the country's student debt. Gokey initially hoped the group's telethon would raise around $5,000, enough to buy $1 million in student debt off the secondary debt market. But his fellow organizers aimed higher: they wanted to raise fifty thousand. On the November night telethon, exactly a year after Occupy protesters were evicted from Zuccotti, Strike Debt raised a quarter of a million dollars. That amount nearly tripled, passing $700,000 by the end of the fundraiser. The organization then proceeded, like any other investor, to buy graduates' debt off the secondary market, Gokey told me, paying "four cents on the dollar, on average, depending what type of debt and how old it was." Over the next several years, Strike Debt purchased more than $30 million in student debt, then "we destroyed it, we abolished it," he said, because "it was our view that this debt shouldn't exist in the first place."

By exposing how the secondary market worked, Strike Debt flipped the debt burden on its head—organizing people to refuse to pay and if debt collectors contacted them, "to call their bluff and dispute the debt" because collectors had only paid a fraction of what they were demanding. The logic was "Why do you owe them anything?" said Gokey. "If they purchased it for four cents on the dollar, why should you pay the full amount for it?" In the process of buying portfolios of student debt, mainly from predatory for-profit colleges like Corinthian Colleges and University of Phoenix, Strike Debt acquired people's names, emails and contact information, which allowed them to send congratulatory letters to each student whose debt had been destroyed.

In 2015, Strike Debt went further by creating a "debtors' union," called the Debt Collective, to organize mass payment refusal. Rather than be in default, the group said, people should be on strike. The debt strike started small with just fifteen members, then grew to two hundred and, later, included more than one thousand graduates who had committed to stop paying their student debt. Organizers of the Debt Collective received help from lawyers who taught them about a little-known rule, passed by Congress during the Clinton administration as a part of the Higher Education Reauthorization Act, called the borrower defense to repayment law. The law asserted that a person had the right to defend him or herself against the forced repayment of a fraudulent debt—when, for example, a school broke the law. No one, not even lawyers from the National Consumer Law Center or the Project on Predatory Student Lending at Harvard Law School, had applied the borrower defense to repayment provision to halt student debt payments. The Debt Collective presented its strategy to members of the Obama administration, who were "extremely reluctant" to take up the measure, Gokey told me. "We had to fight them tooth and nail, every inch of the way, but the law was on our side."

There was no precedent for what Strike Debt was trying to do because the playbook hadn't been written, said Gokey, so "we made it up on our own." The group created its own paperwork, which it sent out to its large list of student debtor contacts, asking them to fill out the forms. Suddenly, in addition to the student debt strike, thousands of borrower defense forms came flooding in, since "a lot of people who couldn't go on strike could still fill out this paperwork and assert a claim." The actions had gotten the attention of the Obama administration, which set up an in-person meeting between representatives of Strike Debt and the undersecretary of education, Ted Mitchell. And at the meeting, Gokey said, "we surprised everybody by presenting them a red box full of thousands of these applications."

The conversation was now in progress, which meant the federal Department of Education could no longer ignore the growing debt claims. Massachusetts senator Elizabeth Warren, a specialist in debt and consumer protection laws, brought further media attention to the issue by pressuring Obama to take action to forgive student debt. After the collapse of Corinthian Colleges, the education department discharged tens of millions of dollars in debt for some fifteen thousand students before handing the process over to Donald Trump's education department, led by Betsy DeVos, who stalled the claims by litigating through the courts. As a result, more than two hundred thousand borrower defense claims sat unprocessed during the Trump administration. Obama's team "could have, with one signature, cancelled all of the debt from

Corinthian Colleges," said Gokey. Finally, after courts forced the administration to process the applications late in Trump's term, the Department of Education denied 94 percent of them, "even though they should have granted close to ninety-four percent of them, if they were to follow the law."

Even in the Trump era, debt resistance efforts started to show results. The movement influenced Bernie Sanders, who in 2017 introduced legislation to make public universities debt-free. In the summer of 2019, when Representative Ilhan Omar of Minnesota introduced a bill in the House to cancel all student debt, Gokey and others from the Debt Collective were invited to Washington to talk about the ways debt impacted their lives. Sanders's call to cancel student debt and fully fund public universities became a central theme of the 2020 Democratic primaries; that same year, the coronavirus spurred Congress to set a temporary moratorium on student debt as part of the CARES Act. Gokey's team, which by then had helped more than ten thousand people submit defense to repayment applications, sought to make the moratorium permanent by urging people to "not send in student debt payments and default."

A parallel debt resistance group that emerged from Occupy Wall Street was RIP Medical Debt, co-founded by Jerry Ashton, author of *End Medical Debt: Curing America's $1 Trillion Unpayable Healthcare Debt*. Ashton, who was seventy-four years old at the time of Occupy, understood precisely what the young protesters were trying to do. He came to Zuccotti Park prepared to help because he had worked in the debt collection industry for forty years. Debt was his career, and he knew his way around all kinds of commercial debt, hospital debt, newspaper debt, payday loan debt. After the Rolling Jubilee in 2012, Ashton said he helped coordinate Strike Debt's initial purchase of $1 million of debt. But for him, tackling medical rather than student debt made more long-term sense. "The low-hanging fruit was medical debt because it was the least controversial," he said. By 2019, his group, RIP Medical Debt, had purchased and abolished more than $500 million of medical debt from the secondary market; by early 2021, the amount had exceeded $3 billion. As a result of Occupy, "we have taken the collections industry and turned it on its head," Ashton told me. "Occupy changed the entire dialogue about debt. They shifted the conversation, they pointed out inequities, they created a change, and we've furthered what they started. We're proving to everybody that doing the right thing not only feels good, but it makes economic sense as well."

By 2020, the debtors' union from Occupy Wall Street had expanded into cities nationwide as it transitioned toward a more traditional membership model for its tens of thousands of student debtor allies. It had also published a second book, called *Can't Pay, Won't Pay: The Case for Economic Disobedience and Debt Abolition*, which argued that all $1.7 trillion in U.S. student debt should be eradicated, and proposed widespread resistance to payment by "a militant debtors' movement." During recent years, the group had discovered new legal tools, like "compromise and settlement" authority, which granted Congress the right to waive or discharge student loans at its discretion. Heading into the 2020 presidential election, Gokey expressed optimism about the trajectory of the student debt movement, which he believed was finally approaching takeoff. "If you look at the narrative during Occupy, the pundits and media were saying student debt cancellation is never going to happen, nobody in Congress is going to do this, this is pie in the sky," he told me. "Now it doesn't seem that way anymore. We've never been closer. These ideas are mainstream now. Especially with a global depression and pandemic, the time is ripe for debt resistance to come into its own. This is our moment."

The financial crash and destruction of the economy in 2008 had lasting impacts on the Occupy generation. "The young college graduates who entered the job market at the height of the Great Recession quickly realized that their degrees were like almost everything else in 2009 America: worth little amid the crisis, and less than they paid for them," wrote Charlotte Alter in *The Ones We've Been Waiting For*. For millennials, the debt trap, like the warming planet, became the crisis of their time. "Kids spent the first eighteen years of their lives training to get into college—and the rest of their lives trying to pay for it." A decade later, according to the Federal Reserve, more than two-thirds of the nation's student debt belonged to people under forty years old, and more than one-third belonged to people under thirty. By 2020, loan defaults were soaring as the student loan delinquency rate topped 11 percent—nearly quadruple the rate of home mortgage delinquencies. The Debt Collective had succeeded in discharging around $1 billion in student debt nationwide. Meanwhile, a consensus was growing among mainstream economists that to discharge the entire $1.7 trillion in student debt would amount to a massive economic stimulus, creating millions of jobs through increased economic activity.

"What might students do differently if they didn't have student debt? Buy a car, buy a house, have kids, start a business," Gokey said. "No student debt should exist at all," he added, which is why "we've got our eyes on the prize of $1.7 trillion." For so many people, Occupy was a transformative experience—not only because of the ways it changed their lives at the time, but because of the ways it kept on changing them a decade later. "For a long time I felt that Occupy didn't really end for me," Gokey said, "and in some ways it still really exists in the future."

BANKING FOR THE PEOPLE: MARC ARMSTRONG

OCCUPY ASSERTED ITSELF ON THE GLOBAL STAGE WITH A RESOUNDing No to Wall Street greed, No to corporations buying political influence, No to illegal foreclosures, and on down the line. At its core, the movement demanded solutions to confront the crises of our time and provide bold fixes to a broken system. Yet to many people, the "No" responses seemed to outnumber and overshadow the "Yeses": Occupy, it was thought, was more effective declaring what it didn't want than articulating proposals to make things better. But this was and is a misconception: a constructive, creative idealism anchored the spirit of a movement that was filled with *solutionaries*, people whose ethos was expressed in the chant "We are unstoppable, another world is possible!"

Devising ways to remake the future is no easy task; building an organization with a successful strategy to change the lives of people and communities requires patience and exacts costs on the individuals who persist in their undertaking. In the case of the artist Thomas Gokey, it meant spending a decade after Occupy in the trenches of Strike Debt and the Debt Collective to bring those projects to fruition. For the Virginia hemp farmer Marc Armstrong, it meant years of his life dedicated to the project of establishing a system of public banks across the United States.

Like millions of Americans, Armstrong's life was practically destroyed in the 2008 financial crisis. He had divorced his wife, with whom he had two sons, and used up all the equity on his California home, so he took out a subprime loan with World Savings, a company later bought by Wells Fargo. Every six months, Armstrong saw his loan payment requirements climb a few hundred dollars higher, "and it got to the point where it was way too high, I couldn't make enough money," so he sold his house in a short sale. "The Great Recession took wealth away from eleven million Americans who lost homes as a result of the crash. I'm one of them," he told me. "I walked away with zero dollars."

In the autumn of 2008, as the economy was in free fall, Armstrong turned on National Public Radio one day and heard a program about local currencies, which piqued his interest. "I asked myself the question, 'Well, what is money, anyway?'" Armstrong held a dual degree in economics and biology from Wheaton College and a business degree from UCLA. He had worked at IBM as a software and systems specialist and arranged service deals with corporate clients like Bank of America and Wells Fargo. He felt at home discussing complex instruments like short-term lending and collateralization, but he still didn't understand what went wrong with the financial system, who was to blame, and why. The more he researched, the more Armstrong sought the answer to a single question: How does money get created?

He found his answer at an Economics of Peace Conference in 2009 where he met the attorney Ellen Brown, author of *The Web of Debt: The Shocking Truth About Our Money System and How We Can Break Free*. Brown's book explored the history of the Federal Reserve and explained the surprisingly simple way that money comes into existence: when a bank lends money, it adds new debt to its ledger. Few Americans, including Armstrong, had ever heard it told so clearly. Banks, he learned, "created" money in the same moment that they loaned it out by merely writing a new dollar amount, known as debt, into their books. Armstrong now understood why high-interest loans were the choke point for Wall Street, because that is the way "they make their money," he told me. "Banks create a loan and they create a matching deposit: that's how money is created." As a result, "If you don't have lending, the money supply contracts and the local economy gets turned upside down."

Armstrong embraced Brown's radical proposal: in order for communities and local governments to take back economic control and break "free" from the "web of debt" incurred by Wall Street lenders, they could borrow from public banks instead. Countries like Germany, China, Japan and India had shown for decades how it was done. The only publicly owned and operated bank in the United States, the Bank of North Dakota, had existed for nearly a century. As a wholesale bank, BND lent money to other banks—not to individual customers—through a process known as participatory lending. It had built a long track record of sound financial management in the people's interest, providing low-interest lending for student loans, farmland repurchases, water infrastructure, flood disaster relief, and a range of public goods and projects across the state. During the financial crisis, BND was among the few American financial institutions that avoided losses and continued to grow and issue loans due to the absence of high-risk derivatives in its portfolio. The bank made an 18 percent return on equity during the Great Recession.

For Armstrong, the public banking model of North Dakota "clearly demonstrated that there's an autonomous, decentralized way to control your economic destiny, by being in charge of your own credit that is issued within your economy, and not being dependent on Wall Street or Washington." In January 2011, eight months before protesters assembled in Zuccotti Park, Armstrong and Brown co-founded the Public Banking Institute. Hardly anyone at the time knew or understood what a public bank was, so their education and outreach efforts started small. But the vision was clear: a network of locally administered, city- and state-level public banks, working not for profit but for lending in the public's interest, would revitalize local economies by shifting the balance of power from Wall Street back to Main Street. Armstrong told me, "We realized public banks were a big part of the solution to the financial crisis."

After seeing the livestream of the young women getting pepper-sprayed on the second Saturday of Occupy Wall Street, Armstrong got on a plane because he "needed to go" see the movement for himself. He spent a few days around Zuccotti Park, where the uprising against Wall Street confirmed what he had hoped he would discover. "We'd been talking about systemic injustices in the economy and wondering if people cared," he said, "and all of a sudden Occupy Wall Street happened and it was like, 'Great, they do!'" In criticizing a financial system wrecked by the big banks, the young people sleeping out to protest corporate greed "were speaking our language, and we were speaking theirs."

Armstrong spent the next year traveling around the country giving talks and educating communities about the benefits of public banks. He liked to contrast the crumbling infrastructure in America with China at the time, which "was building out seventy new airports in the next five years, using their own [public] banks." The difference, he told people, was blunt. "While we were stuck, unable even to get a few hundred billion dollars for infrastructure, they're building out their entire economy using credit issued by these banks." In June 2012, Armstrong organized the first Public Banking Conference in Philadelphia, where twelve-year-old Victoria Grant, from Ontario, Canada, stole the show with "an amazing, barn-burning talk" in which she spoke plainly about big banks, mortgages, debt, and "how you pay until you die." Her eight-minute speech went viral, capturing millions of views. The public banking movement was underway.

During Obama's second term, it became clear to many Americans that the president who once declared that he was the only one standing between Wall Street bankers and "the pitchforks" had recommitted himself to protecting the forces of free-market globalization. Obama stood fully behind the Trans-Pacific Partnership, a global trade pact that threatened to lose more U.S. jobs to cheap, under-regulated Asian markets, while appointing "corporate tribunals" to handle any charges brought against lawbreaking corporations. Armstrong felt the country was at a transitional moment because more people seemed to be moving in the opposite direction—toward a more decentralized economy with renewed focus on Main Street.

"What Occupy did was change the social justice framework to include economic justice, which had been missing from the whole conversation," said Armstrong. The Great Recession "was still fresh in people's minds, and they were earnestly trying to find ways to avoid that kind of credit contraction" happening in the future. "The banks skated free, they left with their franchise intact, and they're still the [only] ones able to issue credit," he added. "I think a lot of people were going through those years, seeing what was happening, and recognizing there needed to be a better way of localizing the economy."

Increasing interest turned a community-led discussion around public banks into a national conversation that garnered mainstream media attention. During Occupy, tens of thousands of Americans had closed their accounts with Wall Street banks and opened new ones with community co-ops, credit unions and other regional banks. The Move Your Money campaign had been popular, but it didn't go further. Instead, a nationwide movement to launch public banks was growing in California, Washington State, New Mexico, Colorado, Pennsylvania, Vermont and elsewhere. In 2016, the monthslong #NoDAPL protests at Standing Rock spurred renewed calls to divest from the Wall Street banks that were funding the Dakota Access Pipeline, pushing more people toward a public banking solution. "A lot of people realized these goddamn banks are controlling everything and we really need to have an alternative" to privately funding fossil fuels, prison corporations, big ag, pharma, and other industries harmful to human health, he said. By that time, people understood that "you can't solve this problem with regulation and legislation against the banks. You really have to create a separate banking system that reflects your values, like clean energy. People were actively looking to public banks as the only approach that a divestment strategy could take."

The movement received another boost in November 2016, when California legalized marijuana. Taxed heavily by the state, cannabis sales topped $3 billion the following year. But federal drug classification laws prevented federally regulated commercial banks from depositing or managing proceeds from cannabis sales. Operating a cash-only business, growers and dispensaries faced an increased threat of crime, raising public safety concerns about the industry. The conversation soon turned to public banks and the possibility that their status as municipally run entities could enable them to handle cannabis-generated receipts. In response to pressure from cannabis advocates, California created a task force, headed by the state's then treasurer, John Chiang, which spent several years debating the merits of a state-run public bank.

Meanwhile, statewide support for the movement was growing and in 2018, a new grassroots organization called the California Public Banking Alliance drafted a proposal for legislation authorizing the creation and licensing of statewide public banks. That fall, Los Angeles voters by a margin of 58 to 42 percent rejected ballot measure B, which would have allowed for the creation of a public bank in America's second largest city. Following the defeat, the advocacy group pivoted and spent the next year working with lawyers to fine-tune the legislation while lobbying lawmakers in Sacramento. Then, in the fall of 2019, CPBA saw its breakthrough when the California state legislature passed AB 857, known as the Public Banking Act. The legislation, signed into law by Governor Gavin Newsom, established the right of cities and other local governing entities to issue licenses for public banks, signaling that California, the world's fifth largest economy, was ready to take on Wall Street.

As states looked less to the federal government for assistance and more to their own tax base, Armstrong said that local- and state-level public banks could become an accepted and widespread solution. "There's a growing recognition that states have to be responsible for their own economies, because the federal government certainly isn't going to help them out," he told me.

"The heart of the economy is a public bank because it puts communities in charge of our credit [and] in charge of our own economic destiny. We're not Congress—we can't mint coins, we can't issue currency—but we can create a bank which has the right to issue loans, using credit as the basis for those loans, which then impact the economy." Armstrong added, "We rarely talk about a democratic economy. But when you realize that the way the economy grows, and is shaped, can be controlled by a bank—and that we can have a democratic governance of that bank—then you realize that your values can be funded through the lending programs of the bank."

WORKERS OWN THE BUSINESS: NATHAN SCHNEIDER

IN THE WAY THAT OCCUPY GALVANIZED NEW MOVEMENTS TO SEEK solutions to student debt and high-interest Wall Street lending, it also inspired a new generation of worker-owned businesses. Worker-run enterprises had been around for decades, but prior to Occupy, the cooperative company model had turned stagnant. According to journalist and author Nathan Schneider, "co-ops were mainly going about their business and not really growing. Legacy cooperative organizations were totally irrelevant." After Occupy, when participation in worker-owned businesses suddenly increased, the number of cooperatives grew nationwide, and their economic impact started to expand. The message after Occupy, Schneider told me, was that "we don't just want democracy in our election every four years—we need to practice it every day," through workplace activism. "Occupy absolutely rejuvenated the co-op movement in this country, there's no question about that."

Schneider was a founding editor of the progressive news site Waging Nonviolence and a freelance journalist who had embedded himself in Occupy Wall Street from its inception, straddling the role between participant and observer. His 2013 book, *Thank You, Anarchy: Notes from the Occupy Apocalypse*, was among the most richly descriptive accounts of the movement, and his interests soon shifted from there to cooperative economics. In *Everything for Everyone: The Radical Tradition That Is Shaping the Next Economy*, Schneider chronicled the evolution of worker-run companies, which he saw as an antidote to economic disempowerment in the gig economy.

In the decade after Occupy, the number of worker co-ops in the country doubled to more than six hundred, according to the U.S. Federation of Worker Cooperatives. Most cooperative businesses were located in urban areas, and often the same liberal cities where Occupy put down strong roots—New York, Oakland, Boston, Denver, Madison—saw the highest participation and funding of shared enterprises. The links weren't a coincidence, Schneider told me. "A lot of people who are circulating between these [co-ops] were involved in Occupy in their cities. Wherever you see this work happening, you see those Occupy connections."

Schneider, who teaches media studies at the University of Colorado Boulder, saw a natural through line from Occupy to the cooperative movement, because "it combined the desire for an economy that is of and by the people—a radical alternative to Wall Street, that [puts] people before profits—and the desire to practice democracy in everyday life." In some ways, he said, the "resurgence in interest and dynamism and participation" around cooperative economics paralleled the rebirth of progressive politics ignited by Bernie Sanders in 2015. After Occupy, "people came out and started doing the long-haul work," because there was "a recognition in the community that this isn't going to happen in two months like Occupy—this is going to be years in the making, so the people who are into it are in deep, and are making a life out of it." Nowadays, old timers in the co-op business mix with the new energy brought by "the radical young kids who came up through Occupy," Schneider said. Occupy in some ways was "a perfect fit" with cooperatives, which had forgotten their "deep radical commitments, so people coming out of Occupy infused the co-op movement more broadly with a reminder of its radical nature, and that process is still going on."

As Occupy started to fade from public view in 2012, the cooperative sector began visibly to grow. The process was perhaps clearest seen in New York City, where many activists transitioned from Zuccotti Park to helping develop worker-owned businesses. The graphic arts group OccuCopy, which produced visual materials for the movement, became one of the first employee-run companies to arise from Occupy. After establishing itself on Bergen Street in Brooklyn, the cooperative merged with Radix Media, which published science fiction among other projects. "OccuCopy may have been one small outfit," Schneider said, "but the vision it represented was sweeping in scope. It was just one of the cooperatives that grew directly out of Occupy as the cooperative wave fanned outward."

The organization The Working World, which had gotten off the ground before the movement and saw a surge of participation after it, helped develop cooperatives in the Rockaways following Hurricane Sandy in 2012 and also assisted in converting a historic window and door factory into a worker-owned enterprise in Chicago. The organization Center for Family Life, based in Sunset Park, Brooklyn, partnered with Occupy organizers to push for city budget laws that helped create the trade association New York City Network of Worker Cooperatives. Credit unions saw a surge in customers after Occupy following the movement's successful Move Your Money campaign; the credit union Brooklyn Cooperative, in Bedford-Stuyvesant, was founded in the post-Occupy period as well. People saw "just how boring and establishment credit unions had become," Schneider observed, "but suddenly there was a new generation of people who said, 'You're actually what we want.'"

Outside New York, the co-op movement grew at a similar pace. In Boston, the New Economy Coalition, a network of co-ops and non-profits, became a nationally recognized organization, in part, because so many people energized by the Occupy movement had recommitted themselves to worker activism. At the same time, cities like Chicago and states like Colorado moved to change laws and encourage greater opportunities for employee-owned businesses to prosper. Even in places as distant as New Zealand—where a group of techtivists from Occupy Wellington developed Loomio, a software tool that enabled co-ops and worker-owned businesses to make digital proposals and decisions through direct-democratic process—Occupy impacted the cooperative economics arena. "Right now it's a scattering of experiments and efforts," Schneider said, and as a result, "the sector is increasingly in a position to make significant gains. It's not exclusively because of Occupy, but there was certainly a contingent of people from the movement who came into this work."

Small worker-run businesses aren't the only ones gaining attention. Large, legacy co-ops began to market themselves differently—in the case of outdoor gear company REI, at twelve thousand employees the country's largest consumer cooperative, worth $2.2 billion, by adding the word "co-op" to its logo—after that branding "became cool" with Occupy. Companies that for decades during the Cold War "were hiding the fact that they were co-ops, suddenly discovered that this is interesting" once young people started flocking to employee-owned firms, Schneider said. The growing popularity of cooperative businesses received federal recognition in 2018 when U.S. Senator Kirsten Gillibrand of New York introduced a bill to Congress, called the Main Street Employee Ownership Act, which won bipartisan support and was signed into law by President Trump, becoming the country's most important piece of federal worker ownership legislation ever. Support for cooperative businesses was also incorporated into the Green New Deal resolution introduced by Representative Alexandria Ocasio-Cortez of New York and U.S. Senator Ed Markey of Massachusetts in early 2019.

For Schneider, worker-run companies may be "still revving up," but at the same time he acknowledged that "it's a struggle to get cooperatives going, because the system is not designed for them." By awakening the idea that collective decision making could empower people in the workplace, Occupy Wall Street helped ignite a movement whose economic impacts continue to grow, paralleling the populist financial efforts of Strike Debt and public banks. Already at Zuccotti Park, Schneider saw among the activists "a clear intuition that technology can be a tool for democracy," and he followed the story. "In this new generation, there's this fascination with worker co-ops, which has been almost entirely absent in U.S. history," he said. In the aftermath of the global economic rupture caused by the coronavirus, American workers are demanding more loudly than ever before to hold a stake in the enterprise. "Yes, we're building new co-ops, but more importantly we're building infrastructure that will make it much easier" to sustain worker-owned businesses in the future, Schneider said. In the realm of workplace democracy, "it's like Occupy spread out."

REINTRODUCING SOCIALISM TO AMERICA: KSHAMA SAWANT

WHEN KSHAMA SAWANT BEAT AN AMAZON-FUNDED CARPETBAGGER to win reelection to the Seattle City Council in late 2019, her victory rewarded a decade of activism that began when protesters at Occupy Seattle moved their encampment from Westlake Park, where they were facing police harassment, to the downtown campus of Seattle Central College, where Sawant taught economics. The thirty-eight-year-old former software engineer, who had immigrated to America as a college graduate from Mumbai, was already engaged in fights to halt tuition hikes and cuts to public education in her adopted city. Suddenly she found herself in a dual role, as teacher and union member, helping lead Occupy protests while battling her school's administration for the public's right to occupy the campus.

"It was a brilliant moment of solidarity: teachers were there, students were there, Occupiers were there, and that's exactly what we needed," she said, "but to take the movement to the next step we needed political demands." Political demands were something Occupy's participants had steadfastly rejected, and Sawant watched as the movement wound down over the course of months without achieving any concrete gains. She felt the energy around Occupy had signaled that Seattle, with its soaring rent costs, wage disparities and rising numbers of homeless, was ready to go further in addressing systemic inequalities. It just needed the right kind of leadership.

In Sawant's mind, the socialist kind.

The following year, in 2012, Sawant ran and was beaten badly—by more than forty points—in a race for Position 2 in the Forty-Third District of Washington's House of Representatives. She came back in 2013 and campaigned for a Seattle City Council seat, running on the ticket of a fringe political party called Socialist Alternative. Sawant eked out the election victory by less than two thousand votes, or one percentage point, to become the first socialist in nearly 140 years to win a seat on that body. Her victory stunned the establishment and represented, in political terms, the first visible sign that Occupy had, in fact, done more than simply protest in the streets. The movement's message of inequality had catapulted an unapologetically far-left voice into citywide office in a coastal metropolis.

"For decades there was a very systematic and calculated program of vilification and demonization of socialist ideas in the United States, along with genuine criticism of the problems of the Soviet Union [with its] bureaucratic dictatorship and many deficiencies," Sawant told me. As a result, "several generations were raised in this atmosphere of [considering] socialism as a very, very bad idea. But I think we are far away from that past because the fact is, entire new generations that weren't raised in the Cold War have come of age in an era when they're facing low-wage jobs, student debt, sky-high rents, absolutely dysfunctional healthcare, and they're drawing their own conclusions that the system that's on offer is not working for us."

Sawant took the fight to her city, immediately tackling inequality as she mobilized the Fight for $15 movement to raise the minimum wage. Within half a year of taking office, Sawant and her Socialist Alternative party scored a seismic win, leading Seattle as the first big American city to pass a $15 minimum wage law. She next turned her focus to strengthening renters' rights as the cost of Seattle housing soared to levels seen in San Francisco and New York, pushing more families and working people out of the city. By marshaling the council's progressive wing, in 2016 she fought for and won a move-in fee cap, which limited the enormous rent and deposit costs that landlords were able to charge new tenants—sometimes totaling as high as $8,000—and forced land-lords to offer renters a six-month payment plan to cover those costs. The victory over the city's powerful landlord lobby put Sawant and her party at "ground zero" of a growing national movement for housing justice.

"We need to fight for not only rent control and a full Renters Bill of Rights in every city, but to tax the rich and big business to fund a massive expan-sion of publicly owned, permanently affordable social housing. I'm emphasiz-ing public ownership," she said, echoing the rationale of Gokey, Armstrong, Schneider and other solutionaries from the Occupy movement, "because the free market has completely failed us. There is no evidence to show that the for-profit market can actually address the housing affordability problems."

For Sawant, like for many millions of Americans, Bernie Sanders's com-petitive candidacy offered the earliest example of the way Americans' views were starting to shift toward a bolder embrace of socialist ideas. "You can just look at the 2016 election results in a place like West Virginia, one of two states where Trump won every county, and draw the conclusion that the people in this state are irreparably right-wing and bigoted and there's no way of reaching them," Sawant said. "But earlier that same year, Bernie was hugely popular in the state's Democratic primaries, and just two years later, every county's school district went on strike because of the kind of support the teachers had in their communities. These are regular working-class people who are looking for a way out of endemic and intergenerational poverty, who have been completely betrayed and left behind by the Democratic Party establishment for decades, and who can be won over if there were actually something that they thought was worth fighting for." She added, "The fact that the labor movement can win victories and bring the Republican legislature in that state to its knees [shows] our potential if we have campaigns that address the real needs of working people."

The core crisis in American democracy that Occupy nakedly exposed was the crisis of capitalism. For the first time in generations, large numbers of peo-ple were asking the forbidden question: is our broken and unequal economic system worth saving, and can democratic socialism be a legitimate alternative? "Socialism was a dirty word before Occupy. You weren't allowed to say it," the filmmaker Abraham Heisler told me. As the economist Richard Wolff put it, "What Occupy did was absolutely crucial in American political history and should be understood as a watershed moment because it broke the spell—it broke the seventy-five-year taboo, after the New Deal, when that debate was shut down by the Cold War. Occupy was the first movement to say, 'We're not running away from the critique of this capitalist system. We're sticking our nose right in it: we're saying this country is destroying itself by dividing between the 1 percent and the 99 percent.'"

After Sanders's run and Trump's victory in 2016, young American social-ists announced themselves by the tens of thousands. Membership in Dem-ocratic Socialists of America exploded over the next four years—climbing from five thousand to more than seventy thousand members—galvanized by Representative Alexandria Ocasio-Cortez's victory in 2018 and the economic impacts of the 2020 pandemic. Even before Sanders's historic candidacy, more than a third of adults under the age of thirty and more than a quarter of Amer-icans overall said they held a "favorable view" of socialism. By December 2019, a series of YouGov polls showed 70 percent of millennials were "extremely" or "somewhat likely" to vote for a socialist candidate, while 21 percent of U.S. voters—and 47 percent of the population under forty-five—said they outright preferred socialism to capitalism.

According to journalist John B. Judis, author of *The Socialist Awakening: What's Different Now About the Left*, today's generation of pragmatic "new socialists" doesn't carry the baggage of Marxist orthodoxy in calling for the de-struction of the capitalist state. Rather, "they see socialism as developing *within* capitalism, the way capitalism developed within feudalism." As young people in the post-Occupy era approached politics through a new socioeconomic lens, the makeup of America's elected officeholders began to change. In the 2018 midterms, DSA members won city council seats from Lansing, Michigan, to Cambridge, Massachusetts, and from Aurora, Colorado, to West Lafayette,

Indiana. Following the 2020 elections, nearly forty democratic socialist candidates had won senate and assembly seats in statehouses nationwide; more than sixty others sat on city councils, while some twenty occupied local positions including school board, county recorder, planning and zoning, board of supervisors, district attorney, criminal court judge, transit board and treasurer. At the federal level, voters in 2020 elected two new democratic socialists to the U.S. House of Representatives—Jamaal Bowman from New York's Sixteenth Congressional District and Cori Bush, who got her political start with Brand New Congress, from Missouri's First Congressional District—bringing the number of DSA members in that body to five.

As Tim Alberta wrote in *Politico* after Joe Biden overtook the Sanders campaign in March 2020 on Super Tuesday, "Socialism is ascendant among ascendant voters, the youngsters ages 18 to 35, not as a short-term political engine to propel Sanders into the White House but as a long-term restructuring of the American social contract." Yet this attitude and entire movement, with Sanders's protégé Alexandria Ocasio-Cortez leading the charge, would never have happened, Richard Wolff argued, had Occupy not opened the door.

"Without Occupy there's no Bernie, no Alexandria Ocasio-Cortez, none of the poll numbers that show that Americans thirty-five and under think we can do better than capitalism and that socialism is an interesting idea," Wolff said. "All of that is a reconnecting of American culture with pre–World War I politics. We've been like a bear in hibernation for a hell of a long time." After bankers ruined the economy in 2008, "we can talk not only about criticizing our education or transportation or energy systems, but we can finally grow up as a nation to realize that if we don't criticize our economic system, we allow it to indulge its worst interests."

SAWANT'S ELECTORAL VICTORY IN 2013, FOLLOWED BY HER SWEEPing legislative achievements, represented a political earthquake in Seattle. Left-leaning operatives "were stunned we would openly run campaigning as socialists, saying, 'Even if you're socialist, just keep it under wraps because there's no way you can win.' It's changed quite a bit from that time." In fact, Matt Taylor wrote in *Vice*, "rather than branding her as a fringe figure, Sawant's loud and proud left-wing views have earned her massive grassroots support—a show of force that has turned heads among local political insiders." Sawant, who won reelection in 2019 after a grueling battle against billionaire donors and multinational real estate corporations, viewed her own constituency as a microcosm of the wealth gap that Occupy decried. "In my district we have many, many renters who are struggling to pay their rent and we also have Howard Schultz, the CEO of Starbucks," she said. As both a socialist and an elected officeholder, Sawant saw no contradiction between renegade activism and using politics to make change from within.

"We don't see a dichotomy between street heat and elected office. The flip side is, when you're elected people say, 'Now you need to stop being an activist, now you need to be a legislator,'" she explained. But, "the challenge isn't just recognizing that you need to build an independent politics. It's a question of how do you use your position in a completely principled way and yet not be ineffectual and marginalized." For Sawant, confronting the power of the 1 percent and addressing deep-seated inequality was what voters elected her to do—not to stay safely within the guardrails of conventional city politics. "We don't accept that the purpose of winning elected office is to treat everyone equally. If we did that, it would mean those who are already powerful would continue to have influence at City Hall. Instead we've flipped that on its head and drawn the line between the interests of working people and the interests of the billionaire class."

In a direct sense, Sawant wrote the new socialist playbook by speaking to the issues raised at Zuccotti Park, and forged a pragmatic framework for her generation's new socialist agenda. "The Occupy message was a complete rejection of status quo politics," Sawant told me, and "I think the people who say that Occupy is long gone and has produced nothing are completely devoid of any analysis or understanding of how social change happens. Occupy is actually an example of how movements develop, because when it first came on the scene it caught a lot of people by surprise, people wondered where it was going, and when it was ending, a lot of the pundits, even in the left establishment, said, 'See, it really doesn't work to build movements. We need to reelect Obama; we need to reignite the faith in the usual process led by the Democratic and Republican Party establishments and limit our expectations of what they can deliver.'"

Donald Trump would shatter the precedent of appealing to the center in this hyper-polarized era. But it was Occupy that paved the ground for reforms that moved in the opposite direction. "We absolutely would not be in City Hall if it weren't for Occupy, and movements like fifteen dollars an hour and rent control wouldn't have won," Sawant said. "I often hear people say, 'What does protesting change?' This is something that people have learned unconsciously through corporate media because corporate media tells you protesting doesn't work. Like hell it doesn't! Look at where we are." She added, "You think we got a fifteen-dollar minimum wage in Seattle because of the largesse of big business and the elite politicians who support them? We got it because we had our own voice in City Hall and we had the momentum on the streets: we protested, we rallied, we marched."

After those legislative victories, Sawant turned her attention to taxing the Seattle-based e-commerce behemoth Amazon. Owned by Jeff Bezos, the richest man on Earth, the company valued at more than $1 trillion had for years avoided paying its share of taxes to the city where it was headquartered since the midnineties. In Sawant's 2019 reelection race, Amazon poured hundreds of thousands of dollars into a candidate it hoped could defeat her, but fell short. As she liked to say, "My race is a proxy for Amazon versus working people," and that time, the people came out on top. In July 2020, as the economy sputtered amid the coronavirus lockdown, Sawant led a 7–2 majority on the Seattle City Council to pass an "Amazon tax," which would generate hundreds of millions of dollars annually—to serve in the short term as emergency assistance for working families hit hardest in the pandemic, and in the long term to fund affordable housing—by levying a payroll tax on Seattle's richest corporations.

Sawant saw Occupy located "on a continuum of social movements," one which had started with the Arab Spring and Wisconsin's public sector uprising, and continued evolving through the decade. The revolution that spread from Cairo to Madison to Wall Street had caught what Sawant called "the inspiring contagion of social movements," and "that is exactly the kind of contagion that capitalism does not want spreading. The movement of the 99 percent allowed people to understand that they were not the only ones feeling outrage about extreme inequality, where three billionaires can own more wealth in the U.S. than the entire bottom half of the population," she said. "It brought to the fore an anger that young people have been feeling for many years now: not only at an economic elite, but anger at a system as a whole."

Now, as the planetary crisis deepens in the 2020s, "more and more people are drawing a conclusion that capitalism is really not working, [particularly] on the question that is most urgently looming over all of us—climate change." Desperate to establish economic and climate stability, today's generation may be ready to embrace policy programs like the Green New Deal that drive free-market capitalism out of business. "Young people are starting to understand that capitalism is fundamentally incapable of delivering any kind of solution to what appears to be now a complete disintegration of our planet unless something is urgently done, and what that something is, based on the science that we know, is a rapid shift away from fossil fuels toward renewable energy on a very massive scale," she said. From the People's Climate March to the Global Climate Strikes, and from the Sunrise Movement to Extinction Rebellion, the resistance is radicalizing as people connect the dual crises of climate and capitalism. "The shift is not going to happen when you have a few billionaires controlling the wealth in the society. In other words, the scientific conclusions are leading toward different political conclusions." By 2021, with Joe Biden and his climate cabinet installed in office, young Americans were ready to join the politics and the science in a bid to save the Earth.

REFORMING THE POLICE: RAY LEWIS

LIKE MOST THINGS THAT HE DID IN LIFE, THE RETIRED POLICE captain Ray Lewis was methodical in planning the protest that led to his arrest. He was at his homestead in the Catskill Mountains of upstate New York, where he and his wife had been living for the past eight years since his retirement from the Philadelphia Police Department. One day in the autumn of 2011, Lewis was watching a documentary called *Inside Job* about the corruption on Wall Street that caused the financial crash. Outraged, "I shouted to my wife, 'Why doesn't somebody do something!'" Then, a week later, he said, "I read about this thing called the Occupy movement. They were living in tents and under tarps in a place called Zuccotti, and I thought, 'Wait a minute, why are they protesting and living in these conditions?'" Eager to learn more, Lewis searched online until he came across the Declaration of the Occupation of New York City. "It had twenty-three bullet points and I read each one of them and wholeheartedly agreed," he told me. "It was a work of brilliance. I was so taken aback." Lewis wanted to help the movement, but thought, "If I'm just another face in the crowd, that won't be contributing enough. Then I had an epiphany—I have a uniform."

On the afternoon of November 13, 2011, a few days shy of his sixtieth birthday, Lewis left his wife and their dogs, cats, chickens and goats on the mountain farm and drove in his 1987 white Plymouth Reliant south to New York City. He rented a cheap apartment that evening in Harlem, and the next morning Lewis went down to Wall Street. Lewis felt the corporate media had been missing Occupy's economic message by marginalizing the protesters. "Fox News was disparaging the movement, interviewing kids with orange hair and piercings and tattoos," he said, depicting activists "as rabble-rousers, dirty hippies who were lazy and didn't have a job and wanted the system to give them everything. I thought I could help minimize that." Lewis sought to shift the public's perception, because "if I go down there in uniform, they won't be able to tell me to take a bath or get a haircut or get a job. I'm not a hippie but I am behind this movement, and instead of changing the channel maybe people will say, 'Wait a minute,' and I can reach white America." As a former police captain with twenty-four years on the force, Lewis had a distinct message for the protesters: "I was on the other side, but now I'm on your side, because everything you're saying is right."

Before coming to Occupy Wall Street, Lewis had done his homework. He suspected there might be a risk protesting while wearing a police officer's uniform, so he phoned the Philadelphia PD's legal team. "I knew there was only one law [violation] they could charge me with—impersonating a cop—but that only holds true if you try to exert legal authority. I asked, 'Is it legal for me to go down there and protest in uniform,' and they said, 'It's never happened before, it's highly unusual—but not illegal.'" Lewis also consulted his lawyer, who confirmed "with 99.9 percent certainty" that the department couldn't touch his pension or benefits. Then, on the morning of November 14, a little over a dozen hours before New York City police would surround Zuccotti Park and violently evict the encampment, Lewis carried his homemade signs, one of which read, "NYPD: Do Not Be Wall St. Mercenaries," and showed up at the park.

For the next few days, including in the aftermath of the camp's closure, Lewis stood on the sidewalk by Zuccotti dressed in full uniform, holding his signs and engaging with anyone who wanted to talk. Slim-waisted, six foot two and one hundred eighty-five pounds, Lewis cut a sharp profile in his officer's cap, black tie and navy suit, with shoulders covered in epaulettes. His square-jawed features and silver toothbrush moustache had the gravitas of a public protector; he reminded me of Chesley "Sully" Sullenberger, who nearly three years earlier had heroically landed a U.S. Airways commercial flight on the Hudson River, saving 155 lives. On his fourth day at the park, November 17, someone invited Lewis to join a large demonstration happening on Wall Street. Dubbed a "mass day of action," the protest drew thousands into the streets to commemorate the movement's two-month anniversary and to express defiance in the face of the park eviction. Lewis walked down Broadway, where he saw hundreds of young people engaging in civil disobedience, sitting down and blocking traffic outside the stock exchange. "I was only going to hold the sign with everybody else and demonstrate. The thought that I'd be arrested never entered my mind," he recalled.

"But then I saw young person after young person being dragged off by police. Just two days after seeing the park brutalized, they were willing to sacrifice for justice to this degree—they had no idea if they'd get beaten or how much time they'd spend in jail—and I was so moved by their conviction, risking their personal freedom and personal welfare, that I said, 'I have to join them, I have to show solidarity.' I am not a spontaneous guy," Lewis said. "I am a planner. I like to think things through. And yet I made this decision in a matter of seconds—the quickest decision in my life. I turned to the woman behind me, a Spanish reporter, and asked her to hold my sign, then I just went and sat down. Two times the police went around me to get [other] people. After the third time, one of the commanders said, 'What do you want?' I said, 'I want to be arrested.'" Lewis was taken away, along with hundreds that day, and booked on charges of disorderly conduct, disobeying a police officer's order and blocking traffic. Standing in handcuffs in a large courtyard in front of the precinct jail, he noticed a female officer studying his ID. "She looked at me and said, 'Oh, I'm sorry, it's your birthday,' and the kid next to me heard that and he shouted to all the others, 'Mic check! It's Captain Lewis's birthday today!' Next I know I have a hundred people singing happy birthday," he said. "It was the most moving birthday of my life."

Overnight, Lewis became an unlikely icon of the movement. The image of a tall, dignified, retired cop in uniform being handcuffed and hauled away from the Occupy protests struck a chord. His face showed up in newspapers, blogs, magazines. His photo even took up a page in *Time*'s 2011 "Person of the Year" issue, which it awarded in montage to "The Protester." "Walking across that intersection handcuffed was the proudest moment of my life," read the caption. But beyond the media attention he received, Lewis's actions had also touched individuals' lives. In one instance, a student from the University of Massachusetts had left school that fall to join Occupy Wall Street, and her parents, appalled by her decision, had cut off her college funding. But after the student sent her sister a link to the video showing Lewis's arrest, her sister shared the clip with their parents. Disarmed by the footage, they decided to read further about the movement. They then not only resumed supporting their daughter financially, but contributed $500 to the Occupy Wall Street food bank. "That's the epitome of what I wanted to do," Lewis told me, "to reach Americans who were against the occupation, who didn't understand it, but seeing me made them want to learn more. I wanted mainstream America to get involved and understand what's going on."

Not everyone responded so favorably to Lewis's actions. He realized that a lot of Americans saw him as "a nut, a whacko, a traitor, a commie." His former colleagues back in Philadelphia were indignant, and both the police commissioner and the head of the police union threatened him. "Unions fight for cops to keep their pensions when the city tries to take them away," Lewis said, but in his case, "my union, the Philadelphia Fraternal Order of Police Lodge #5, wanted to take away my pension." The union boss knew it wasn't possible, "but he used the threat to bully and intimidate me to stop using my uniform to protest." He even sent Lewis a letter warning him that if he ever stepped foot back in Philly he'd be arrested, writing, "I will take *any* and *all* necessary action to stop you." Lewis told me, "What, am I going to find a horse's head in my bed? That's mafia language."

In fact, Lewis had never quite fit in with his crew of mostly white, and, in many cases, racist Philadelphia police officers. After joining the force at twenty-nine, he had spent his first ten years as a patrol officer working in poor parts of the city, where Black communities "saw us as the enemy, as an occupying army, not as their friend or helper. They knew how brutal the police were, they had seen [violence] done to their brothers, their nieces and nephews and parents." Lewis witnessed "repulsive" episodes when his fellow white cops would indiscriminately beat up Black men (they called it "party time"). He said it was common for cops to arrest Black people just to boost their monthly quotas, which meant a higher take-home pay.

Lewis told me, "Arrests aren't done to protect people, they're done for one reason: arrests equal money, through overtime and court time. See how many drug arrests are made a half hour before the term ends—that means the paperwork will take an hour overtime, and court appearances are in the daytime, which for many cops means automatic overtime. Cops want that overtime, they want the cabin up in the mountains, they want that new car like their neighbors." He added, "White people didn't believe this brutality goes on because they only had good interactions with the police; they had 'Officer Friendly' who came to school every year and would teach people how to cross the street. In my family, the police were next to God. 'If you ever need any help, have any trouble, ever get lost, go to the police,' my dad said, 'they'll save you.' The Black community knew different."

Lewis's attitudes didn't make him an especially popular figure on the PPD, so instead of working under sergeants he didn't respect, he decided to become one himself. After four years he made lieutenant, and with four sergeants and about sixty officers working under him, Lewis found that he had power to impact communities in a positive way. As someone who saw himself on "the empathetic side" as opposed to "the militaristic side" of law enforcement, he focused on rewarding officers for what they did well rather than punishing them for their mistakes. He tried to direct them into a role of helping people, not treating them as adversaries. In 1995, Lewis made captain, a position he held until his retirement, in 2003, which was the day before he and his wife made their way to their new life in the Catskills.

Even as the Occupy movement faded from public view, Lewis remained for months, dressed in uniform, standing alone outside the barricades around Zuccotti Park where he continued to share his message. In the years that followed, he would show up at protests in different cities, "any place where I felt there was injustice," he said. Lewis traveled twice to Flint, Michigan, to protest the city's poisoning of its majority Black population with lead-tainted water; to Indianapolis, where he protested then governor Mike Pence's effort to pass a law allowing businesses to deny service to LGBTQ people; and twice to Ferguson, Missouri, once after Michael Brown was killed, "to tell the people, 'I know this was murder,'" then again after Officer Darren Wilson's acquittal. Lewis attended other Black Lives Matter protests—in Chicago, after police shot and killed the teenager Laquan McDonald, and in Cleveland, after the police killing of twelve-year-old Tamir Rice—despite being aware that most of the protesters did not accept him.

"They could not get over the fact that I was a white cop. People wanted nothing to do with me, and I understand that," Lewis said. But he felt it was important to be there, drawing the connections between Occupy Wall Street and Black Lives Matter, because "you won't ever have racial justice without economic justice. Economics is the bottom line to justice, and then the police departments have to be held accountable. You will not have equality in this country until you have a Black man sitting in an office with three other white men, waiting to get interviewed for a job by a white supervisor, and the Black man feels he has just as equal an opportunity to get that job as the three white men."

After white Minneapolis police officer Derek Chauvin killed George Floyd in May 2020, the national conversation around policing reform echoed a lot of what Lewis had been saying for years. But there were other, more specific recommendations that he thought police departments should consider. Lewis wanted to see mandatory psychological tests to determine a police applicant's mental and emotional health, ensuring that the right people are hired as officers to begin with. The industry standard, known as the Minnesota Multiphasic Personality Inventory, measures qualities such as sensitivity, empathy, compassion and aggression. People deemed too sensitive or empathetic are usually rejected under the assumption that they won't last long enough on the job to be worth the investment involved in training them. On the flip side, said Lewis, "if you hire the aggressive guy, you're going to be paying millions of dollars in police brutality cases." In his view, training officers to approach their jobs with more of a "social worker–type mentality" is critical to any serious police reform efforts, and should be accompanied by mandatory annual counseling, because "they're not going to go voluntarily, but if they're made to go, and it's behind closed doors, they're much more open" to discuss the problems they're facing on the job.

Just as important, said Lewis, is the need to hold police department leadership accountable. Like millions of Americans, Lewis was appalled that Chauvin had been allowed to remain a beat cop after eighteen complaints had been filed against him. It's inevitable that police receive complaints, given the work they do, Lewis said, but eighteen is "beyond the pale. You should be monitoring after three, four, five complaints, so it means the commissioner wasn't doing his job and holding officers accountable. They should be disciplined for failure to supervise." Lewis added, "That police commissioner in Minneapolis took a stand and fired four [officers] immediately. Well, I've got news for you: he should have fired himself. He had an officer that had eighteen complaints and he should have taken action. That man should have never been on the street, in a patrol car, dealing with Black men who had filed complaints against him. He should have been in a desk job somewhere."

Based on what Lewis saw during his decades of law enforcement in Philadelphia, police violence isn't the only crisis plaguing law enforcement. Often, he said, apathy among officers also has long-term damaging effects on communities. "The root of this problem goes back to what types of people you are hiring," he said. "You don't only want to weed out people who are brutal, but also weed out the people who don't care. A lot of them don't care about the living situation of some people, the horrors of people's lives, and then they treat people like they don't care, and that has a lasting image." Giving lip service is "the lowest level of police abuse" because it means essentially doing nothing. "Somebody calls in with a problem and police answer and say, 'I'll check into it, I'll take care of it, I'll get back to you,' and that's the end of it. They don't check it out, they don't look into it, they don't send somebody out—they don't care. If they cared they'd look into it and solve the problem. That's the other type of cop you don't want: he might never be brutal, but he doesn't give a shit."

For Lewis, the overdue debate around police reform happened in large part because of the singular piece of technology that most of us now carry around in our pockets. "The cell phone camera is the greatest invention for justice. It brings out the truth," he said. "White people before never believed Black people. They believed their own police department, their own politicians. With cell phones, white people are now saying, 'My God, I'm seeing this with my own eyes, I'm hearing it, I can't deny this anymore—I cannot deny that police are brutal, I cannot deny white privilege.' People seeing the atrocity can no longer say, 'Well, he must have deserved it.' George Floyd did not deserve it." And yet, added Lewis, even the ubiquity of cell phones hasn't prevented tragedies like the killing of Floyd. "Every single cop knows that every citizen has a cell phone, and yet they still commit brutality in front of these cell phones. That's how ingrained police brutality is," he said. "Even Derek Chauvin had his cell phone on him and he knew it. He still continued to kill [Floyd] and he kept his left hand in his pocket while he was doing it—he did it so nonchalantly, kneeling on this guy like he did it every day, it was that easy for him."

Lewis was inspired watching the large numbers of white people who came out to participate in the 2020 racial justice protests. One place that especially gave him hope was Ocean City, New Jersey, a white, religious, conservative town that he used to visit on weekends with his buddies during college. In Ocean City, "you can walk around all day and not see a Black person," he recalled. Yet in June 2020, "most stunning to me was a photo of Ocean City, outside city hall, with two hundred white people lying down in the middle of the street blocking traffic, saying 'I Can't Breathe.' If this hit the white people of Ocean City, New Jersey, that tells you how far reaching it is. This is waking up white people, and I'm seeing more and more understanding, although it's going to take a lot of work and a lot of time."

A decade after holding up signs at Zuccotti Park to protest Wall Street greed, Lewis saw the movement's evolution playing out in perhaps its most meaningful sense: demanding equality for all. Echoing an analogy used by many, he said, "Occupy was a seed. It didn't sprout as quickly as we wanted, and it didn't grow as fast as we wanted, but I see it turning into a justice movement not only against police brutality, but against white privilege."

COURAGE IS CONTAGIOUS

AN EXPRESSION CAME UP OVER AND OVER DURING MY CONVERSA-tions with people about Occupy and its legacy. "Courage is contagious," they would say, meaning, when we see others act in protest, we feel emboldened to do the same. One person who helped to popularize the phrase and was perhaps the most courageous of them all was the former NSA contractor and whistleblower Edward Snowden, whom the United States Justice Department charged in 2013 with violations of the Espionage Act for revealing illegal mass surveillance programs being carried out by the American government against its people. In 2016, Snowden tweeted those three words—"courage is contagious"—in response to the leaks that led to the publication of the Panama Papers, which exposed systemic tax evasion on a global scale. Indeed, in recent years, courage appears to be having a renaissance. As Ray Lewis told me: "You can't instill courage. It's got to be in the person. What you can do, though, is bring them information to help them utilize that courage. There's a lot of courageous people out there who don't know how to use it." A decade after Occupy, he said, "Now they do."

Occupy Wall Street introduced America to a new spirit of defiance and resistance, not only in the hundreds of thousands of individuals who had participated in the movement but in the many millions more who had observed it from a distance and considered themselves part of the 99 percent. "I'm not going to say courage didn't exist before Occupy, but Occupy showed people in a grand form what it looked like to protest outside the norms and permits of society," said the comedian and news show host Lee Camp. "Courage often comes in community—it's easier to have courage as a group—and that's another reason Occupy was so threatening to the ruling powers, because people showed up and found a community of people wanting to change the system." During the Trump presidency, that courage found new expression in the struggle to *preserve* the system in the face of a lawless executive whose attack on constitutional norms threatened the foundations of American democracy.

In fact, people's loss of fear may count among the lasting legacies of the Occupy movement. In the words of the derivatives analyst turned Occupy activist Alexis Goldstein: "Courage is the thing Occupy gave me. I felt brave around all these other people who were being brave." The inequality and social movement analyst Sara Burke understood Occupy as an expression of "both courage and clarity" from a generation that had finally found its voice. "I think in many different ways now we're able to speak truth to power," Burke said. "Black Lives Matter has been able to speak the truth about what it means to be in a Black body under the gun of the armed police, and #MeToo is [enabling] women to speak the truth of male domination." The pediatrician and movement organizer Margaret Flowers, who along with her late partner Kevin Zeese helped to launch Occupy D.C., believed that many people had discovered their courage by observing the actions of those around them. "When you see other people standing up, it gives you the confidence to say, 'Oh, I can do that too,'" she said.

In our conversation the year before his death, Zeese told me that the heavy police violence meted out against Occupy protesters had backfired because it exposed the failure and weakness of the State to address legitimate grievances of the population. As people saw their fellow peaceful citizens unconstitutionally assaulted by law enforcement, it awakened a popular spirit of courage to join them. "When police crack down in an aggressive way like they did at Occupy, it spreads across the country because people are supportive of nonviolent protest," Zeese said. The police killing of Michael Brown three years later in Ferguson, Missouri, which launched Black Lives Matter, represented "a tipping point, where people aren't going to take it anymore. There was a time when people thought we'd solved that racial violence problem, but now they realize no, we actually haven't." In the years since Occupy, "more and more movements [have] galvanized people to see that they have to do something about it," Zeese added. "It's a question of who we are as people."

The movement on Wall Street injected activists with a new sense of courage because it revealed the feeling on a mass level that people were not alone. "For a country like ours where loneliness is a disease of virtually everyone, the isolation of the American people is already debilitating for activism on the left. You put that together with anti-left persecutions since the end of the Second World War and you have a really heavy one-two punch that makes it difficult for people on the left to get their heads up," said Richard Wolff. People's rediscovery of their collective power through activism represented a sea change. In the aftermath of Occupy, "if you had instincts in the direction of economic radicalism, if you were in the labor movement, or were an anti-poverty or anti-racism activist, it was easier to initiate and sustain [that activism] because suddenly there was reason to believe other people were there—you just hadn't found them yet." In 2018 and 2019, Wolff added, "there was more labor unrest and people that went out on strike than happened in thirty years, and I think Occupy was a very important boost to all of them."

Among the slogans and chants that resonated at Occupy Wall Street, one in particular has echoed through the decade: *This is what democracy looks like.* The courage to confront power and demand justice is now an ingrained part of our political culture. Workers demand a living wage. Youth demand a livable planet. Black and Brown people demand safety from law enforcement. The country recognized in the powerful civil rights movement that coalesced around the police killing of George Floyd that denial and intimidation are no longer acceptable responses to injustice.

Occupy was like a great wave hitting shore: a wake-up call and a warning of more inundating future waves to come. During recent years we have learned that to ignore threats to our democracy is not an option. The question that looms over the future of the country and, of greater consequence, over the future of the planet, isn't whether or not we choose to resist, but what form our resistance will take. As the turbulence of the last decade has shown, systemic crises must be confronted. In the words of Greta Thunberg: "Change is coming whether you like it or not."

To secure democracy and achieve some of the victories that would constitute a Second Progressive Era, America will require new ground rules to ensure justice, accountability and equality under the law. Above all, it will need fresh forms of leadership that are beginning to reveal themselves in the post-Occupy era. The new generation that has arisen is acutely aware of the task at hand: to repair the climate, to restore the dignity of work and the promise of opportunity, to create a fair and secure future for all. In marching for our lives we create the conditions for our survival. Showing up is where it begins.

AFTERWORD

ON APRIL 20, 2021, A JURY IN MINNEAPOLIS CONVICTED FORMER police officer Derek Chauvin on all three counts in the murder of George Floyd. It felt as though the nation, traumatized by the past year, could finally breathe a sigh of relief. Significant reforms had yet to arrive; the country's political direction remained clouded in uncertainty, and I hesitated to write an afterword for fear that the ground would keep shifting beyond recognition. But to more fully measure the distance we had traveled in the decade since Occupy—and in the tumultuous six months since Joe Biden defeated Donald Trump by more than seven million popular votes, beating him 306–232 in the electoral college to win the U.S. presidency—a closing statement seemed unavoidable.

For nine weeks following the November 2020 election, Trump peddled the Big Lie that states and counties had rigged the process. More than eighty judges across the nation's judiciary, including at the Supreme Court, tossed out his baseless claims of voter fraud. Even after the New Year, Trump sustained pressure on local and state election officials, whom he urged to "find the votes" needed to overturn the results. Late on the night of January 5, 2021, Jon Ossoff and Raphael Warnock pulled off a stunning pair of victories in Georgia's run-off elections, delivering Senate control to the Democrats. Then the fateful day arrived, January 6, eight months shy of the twentieth anniversary of 9/11, except this time the attack on America came from enemies not foreign but domestic: homegrown, white nationalist, right-wing extremists who were ready to kill to keep their president in power. That afternoon as the Senate convened to count the electoral college votes and make Biden's victory official, Trump told thousands of his supporters, who had driven and flown in from across the nation and assembled for his "March to Save America" rally outside the White House, to walk down Pennsylvania Avenue to the Capitol and "fight like hell" to "stop the steal." In the violent act of sedition that followed, Trump's people invaded and ransacked Congress—an attempted coup that the president, watching on live TV from the West Wing, failed for three hours to call off.

The insurrection caused the deaths of five people, including a Capitol Police officer, and marked the gravest assault on the seat of Congress since British troops set fire to the Capitol in the War of 1812. One week later—exactly seven days after the attack and seven days before his term ended—Trump became the first president to be impeached twice by the U.S. House of Representatives. The first time for abuse of power and obstruction of Congress after he sought Ukraine's help to win the election; the second time for igniting a treasonous rebellion to overthrow the American government, its elected leaders, and our constitutional democracy. The shock of that seminal event will remain a dark landmark in the nation's history, akin to the September 11 attacks two decades prior and perhaps even comparable, in national security terms, to the bombing of Pearl Harbor six decades before that.

Yet in the context of this story, Trump's bid to alter the results of a free and fair election and halt the peaceful transfer of power resulted in something else unexpected: it revealed how deeply the images and rhetoric of Occupy had become embedded in the nation's culture. The bloody right-wing mobs in paramilitary gear who stormed Congress borrowed from the language of Occupy Wall Street, calling their action "Operation Occupy the Capitol." But beyond the name, the fascist uprising couldn't have been more different in style and substance. Led by anti-government militia groups like the Oath Keepers, Three Percenters, and boogaloo boys; violent white nationalist Proud Boys; neo-Nazis; Confederate racists; lunatic conspiracy theorists of QAnon and a diverse array of Trump supporters, the armed red-hatted rioters transformed the act of resistance into a new, more lethal beast.

By April 2021, more than four hundred people involved in the attack would be arrested on federal charges as President Biden's attorney general Merrick Garland—who led the Justice Department's successful prosecutions after the 1995 Oklahoma City bombing and was considered the nation's top expert in domestic terror–related cases—declared tackling violent right-wing extremism his top priority. Following the failed coup of January 6, it became ominously unclear who held the reins and momentum of popular dissent in the country: the left or the right. But Occupy seemed to have framed the positions. There will be a peaceful way and a violent way to resolve political conflict in the years ahead, and America's future hinges on the power struggle between those diametrically opposed forces.

FACING UNPRECEDENTED HEALTH, ECONOMIC, RACIAL, CLIMATE and civil crises, Joe Biden wasted no time getting to work. Biden had campaigned as the candidate who could govern from the middle, preaching unity after the divisive years of Trump. He rejected calls for radical change: this was not the political revolution's candidate. The two Democratic challengers who could most closely claim that mantle, Bernie Sanders and Elizabeth Warren, had strong support from progressives but lost decisively to Biden. And yet, something had shifted.

On January 20, the day he took office, Biden signed seventeen executive orders and directives that, among other things, canceled the Keystone XL pipeline, reentered the United States into the Paris Agreement, extended a freeze on student loan payments and a nationwide moratorium on evictions and foreclosures, fortified DACA to strengthen protections for Dreamers, reversed Trump's travel ban targeting seven Muslim-majority countries, ended gender-based discrimination in the workplace and halted construction of the border wall with Mexico. On Day 2, Biden launched a national strategy to contain the Covid-19 pandemic. America's death toll from the coronavirus had by that point surpassed four hundred thousand as the country registered nearly a quarter of a million new cases a day. Biden began his presidency with a raft of executive orders that required masks in airports, safeguarded workers' health, improved pandemic treatment and care, introduced a plan to safely reopen schools, activated the Defense Production Act to manufacture more personal protective equipment and started a national vaccination campaign to get one hundred million doses into Americans' arms in the first hundred days (a goal surpassed on Day 58 of his administration). By the end of his first week Biden had bolstered food aid for millions in need, restored collective bargaining power and protections for federal workers, ordered the Justice Department to end all federal contracts with private prisons and directed the Department of Housing and Urban Development to abolish discriminatory housing practices. Encouraging signs abounded, and what had been considered progressive priorities were starting to look like the presidential agenda.

The GameStop saga that gripped Wall Street in the final days of January seemed to resurrect the spirit of Occupy. Masses of young people—using the stock trading app Robinhood and spurred by the Reddit page wallstreetbets—had banded together to buy up shares of the brick-and-mortar video game retailer GameStop. The army of renegade investors drove the company's stock price to outrageous heights: from $65 to $483 over several days. Their subversive campaign made some investors rich, creating $30 billion in overnight wealth, and dealt a costly blow to hedge funds that had profited off the stock's short sale. The event rattled Wall Street and Washington, causing Robinhood to halt sales of GameStop and other volatile "meme stocks" in an effort to stanch the bleeding. The rebellion was brief, but it seemed to send a message: the swarming tactics developed a decade ago at Zuccotti Park had found new form within the financial establishment. "You can't deny this is a major moment. Occupy Wall Street 2.0," declared Kelly Evans on CNBC.com. "It's Occupy Wall Street, the sequel," wrote Lisa Lerer and Astead Herndon for *The New York Times*. Drawing attention to former Occupy protesters who had become influential penny-stock traders helping drive the movement, Joan Donovan wrote in *Politico* that to see the link between Zuccotti Park and GameStop was "the key to appreciating how broad social disruptions work now." Whether the activists' insurgent investment strategy would be consequential in the long run was yet to be seen.

Popular wage demands took center stage the next month as workers reinitiated calls for a $15 minimum wage. By this time some thirty million Americans—disproportionately Black, Brown and female workers—were earning less than $15 an hour, down from nearly forty million in 2019 before the pandemic imploded the low-wage sector. In mid-February, nurses and homecare workers joined fast-food chain employees in strikes for $15 across fifteen states. A raise of the minimum wage would fail to make it into the Democrats' defining first piece of economic legislation. But in early March, the House of Representatives passed the most pro-union bill in decades—the Protecting the Right to Organize, or PRO Act—which sought to strengthen labor protections, expand collective bargaining rights, penalize employers who violated labor laws and weaken right-to-work laws. Biden's pick to head the labor department, Marty Walsh, became the first union leader in forty years to hold the nation's top job responsible for protecting America's workers. In Bessemer, Alabama, Amazon warehouse workers led a historic effort to join the Retail, Wholesale and Department Store Union; although their vote to unionize fell short, employees of the world's richest man declared the fight had only begun. Even in the highest echelons of the Bay Area technology market, at Google, hundreds of workers launched a union to establish stronger ethical standards and fairer labor practices. Across the labor landscape, workers' demands were more robust than they had been in a generation, reflecting the distance the country had traveled since Occupy issued its clarion call for economic justice.

A severe freeze that winter had laid bare parts of the South as failed power grids and water systems from Texas to Mississippi revealed the human costs of privatizing and deregulating vital public goods. In places where tax-starved city and state governments were no longer capable of safeguarding people's health and well-being, the bill was coming due: large parts of America stood in need of an overhaul. The earliest sign that help might be on the way occurred on March 11, halfway through Biden's first hundred days, when he signed the American Rescue Plan into law. Hailed as the most progressive economic package since the Great Depression, the $1.9 trillion coronavirus stimulus bill passed by the new Democratic Congress issued $1,400 immediate direct payments to most Americans—families of four would receive checks for $5,600—and expanded food support while boosting pandemic unemployment benefits. Notably, the bill offered an extended child tax credit through 2021; families earning less than $150,000 would receive $300 a month for every child under six and $250 for every youth under eighteen, a measure that experts predicted would cut child poverty in half within the year.

The American Rescue Plan eclipsed the $800 billion Recovery Act passed by Obama during his first month in office and did what no major economic law since Lyndon Johnson's Great Society had attempted: it began moving money back down the economic ladder. The package provided $170 billion in relief and reopening funds for K–12 schools and colleges, distributed tens of billions of dollars in grants to keep restaurants afloat, covered six months of health insurance costs for Americans on post-employment COBRA plans and provided $5 billion to small farmers, most of them Black and historically discriminated against, in what Tracy Lloyd McCurty, the executive director of the Black Belt Justice Center, called "the most significant piece of legislation with respect to the arc of Black land ownership in this country."

The rescue bill also sent hundreds of billions of dollars to state and local governments to fill emergency budget holes helping sustain vital services like water, sewage, and broadband while avoiding mass layoffs of administrators, firefighters, emergency crews and health workers. Mark Ritacco, director of government affairs for the National Association of Counties, called the stimulus "a historic investment in local government," and Svante Myrick, the mayor of Ithaca, New York, which received $17 million from the bill, asserted, "If the federal government sent every community this amount of money every year we'd be living in a cleaner, safer, more prosperous country." Could it be that Washington had learned the lesson from 2009 and the Great Recession? This time Main Street, not Wall Street, was getting a bailout. Progressive congressman Ro Khanna called the law "an ideological revolution on behalf of justice," while Nicholas Lemann wrote in *The New Yorker*, "The side that always seemed to lose the argument within the Democratic Party has finally won . . . It feels as if half a century's effort to reorient the political economy away from the state and toward the market may finally have run its course."

As they leveled up from the bottom, Democratic legislators also sought to level down from the top, taxing the rich and laying the groundwork for broader wealth redistribution in ways that echoed some of Occupy's earlier demands. The stimulus bill promised to raise $60 billion by eliminating companies' deductions through executive compensation, revising tax rules on interest expenses for multinational corporations and setting new limits on how much unincorporated "pass-through" businesses could account for losses. Senators Sanders and Warren led Democrats in unveiling an Ultra-Millionaire Tax Act that would impose a 2 percent annual tax on wealth above $50 million and a 3 percent tax on billionaires to generate $3 trillion in federal revenue over ten years. Raising taxes on corporations and the wealthy anchored Biden's $2 trillion "build back better" clean energy and infrastructure bill known as the American Jobs Plan, the centerpiece of his economic agenda. And in April, treasury secretary Janet Yellen called for a global minimum tax on corporations to, as she put it, "raise sufficient revenue to invest in essential public goods [so] that all citizens fairly share the burden of financing government."

A decade after Occupy Wall Street, the conversation was circling back to where it had started: economic inequality and corporate greed. As those and many other battles played out in Congress—to protect and expand voting rights, to clean up corruption and reduce the influence of money in politics, to reform criminal justice and laws governing police—public opinion shifted what people thought to be politically possible. Measures to cancel student debt, fund affordable housing and transform the energy economy had begun to re-shape the debate in Washington. Bold economic solutions were also emerging on a local level as sixteen new bills, introduced across eight states between January and March 2021, sought to establish city-owned public banks as an alternative to the private, debt-based financing system of Wall Street.

During his first address to Congress on the ninety-ninth day of his presi-dency, Joe Biden struck a remarkably progressive, populist tone as he laid out his "blue-collar blueprint to build America." Promising to eliminate havens and loopholes to "crack down on millionaires and billionaires who cheat on their taxes" and force "the wealthiest 1 percent to pay their fair share," Biden employed language that could have once been heard echoing through the peo-ple's mic at Zuccotti Park. "Fifty-five of the nation's biggest corporations paid zero federal tax last year [and] made in excess of forty billion dollars in profit," he told the country. "It's not right. The pay gap between CEOs and their work-ers is now among the largest in history." Biden added that during the pan-demic, "roughly 650 billionaires in America saw their net worth increase by more than one trillion dollars, and they're now worth more than four trillion dollars." Occupy Wall Street had crystallized the struggle between democracy and plutocracy. By the start of the Biden era, the nation appeared poised to confront its existential socioeconomic crisis.

As I write this afterword, America stands at a crossroads. The ideals and lessons of Occupy, hatched ten years ago in the blustery autumn encamp-ment in lower Manhattan, have spread through the country. Now the political upheaval that the movement had advocated may be on the verge of becom-ing a reality. Substantive changes feel close at hand, yet laws remain far from enactment, raising eternal questions: Can bold initiatives lead to meaningful societal change? Will popular social and economic demands produce last-ing impacts, upending a system by which wealth and power have historically squeezed out the 99 percent? Four decades after Ronald Reagan entered office, the age of laissez-faire, trickle-down economics seems to be giving way to a new period of muscular, more expansive government that seeks to protect the rights and interests of people, not merely capital. A national consensus calls for inequalities to be addressed and rules constraining corporate power to be created and finally enforced. The pendulum will keep swinging. Reactionary forces will persist. But a decade after the Occupy movement, I remain hopeful that justice and economic security will be extended to a greater number of people. The fight will go on as it has always gone on. Occupy is not over. The Occupy story is never-ending.

May 1, 2021, International Workers' Day
El Cerrito, California

ACKNOWLEDGMENTS

MY GREATEST THANKS AND RESPECT GO TO ALL THE PEOPLE WHO have fought and will continue to fight for economic and social justice in our time. I am inspired and humbled by your courage, creativity and enduring commitment to make the world a more just and livable place for future generations. Your work compelled me to tell this story.

A giant thank-you to those friends and companions on the front lines who shared all that they had and taught me so much, in no particular order: Buddy Bolton, Theo Talcott, Deirdre Day, Gary Roland, Melina Hammer, Elektra Buhalis, Alphonzo Terrell, Jed Brandt, Matt Stannard, Eleanor Goldfield, Ted Hall, Amy Roberts, David Suker, Karina Stenquist, Mark Bray, Carl Gibson, Allred Todorojo, Ariel Zevon, Chris Hedges, Amy Hanks, Ted Schulman, Matthew Darcey, David Cobb, Ana Horta, Peter Rugh, Laura Gottesdiener, Nick Papadopoulos, Trinity Tran, Jim Lafferty, Gayle McLaughlin, David Sauvage, Ben Cohen, Amin Husain, Liesbeth Rapp, David DeGraw, Anna Callahan, Mark Provost, Leah Feder, Joel Serino, Rebecca Manski, Nelini Stamp, Devin Balkind, Bill Dobbs, Tracie Williams, Nate Kleinman, Alex

Fradkin, Sofia Gallisa Muriente, Arun Gupta, Jesse LaGreca, Susan Harmon, Priscilla Grim, Alnoor Ladha, Yotam Marom, Jonathan Smucker, Drew Hornbein, Bjorn Larsen, Linnea Paton, Ed Sutton, Astra Taylor, Stan Williams, Harmony Goldberg, Stacco Troncoso, Kobi Skolnik, Marine Perez, Adriel Hampton, Judith Iam, Will Jesse, Ryan Elwood, Abby Martin, Sandy Nurse, Catherine Hurd, Nicholas Mirzoeff, Bryan Farrell, Hilary Bettis, Evan Wagner and Begonia Santa-Cecilia. Thank you especially to Julien Harrison, Alessandro Cosmelli and Noah Fischer for your ideas, humor and collaboration.

Dear thanks to Lauren Taubman for your friendship, support and lifelong role helping to advance social justice. Thank you to Noah Gaynin and Jennifer Mascia for the hard work we shared and the unexpected road we traveled. Thank you to Steve Rushton, Gabrielle Pickard-Whitehead, Andrew Gavin Marshall, Paromita Pain, Chris Paulus, Steve Horn, Charlotte Dingle, Tom Lawson, Matt Hunger, Nafeez Ahmed, Manar Ammar, Ashton Pittman, Bryan Henry, Michele Oberholtzer, Dan Sisken, Kevin Limiti, Eric Moll, Jabeen Bhatti, Aaron Fountain Jr., Graciela Razo, Nicholas Goroff, Derek Royden, Lainey Hashorva, Emily Ludolf, Matt Higgins, Jonas Hansen, Jonah Raskin, Diego Cupolo, Dina Rasor, Devon Douglas-Bowers, Senka Huskic, Mark Vorpahl, Justine Browning, Ruby Russell, Chris Gay, Brad Poling, Katharina Wecker, Maria and Konstantine Paradias and the other passionate writers and storytellers I had the honor of working with at Occupy.com.

Thank you to my first journalist mentor and teacher, Pamela Porter, and to my early editor, Stephen Kessler, for the confidence you injected into my writing. Thank you to Peter McFarren for giving me my first newspaper job and to Sam Freedman at Columbia Journalism School for the narrative craft and vision you helped instill. My lifelong thanks to John Schak, Jim Mascolo and Mike Tozer, whose own generational wisdom and attitudes continue to provide guidance. Irene Pascual, you taught me what persistent creative work looks like and the value of seeing hard projects through.

I am grateful for the warmth, wit and company of friends who have, like me, committed countless hours to building words and telling stories on the page: Eric Marx, Yaotzin Botello, Joe Lamport, Michael Dumiak, Ken Nash, Gellert Tamas, Dave Graham, Alexa Dvorson, Rachel Rabkin Peachman, Sam Loewenberg, Itai Lahat, Jacek Slaski, Carmen Eller, David Gawthorpe, Kevin McAleer, Tim Wilson, Charlynne Curiel, Elad Lapidot, Jacek Duchownik, Florian Werner, Audrey Mei, Santiago Solari, Ethan Vlah, Carlos Jesus Gonzalez, Hilmar Poganatz, Peter Zilahy, Ian Olds, Philipp Lichterbeck, my mates on the Deutsche Autoren-Nationalmannschaft, Brian Platzer, Matti Rautkivi, Beagan Wilcox, Michael Scott Moore, Noah Haglund, Vince Beiser, Scott Lettieri, Jonathan Greenberg, Riki Rebel and Michael Stoll. I feel so fortunate to find myself in this purposeful sliver of humanity.

Thank you to my comrade Shelly Browning, who never stopped occupying, and to the friends out West who have been my community through thick and thin: Brian Dowd-Uribe, Dustin Luther, Heather Rawson, Marilyn Cannon, Benoit Brisbois, Lila LaHood, Kenn Burrows, Nancy Hayssen, Julian Kissman, Jamison Hollister, Blake More, Sara Green, Dave Hauser, Juan Reardon, George Abrams, the Cohans, the Schneiders, Max Rosenblum, Jonathan Wettstein, Ryan Stone, Gabe Wallace, Scott Bullis, Peter Phillips, Taylor Knoop, Perry Mayfield, Manj Benning, Diego Aristizabal, Zan Rubin and John Luna. Thank you to Obed Vazquez, Mickey Huff, Adam Bessie and the terrific community of teachers and students at Diablo Valley College. Also thank you to Pamela Balls Organista and John Zarobell at University of San Francisco.

A special thanks to editor Yoni Appelbaum for allowing me to tell the genesis of this story in a 2015 article for *The Atlantic*. Thank you to photographer and soccer captain Clara Rice, and to my reliable web man Karl Sandoval.

Heartfelt thanks to writer-editors Michael Howerton, Jacob Resneck, and Joe Sherman, who diligently read and offered valuable insights that sharpened the manuscript.

I want to thank my agent, Andy Ross, who understood and believed in this project from the start and worked energetically to ensure its publication. Thank you to Jack Shoemaker at Counterpoint Press, whose vision, encouragement and steady hand produced this book on a tight deadline, steering it through the turbulent year of the coronavirus. My gratitude to Megan Fishmann, Jennifer Alton, Jordan Koluch, Lexi Earle, Yukiko Tominaga, Rachel Fershleiser, Selihah White and the entire editorial and production team at Counterpoint, whose attuned suggestions, artistry and flexibility brought this project to completion.

In the early days of September 2020, as I was finishing the first draft of this book, the world lost two great thinkers and activists without whom Occupy, in some way, would have been unimaginable: the anthropologist and author David Graeber, and the lawyer and movement organizer Kevin Zeese. May this work serve as a tribute to these two outsize figures of the left whom the descendants of Occupy will dearly miss.

Thank you to Daniel Polley, the Meyerings and a sturdy contingent of Levitins from Boston to Galway and from New Jersey to Lake Champlain, for your love and encouragement. My loving thanks to Karina Ioffee, whose remarkable patience and support sustained me through the pandemic writing year of 2020. To my little ballerina Hannah Simone, you have given me all the reason I need in this world to be happy.

Finally, profound thanks, appreciation, and love for my incredible trio of parents who made it all possible: novelist Barbara Baer, historian Michael Morey, and translator Alexis Levitin. The moral and intellectual foundation you gave me laid the groundwork for so much that I was able to say in this book, and your collective edits brought out the best in the manuscript. Were we all so lucky to have parents like these.

NOTES ON SOURCES

THIS BOOK DRAWS FROM MY OWN EXPERIENCE, OBSERVATIONS AND research over the course of nearly a decade, and is based on more than fifty interviews I conducted between 2019 and 2020 with movement organizers and activists, journalists, economists, historians, union workers, authors, filmmakers, lawmakers, policy analysts and others. Their rich insights and personal stories provided the flesh and blood of this narrative; the historic legacy of Occupy Wall Street could not have been told without them.

In addition, I relied on a trove of books about Occupy, social movements, economic inequality and related topics. I want to recognize and thank those authors whose works I especially benefited from and, in some cases, quoted at length.

Charlotte Alter, *The Ones We've Been Waiting For: How a New Generation of Leaders Will Transform America* (New York: Viking, 2020)

Ellen Brown, *The Web of Debt: The Shocking Truth About Our Money System and How We Can Break Free* (Baton Rouge: Third Millennium Press, 2007)

Chrystia Freeland, *Plutocrats: The Rise of the New Global Super-Rich and the Fall of Everyone Else* (New York: Penguin Press, 2012)

Todd Gitlin, *Occupy Nation: The Roots, the Spirit, and the Promise of Occupy Wall Street* (New York: itbooks, 2012)

Michael A. Gould-Wartofsky, *The Occupiers: The Making of the 99 Percent Movement* (New York: Oxford University Press, 2015)

Chris Hedges, *Death of the Liberal Class* (New York: Nation Books, 2010)

Sarah Jaffe, *Necessary Trouble: Americans In Revolt* (New York: Nation Books, 2016)

John B. Judis, *The Socialist Awakening: What's Different Now About the Left* (New York: Columbia Global Reports, 2020)

Jane Mayer, *Dark Money: The Hidden History of the Billionaires Behind the Rise of the Radical Right* (New York: Doubleday, 2016)

George Packer, *The Unwinding: An Inner History of the New America* (New York: Farrar, Straus and Giroux, 2013)

Emmanuel Saez and Gabriel Zucman, *The Triumph of Injustice: How the Rich Dodge Taxes and How to Make Them Pay* (New York: W. W. Norton, 2019)

Nathan Schneider, *Thank You, Anarchy: Notes from the Occupy Apocalypse* (Berkeley: University of California Press, 2013)

Joseph E. Stiglitz, *The Price of Inequality: How Today's Divided Society Endangers Our Future* (New York: W. W. Norton, 2012)

Matt Taibbi, *The Divide: American Injustice in the Age of the Wealth Gap* (New York: Spiegel & Grau, 2014)

Micah White, *The End of Protest: A New Playbook for Revolution* (Toronto: Alfred A. Knopf Canada, 2016)

Finally, I drew from the published work of many reporters, editors, analysts, think tanks, pollsters and a variety of reliable media sources to reinforce the accuracy and context of this story. Often I quoted and cited those sources directly; other times I presented facts and information based on a consensus of reports that are freely accessible online. In instances with variable numbers—

for example, concerning crowd size—I used a range of data to reflect both high and low estimates. I tried throughout the book to be as honest, accurate and faithful to the facts as possible; for any potential mistakes that I have made in my reporting or my depictions, I bear full responsibility.

In almost all of the narrated scenes and character accounts from the Occupy movement, I used people's real names; in only a few rare instances did I use pseudonyms to protect the privacy and identity of individuals.

INDEX

© Clara Rice

MICHAEL LEVITIN is a journalist and co-founding editor of *The Occupied Wall Street Journal*. He started as a reporter covering the Cochabamba Water War in 2000 for the English-language newspaper *Bolivian Times*. He earned his master's degree from the Columbia Graduate School of Journalism and later worked as a freelance correspondent in Barcelona and Berlin covering politics, culture, and climate change. His writing has appeared in *The Atlantic*, *The Guardian*, *Financial Times*, *Newsweek*, *Time*, and the *Los Angeles Times*, among other publications. His debut novel, *Disposable Man*, was published in 2019. He teaches journalism at Diablo Valley College in the San Francisco Bay Area, where he lives with his partner and daughter. Find out more at michaellevitin.com.